809·916 MOE
3wk

City and Islington Sixth Form College
The Angel 283-309 Goswell Road
London EC1V 7LA
020 7520 0652

CITY AND ISLINGTON
COLLEGE

This book is due for return on or before the date last stamped below.
You may renew by telephone. Please quote the Barcode No.
May not be renewed if required by another reader.

Fine: 5p per day

0 9 NOV 2011

CPD6017

Sean
with Tony Coult

City
SFC13499

1

ACKNOWLEDGEMENTS

Written by Sean McEvoy with Tony Coult and Chris Sandford

Edited by Barbara Bleiman and Lucy Webster

Design: Sam Sullivan

Cover shows Chorus Mask from Euripides' *Bacchae* at the National Theatre of Iceland, 2007. Mask design: Thanos Vovolis. Stage director: Giorgos Zamboulakis

Published by the English and Media Centre, 18 Compton Terrace, London, N1 2UN

© English and Media Centre, 2009

ISBN: 978-1-906101-06-0

Printed by Gutenberg Press

The authors
Dr. Sean McEvoy teaches at Vardean College, Brighton. He is the author of *William Shakespeare's 'Hamlet': A Sourcebook* (2006); *Shakespeare: The Basics* (2006) and *Ben Jonson, Renaissance Dramatist* (2008). Tony Coult co-directs an Arts in Mental Health project at the Snowsfields Unit at Guy's Hospital and is the author of *About Friel* (2003) and *The Plays of Edward Bond: a Study* (1980). Chris Sandford is a freelance writer and editor of *Beckett's Women*, a collection of essays to accompany Limerick's Beckett Centenary Festival 2006. All three authors are regular writers for *emagazine*.

CITY AND ISLINGTON
SIXTH FORM COLLEGE
283 - 309 GOSWELL ROAD
LONDON
EC1
TEL 020 7520 0652

Thanks to the following publishers, authors and agents for giving permission to reproduce copyright material:

Palgrave Macmillan for Bate, Jonathan (2007), *Introduction to the RSC Shakespeare*, Dollimore, Jonathan (1984), *Radical Tragedy* (3rd edition, 2000), McDonald Ronan (2001), *Tragedy and Irish Literature: Synge, O'Casey, Beckett*, Ryan, Kiernan (2002, 3rd edition), *Shakespeare*, Eaton, Sara (1991), 'Beatrice-Joanna and the Rhetoric of Love', in *Staging the Renaissance*, ed. David Scott Kastan and Peter Stallybrass; Edinburgh University Press (www.euppublishing.com) for Hopkins, Lisa (2008), *Christopher Marlowe, Renaissance Dramatist* and O'Callaghan, Michelle (2009), *Thomas Middleton, Renaissance Dramatist*; Granta Books for O'Toole, Fintan (2002), *Shakespeare is Hard, But so is Life*; Taylor and Francis Books UK for Jardine, Lisa (1996), *Reading Shakespeare Historically* (Routledge), Ewan, Fernie, (2002), *Shame in Shakespeare* (Routledge), Hadfield, Andrew (2003), *William Shakespeare's 'Othello': A Sourcebook* (Routledge), McEvoy, Sean (2006), *Shakespeare: The Basics*, second edition, (Routledge); Cambridge University Press for Boon, Richard (2003), *The Cambridge Companion to David Hare*; Wallace, Jennifer (2007), *The Cambridge Introduction to Tragedy*, Dodds, E. R. 'On Misunderstanding the *Oedipus Rex*', *Greece and Roman Journal Volume 13* (1966) © The Classical Association (reproduced in *Oxford Readings in Greek Tragedy*, ed. Erich Segal, 1983, OUP), Bigsby, C.W.E., 'Entering *The Glass Menagerie*', Devlin, A.J., 'Writing in 'A Place of Stone': *Cat on a Hot Tin Roof*' and Londré, Felicia Hardison, 'A Streetcar Running Fifty Years' in *The Cambridge Companion to Tennessee Williams*, ed. Matthew C. Roudané (1997), Easterling, Pat (1997), 'Form and Performance' in *The Cambridge Companion to Greek Tragedy*, Grene Nicholas (1999) *The Politics of Irish Drama: Plays in Context from Boucicault to Friel*, Goldhill, Simon (1986), *Reading Greek Tragedy*, Winnington-Ingram, R.P. (1980), *Sophocles: An Interpretation*, Shakespeare, William *Antony and Cleopatra*, ed. David Bevington (2nd edition, 2005), Shakespeare, William, (2nd edition, 2003), *King Richard II*, ed. Andrew Gurr; Duckworth Academic and Bristol Classical Press for Mills, Sophie (2002), *Euripides: 'Hippolytus'*; Oxford University Press for Kerrigan, John (1996), *Revenge Tragedy: Aeschylus to Armageddon*; Charlotte Sheedy Literary Agency for French, Marilyn (1992), 'Macbeth and Masculine Values', in *New Casebooks: 'Macbeth'*, ed. Alan Sinfield; The University of Toronto Press for Conacher, D.J. (1983), 'The Trojan Women' reproduced in *Oxford Readings in Greek Tragedy*, ed. Erich Segal; Thomson (Cengage Learning) for Bate, Jonathan (ed. 1995), *Titus Andronicus* and Hadfield, Andrew (2004), *Shakespeare and Renaissance Politics;* Belsey, Catherine for 'Making histories then and now: Shakespeare from *Richard II* to *Henry V*' (1991), in Barker, F., Hulme, P. and Iversen, M. (eds), *Uses of History: Marxism, Postmodernism and the Renaissance* and Belsey, Catherine (2007), *Why Shakespeare?*; Faber and Faber Ltd/© The Estate of T.S. Eliot for Eliot, T. S., *Selected Essays* (1951); The University of Exeter Press for Carter, D. M. (2007), *The Politics of Greek Tragedy*; Blackwell Publishing for Eagleton, Terry, *William Shakespeare* (1986) and Eagleton, Terry (2003), *Sweet Violence: The Idea of The Tragic*; Mary Nuttall c/o Writers' Representatives LLC for Nuttall, A. D. (2007), *Shakespeare the Thinker* published by Yale University Press; Yale Classical Student Journal for Knox, Bernard M. W. (1983), 'The Hippolytus of Euripides' reproduced in *Oxford Readings in Greek Tragedy*, ed. Erich Segal; Verso for Williams, Raymond (1979), *Modern Tragedy*; Hodder for Goldhill, Simon (2004), *Love, Sex and Tragedy: Why Classics Matters*.

Every effort has been made to trace and obtain appropriate copyright clearance but if any accidental infringement has been made, we would welcome the opportunity to redress the situation.

CONTENTS

CONTENTS

INTRODUCTION

This book is an introduction to tragedy for students at advanced or undergraduate level. It provides an overview of key concepts and developments in tragedy, major dramatists in the genre of tragedy and their most significant plays. Critical perspectives on the genre, on individual writers and plays, are incorporated into the text, offering a sense of some of the major strands of thinking about tragedy over time.

Although the book is broadly chronological, some chapters giving an overview of a playwright or period (for example, Modern British tragedy and Arthur Miller) deal with plays in a different sequence considering the treatment of the tragic genre more holistically.

References within the text

The date given to both play extracts and critical quotations refers to the date of writing or first publication. The page reference is to the edition from which the quotation has been taken. Where there may be confusion, the reference gives both the original date of writing and the date of the edition from which the extract has been taken. For full details of the critical texts quoted from, including the edition used, see the bibliography on pages 248.

Editions of play texts used for quotations included in *Tragedy: A Student Handbook* are listed on pages 9-10.

Dates for Shakespeare's plays are taken from Andrew Gurr's *The Shakespearean Stage 1574-1642*.

Terms and concepts emboldened in the text are glossed on pages 236 to 239.

Bold page numbers are used to cross reference to other sections of this publication.

The index

Page references in bold indicate a substantial discussion of the play, playwright or concept. Page numbers in italics refer to the glossary.

The texts

Quotations in *Tragedy: A Student Handbook* are taken from the following editions. For a full bibliography, see pages 248 to 256.

Beckett, Samuel (1986), *The Complete Dramatic Works*, Faber and Faber.

Bond, Edward (1977), *Plays: One*, Methuen.

_____ (1983), *Lear*, ed. Patricia Hearn, Methuen.

_____ (1987), *Plays: Three*, Methuen.

Chaucer, Geoffrey (1957), *The Complete Works*, ed. F.N. Robinson, Oxford University Press.

Chekhov, Anton (2002), *Plays: 'Ivanov', 'The Seagull', 'Uncle Vanya', 'Three Sisters', 'The Cherry Orchard'* ed Richard Gilman, Penguin.

Churchill, Caryl (1982), *Top Girls*, Methuen.

Euripides (1998), *'Medea' and Other Plays*, trans. James Morwood, Oxford University Press.

_____ (2004), *Women of Troy*, trans. Kenneth McLeish, Nick Hern Books.

Friel, Brian (1990), *Dancing at Lughnasa*, Faber and Faber.

_____ (1988), *Making History*, Faber and Faber.

_____ (1980), *Translations*, Faber and Faber.

Hare, David (1995), *Skylight*, Faber and Faber.

_____ (1984), *The History Plays*, Faber and Faber.

_____ (1988), *The Secret Rapture*, Faber and Faber.

Homer (1987), *The Iliad*, trans. Martin Hammond, Penguin Books.

Ibsen, Henrik (1965), *A Doll's House and Other Plays*, Penguin.

Marlowe, Christopher (1964), *Dr Faustus*, ed. John D. Jump, Manchester University Press.

_____ (1997), *Edward II*, ed. Martin Wiggins and Robert Lindsey, Manchester University Press.

_____ (2003), *Tamburlaine Parts I and II*, ed. Anthony B. Dawson, Methuen.

Middleton, Thomas and Rowley, William (1964), *The Changeling*, ed. Patricia Thomson, Manchester University Press.

Middleton, Thomas/Tourneur Cyril (1996), *The Revenger's Tragedy*, ed. R.A. Foakes, Manchester University Press.

Middleton, Thomas (2007), *Women Beware Women*, ed. J.R. Mulryne, Manchester University Press.

Miller, Arthur (1961), *Death of a Salesman*, Penguin Books.

_____ (1968), *The Crucible*, Penguin Books.

_____ (2000), *A View from the Bridge/All My Sons*, Penguin Books.

Seneca (1966), *Four Tragedies and 'Octavia'*, trans. E.F. Watling, Penguin Books.

Shakespeare, William (2007), *Complete Works*, ed. Jonathan Bate and Eric Rasmussen, Macmillan.

Sophocles (1982), *The Three Theban Plays: 'Antigone', 'Oedipus the King', 'Oedipus at Colonus'*, trans. Robert Fagles, Penguin Books.

Webster, John (1996), *'The Duchess of Malfi' and Other Plays*, ed. René Weis, Oxford University Press.

Williams, Tennessee (2000), *A Streetcar Named Desire and Other Plays*, Penguin Books.

Williams, Tennessee (2001), *Cat on a Hot Tin Roof and Other Plays*, Penguin Books.

INTRODUCING TRAGEDY

WHAT IS TRAGEDY?

The word **tragedy** is in common usage in everyday life. In any one day you may hear it used in casual conversation, or in the media, to describe everything from a missed penalty in a football match to the death of a child, from the pain caused by man-made or natural disasters to a pop star's ill-advised haircut. While the light-hearted and exaggerated use of the term (missed penalties, break up of celebrity relationships) may have little to do with literary concepts of tragedy, descriptions of real life suffering as a tragedy reflect our need to make sense of, and dignify the unimaginable, unspeakable, inexplicable and unfair. These aspects of life are at the heart of tragic drama.

The critic Raymond Williams wrote that to restrict the term tragedy only to literature, as some literary critics have sought to do, is to deny to real events the understanding which tragic drama can confer on them. Throughout history one of the roles of tragedy has been to provide a means of understanding our real lives through fictional representation. Tragedy is not just an artistic exercise, but a way of dignifying and making sense of suffering. For this reason some people suggest tragedy is a genre unsuited to Christian societies in which human suffering is seen in the context of God and the afterlife.

> I have known tragedy in the life of a man driven back into silence, in an unregarded working life. In his ordinary and private death, I saw a terrifying loss of connection between men, and even between father and son: a loss of connection which was, however, a particular historical and social fact.
>
> *Raymond Williams 1979: 13*

How can art help us to cope with suffering? How can it make sense of pain and death, and of the sense of injustice that often accompanies these central human experiences? Why does seeing suffering represented on stage in a tragic drama produce a sense of enjoyment rather than merely add to our sense of pain or awareness of the suffering in the world?

The word tragedy itself was coined by the ancient Greeks who first chose to put these crucial questions about human suffering on the public stage almost 2500 years ago in democratic Athens, a non-Christian society. Translated literally the word means 'goat song' which may refer to the prize awarded to the playwright whose play took first prize in the annual competition.

Pleasure and pain

One of the paradoxical characteristics of tragic drama – and a defining difference between the literary and everyday concept of tragedy – is that at the same time as feeling sorrow and pity for those whose suffering we see on stage, we also take pleasure in the representation of suffering. This pleasure comes partly from the delight we take in beautifully crafted works of art in general. It also comes from our response more specifically to the tragic nature of the play and what we feel we have gained from the experience: emotional solace, perhaps a greater political understanding of our world, or perhaps a sense of striving to understand something almost beyond words. Art itself survives death and goes on speaking to generations whose sufferings could not even be imagined by the people for whom a tragedy was originally written. In this sense the existence of tragedy as a literary concept seems to defeat suffering and even death:

> Tragedy is the art form created to confront the most difficult experiences we face: death, loss, injustice, thwarted passion, despair.
>
> *Jennifer Wallace 2007: 1*

The scope of this book

Although tragedy as an art form has also developed in genres such as the novel and films, it has been predominantly a theatrical form, and that is the main focus of this book.

Art and literature dealing with the common experience of human suffering and recognised as tragic is found in cultures throughout the world. This book focuses on the Western tradition, tracing its origins from classical Greek tragedies through the Renaissance to the late 19th and early 20th-century European tragedies. It also considers modern Irish, American and British concepts of tragedy, and what the term has come to mean at the beginning of the 21st century.

CONCEPTS OF TRAGEDY

Tragedy has been important in Western art for two and a half thousand years. Theories about its nature have inevitably changed and developed over that time. There are, however, certain concepts which have remained more or less central to what we understand the term to mean. These concepts have their origin in *The Poetics* of the Greek philosopher **Aristotle** who wrote in about 330 BC. They can be summarised as follows:

1. The drama is usually centred upon one or more main character (**the protagonist**) who acts in a way which proves disastrous.

2. The scope of the play's action is limited in terms of plot (which should not be too complex). The time the action takes to elapse should also be limited, as should the location of the action (**the unities**).

3. There is a calamitous outcome (**the catastrophe**) which causes an emotional response in its audience.

TRAGEDY IN ANCIENT GREECE

In Greek the word **protagonist** meant the first of the three professional actors who played all the speaking roles in the drama. It has come to mean the individual whose suffering constitutes a central part of the tragedy. Sometimes he or she is known as the **tragic hero** (or heroine), but since these terms tend to carry with them the suggestion of virtue, and since not all **tragic protagonists** can uncontroversially be called virtuous, it makes sense to use the older Greek word.

The classical protagonist

When Aristotle wrote *The Poetics* he was thinking of the kind of central character to be found in the plays of **Sophocles (p.43)**. The protagonist was a man who had a certain nobility about him, a man of high birth who was courageous and generous in character. The Greek word Aristotle used is **megalopsychia**, 'greatness of soul'. The protagonist could not be a man who was totally good, or else the audience would feel only disgust at the injustice of his destruction in the play's catastrophe. Neither could he be someone wicked, for then the audience would rejoice at his fall.

> There remains an error between these two extremes. This is the sort of man who is not conspicuous for virtue and justice, and whose fall from misery is not due to vice and depravity, but rather to some error, a man who enjoys prosperity and a high reputation, like Oedipus or Thyestes and other famous members of families like theirs.
>
> *Aristotle c.330 BC: 48*

Hamartia – the fatal error of judgement

The protagonist is a character with whom the audience can identify, someone who makes a wrong decision for good reasons or with the best of intentions.

Aristotle called the protagonist's error of judgement **hamartia**. It is often the result of a condition called by the Greeks **hubris**, the excessive pride which brings down divine punishment upon the head of the protagonist. Conventional Greek religion in the classical period saw the gods as selfish and vengeful. They guarded their status jealously, and would punish any mortal whose sense of personal pride and self-importance seemed to them to exceed what was proper to humans. In a text that Greeks regarded as a guide to their culture's values, Homer's epic poem *The Iliad*, the goddess Hera explains to Zeus why she always takes action against any mortal who offends her – because that is what makes her a god:

> Even men will achieve their purposes for other men, though they are mortal and without the knowledge that we have. How then, when my claim is to be the greatest of the goddesses ... how could I not weave trouble for the Trojans, when they have angered me?

Homer c.700 BC: 304

The story of Oedipus exemplifies the concept of hamartia. According to Greek myth, Oedipus is the man who, having been abandoned to die at birth, grows up to kill his father Laius, King of Thebes. He then take over both his crown and his widow, Jocasta – Oedipus's own mother.

At the beginning of Sophocles' *Oedipus Rex* Oedipus is at the height of his powers: he has slain the Sphinx, the monster which terrorised the people of Thebes, and is attempting to find out the cause of the plague afflicting his city:

> Now we pray to you. You cannot equal the gods,
>
> Your children know that, bending at your altar.
>
> But we do rate you first of men,
>
> Both in the common crises of our lives
>
> And face-to-face encounters with the gods...

Chorus to Oedipus, Sophocles: Oedipus Rex 429? BC: 161

Oedipus discovers that Apollo has sent the plague because Thebes still harbours the man who killed the previous king, Laius. In trying to save the city from the plague, he uncovers the truth: that he is the man who killed the king, his own father, and therefore is also married to his mother. Jocasta commits suicide and Oedipus blinds himself. His unwitting error of judgement and the terrible punishment he suffers demonstrate both the power of the gods and man's lack of power over his life and destiny.

Hubris and anagnorisis

The protagonist in classical tragedy commits **hubris** by choosing to defy the claims of the gods. In Sophocles' play *Antigone*, Creon, King of Thebes commits hubris when he refuses to bury the body of Antigone's brother Polynices, who was killed fighting against his city. Following the suicides of his wife and son, Creon comes to realise that he has made a mistake in defying the gods of the underworld. He recognises he has committed hubris, and so reaches a state of **anagnorisis** – recognition of his tragic error of judgement:

> The mighty words of the proud are paid in full
>
> with mighty blows of fate, and at long last
>
> those blows will teach us wisdom

The final words of the Chorus, Sophocles: Antigone 441? BC: 128

TRAGEDY IN THE MIDDLE AGES

Tragedie is to sey a certayn storie,

As olde bookes maken us memorie,

Of hym that stood in greet prosperitee,

And is yfallen out of heigh degree

Into mysterie, and endeth wrechedly.

(Tragedy is a type of story found in ancient books in which is preserved the glory of one who had high status but fell into a terrible state and ended his days wretchedly.)

Chaucer: The Monk's Tale late 14th century

Tragedy in a Christian age?

In the Middle Ages ideas about tragedy became rather simplified. Some people argue that tragedy is not possible in Christian societies: if it is believed God's providence will ensure that ultimately the wicked are punished and the good rewarded, there is no urgent need for art to make sense of human suffering and those men who seek earthly power are deluded. At the end of *The Monk's Tale* (c.1400), Geoffrey Chaucer suggests tragedy is nothing more than the inevitable turning of the Wheel of Fortune:

> But that Fortune alwey wole assaille
>
> With unwar strook the regnes that hath been proude;
>
> For whan man trusteth hire, than wole she faille,
>
> And covere her brighte face with a cloude.

(Fortune will always assault with an unexpected blow the kings who have been proud; whenever a man trusts her, then will she let him down, covering her bright face with a cloud.)

Chaucer: The Monk's Tale late 14th century

Tragedy during this period shrunk in scope to a moral message about how the turning of the Wheel of Fortune will bring about the fall of kings and princes who put their faith in earthly power rather than God.

TRAGEDY IN THE RENAISSANCE

A royal protagonist

By the Renaissance this was still the basis of the view of a theorist such as Sir Philip Sidney, but there was also a new, more sceptical and more political slant. Sidney, writing in around 1581 was sure that tragedy

> teacheth the uncertainty of the world, and upon how weak foundations guilden roofs are builded.
>
> *Sir Philip Sidney c.1581: 45*

That is, tragedy also showed tyrants that their crimes would be revealed and punished by God.

It was the dramatists, however, who decided that kings and princes were not the only candidates for the role of protagonist. Although Shakespeare's tragedies typically concern noble figures such as *Hamlet* (**p.87**) and *Othello* (**p.94**), Shylock the Jewish moneylender in *The Merchant of Venice* can certainly also be seen as a tragic figure. Christopher Marlowe's *Dr Faustus* was a scholar (**p.67**), and Tamburlaine originally a shepherd. John Webster's tragic protagonists in *The Duchess of Malfi* (**p.132**) and *The White Devil* are women, albeit aristocrats. Early modern English tragedy looked beyond the protagonist – the noble individual – showing not only a wider interest in society, but also questioning whether the universe is ruled by divine justice, a radical, even dangerous perspective at the time. In *King Lear* (**p.103**), the play's ending notoriously defies any notion that God has rewarded the just. The innocent Cordelia cannot be rescued in time and is hanged; the most senior surviving nobleman, Albany, proposes a division of the kingdom, the very policy which began the descent of the kingdom into chaos; the king's most loyal retainer, Kent, declines the offer of the crown for an obscure but ominous reason, hinting at his intention to commit suicide; and there is no clear resolution about what will happen next as the survivors stand on a stage littered with noble corpses.

ALBANY	Friends of my soul, you twain to Kent and Edgar Rule in this realm, and the gored state sustain.
KENT	I have a journey, sir, shortly to go: My master calls me, and I must not say no.
EDGAR	The weight of this sad time we must obey: Speak what we feel, not what we ought to say. The oldest hath borne most: we that are young Shall never see so much nor live so long.

Exeunt with a dead march

5.3.340-47

THE ROMANTICS

> Tragedy delights by affording a shadow of the pleasure which
> exists in pain.
>
> *Percy Bysshe Shelley: A Defence of Poetry 1821*

Reinterpreting the Shakespearean protagonist

After the great days of Elizabethan and Jacobean theatre tragedy in England, fell under the influence of neo-classical ideas (**p.62**). By the end of the 18th century it was German thinkers such as Goethe who were most significant. A key idea in the Romantic movement, of which Goethe was an important part, was that the world of the imagination offered a liberating vision against the constraints of society, with its hierarchies of power and organised religion.

The tragic protagonist in the Romantic period was a sensitive individual striving for self-expression in a world which did not recognise the validity of personal feeling and vision. Sensibility, not royal blood, was what made an individual a potentially tragic protagonist. In England, Romanticism expressed its tragic vision in critical and theatrical interpretations of Shakespeare. Hamlet, according to the poet and critic Samuel Taylor Coleridge, was a man who gave too much weight to the life of the imagination and could not engage successfully with the real world. The tragedy of the Romantic protagonist lay in the failure of the world to fulfil the emotional and creative vision of the sensitive individual. Some fulfilment could happen in the private act of reading, inside the world of the imagination. Indeed, Charles Lamb suggested that Shakespeare ought only to be read since the plays lived best in the imagination, not on stage where they were constrained by the practicalities of performance. For the Romantics:

> man could free himself only by rejecting or escaping from society, and by
> seeing his own deepest activities, in love, in art, in nature as essentially
> asocial and even anti-social.
>
> *Raymond Williams 1979: 73*

In continental Europe Romantic works such as Goethe's *Faust* (completed 1832) and Ibsen's *Peer Gynt* (1867) are almost unstageable in their entirety, but feature heroes striving mightily for emotional and spiritual fulfilment. The protagonists of Chekhov and Ibsen are often sensitive 'Romantic' individuals: in Ibsen's *Hedda Gabler* (1890; **p.149**) Hedda is a woman raging against the world which traps her. However, by the end of the 19th century, the Romantic instinct had become something obscure and, in her case, merely self-destructive as she kills herself:

> Hedda longs for beauty, for some different kind of perspective upon her
> world. 'It's a release to know that in spite of everything the unpremeditated
> act of courage is still possible. Something with at least a spark of instinctive
> beauty' (Act 3) ... But her motivation ultimately remains opaque, both to
> those around her and to her audience.
>
> *Jennifer Wallace 2007: 68-9*

20TH-CENTURY INTERPRETATIONS

The tragic flaw

In the late 19th and early 20th centuries the Romantic focus upon the uniqueness of the character of the individual protagonist, combined with the beginnings of the study of psychology, encouraged close scrutiny of the character of the protagonist as a means of understanding the nature of tragedy. A further factor was the contemporary belief in the ability of 'great men' to transform history on their own, an idea found in writers such as Thomas Carlyle.

A.C. Bradley's *Shakespearean Tragedy* (1904) proposed the idea of the **tragic flaw** in the psychological make-up of the protagonist. (This is not to be confused with Aristotle's notion of **hamartia**, which is a matter of action, not character.)

> What we do feel strongly, as tragedy advances to its close, is that calamities and catastrophe follow inevitably from the deeds of men, and that the main source of these deeds is character.
>
> *A.C. Bradley 1904: 29*

Bradley drew on the ideas of the German philosopher G.W.F. Hegel (1770-1831) who argued that political and social progress is made by the synthesis of opposing and conflicting forces. The character of the protagonist embodies just such a conflict: greatness in conflict with evil. According to this view, the protagonist is noble (not necessarily 'good'), but possesses a flaw which means that their downfall is inevitable. External factors are significant, but nothing like as significant as a conflicted individual moral psychology which brings about the opposite of what the character intends. According to Bradley, Hamlet's moral nature (**p.87**) is fragile, and the shock of his mother's re-marriage causes him to subside into melancholy. Othello's flaw is jealousy (**p.94**). When his lieutenant Iago falsely informs him that his wife Desdemona is having an affair:

> such jealousy as Othello's converts human nature into chaos, and liberates the beast in man.
>
> *A.C. Bradley 1904: 169*

Othello murders his wife and commits suicide. Bradley's view of Othello's character is also inflected by the 'scientific' racism propounded by many in the era in which he wrote.

TRAGEDY FOR THE 20TH CENTURY AND BEYOND

The tragedy of the common man

In the 20th century the protagonist came to be any man or woman. Partly this was a political assertion of the rights of the individual, particularly for American dramatists.

> It is time, I think, that we who are without kings, took up this bright thread of our history and followed it to the only place it can possibly lead in our time – the heart and spirit of the average man.
>
> *Arthur Miller: 'Tragedy and the Common Man', New York Times 1949*

But the tragic protagonist in contemporary drama does not quite seem to be anybody. A residue of Romanticism insists that the tragic protagonist must be someone who is prepared to devote themselves to some idea or notion, which may range from a political or economic belief to the simple need for utter personal integrity in a world which demands compromises. In the case of the former, the political and economic belief may be wrong, and this is the source of the tragedy. In the case of Arthur Miller's Willy Loman in *Death of a Salesman* (**p.215**), it is Loman's dedication to American capitalism that leads to his destruction: he fails to see that men themselves become products with market value, and that once he can no longer behave convincingly as a salesman he too will be discarded as unsaleable stock.

Alternatively the dramatist can present the protagonist as fundamentally good, but doomed in attempting to be virtuous in a world where selfishness is what society values. One such example is Isobel, the protagonist of David Hare's *The Secret Rapture* (**p.225**).

In both cases, however, there is a refusal of the protagonist to surrender: rather than compromise their sense of who they are, they choose death or destruction. While we, the audience, may recognise the futility of this uncompromising and fatal view of life, the plays encourage us also to admire the man (or woman) who takes to its logical extreme the right to assert an individual belief in the face of an uncomprehending or unsympathetic society.

> The commonest of men may take on … stature to the extent of his willingness to throw all he has into the contest, the battle to secure his rightful place in the world.
>
> *Arthur Miller: 'Tragedy and the Common Man', New York Times 1949*

It could be argued of classical and early modern tragedy that the nobility of the protagonist increases the tragic impact, since their fall, as a ruler or aristocrat, greatly affects the society around them. But in modern tragedy the protagonist's very ordinariness may also make him or her able to stand for a wider class of people, and their political views: women, the working class, and other racial groups who have struggled for emancipation during the 20th century. Marlene and her sister Joyce in Caryl Churchill's *Top Girls* (1982; **p.227**) come to stand for the different political and personal choices faced by women in Britain in the 1980s. Donal Davoren, the protagonist of Sean O'Casey's *The Shadow of a Gunman* (1923; **p.169**), dramatises the self-mythologising of Irish nationalism. Davoren, an impecunious poet, is happy to be seen as an IRA gunman in order to impress a young woman in his tenement house, but his deception leads to the shooting of the impressionable Minnie Powell by the British army. This gives Davoren's romantic self-promotion a bitterly ironic edge:

> To the people the end of life is the life created for them; to the poet the
> end of life is the life that he creates for himself; life has a stifling grip upon
> the people's throat – it is the poet's musician.
>
> *Sean O'Casey 1923: 107*

The 20th-century protagonist is devoted to the fulfilment of his or her own personal ideal or the following of his or her own beliefs. The cost of that fulfilment upon themselves and society is often at the heart of the tragedy.

THE SCOPE OF TRAGIC ACTION

CLASSICAL TRAGEDY

The unities

For Aristotle, writing in 330 BC, a century after the flourishing of Greek tragedy, the action of a tragedy must be self-contained, with a beginning, a middle and an end. It is in fact:

> the representation of an action that is worth serious attention, complete in itself, and of some amplitude.

> *Aristotle 330 BC: 38-9*

The action of all Greek tragedies takes place in a single day (the **unity of time**). Aristotle insisted that all the events of the plays should also be part of a single plot line, with only what is essential presented (the **unity of action**). The play's action should also be located in a single place (the **unity of place**). For Roman tragedians such as Seneca, and for those early modern tragedians who followed classical models such as Ben Jonson and the French playwright Jean Racine, the unities were a benchmark of genuine tragedy.

The unities work to provide an intensity of experience by concentrating the emotional impact of the tragedy into a tight space. Characters do not have their experience of suffering broken by sleep; the audience do not have their response distracted by a sub-plot. Nor are they invited to make intellectual connections between temporally episodic scenes. The limits imposed by the unities concentrate emotional reaction and encourage us to think about that emotional response. In Aristotle's opinion, this intensity of audience reaction is what tragedy is about. Aristotle's opinion has been influential, but should not necessarily be taken as what Greek tragedians themselves aimed at. They were certainly also concerned with deliberately provoking moral, religious and political reflections (p.38-40). Aristotle wrote of tragedy's production of 'pity' and 'fear' in the audience (p.25), without necessarily involving any reflection upon the social and religious context of those emotions. The tragedians seem also to be concerned with producing reflection upon the underlying principles of those contexts, or perhaps with political ideas both conservative and radical in nature.

EARLY MODERN TRAGEDY

The unities and tragic action

Early modern English tragedians wilfully broke from the unities and also chose to present a much wider view of the world, demonstrating how social and political forces also work to produce tragedy, and asking their audience to work at making connections between scenes and events. In Shakespeare's *King Lear* (**p.103**) the sub-plot involving Gloucester's sons echoes and comments upon the story of Lear and his daughters. The play's very structure asks the audience to make thematic and moral contrasts. *King Lear* also shows the ordinary British people involved in the tragedy, from Cornwall's servant who dies heroically protesting against the blinding of Gloucester (3.7.76-87) to the old man who helps him after he is turned out of his own home (4.1.1-57). Not only emotional intensity, but moral and political reflection are deliberately sought out here.

IDEALIST TRAGEDY

Beyond the real, material world

In the early 20th century literary criticism drew on the ideas of the philosophers G.W.F. Hegel and Karl Marx. Hegel's influence is particularly clear in the literary criticism of the Shakespearean scholar A.C. Bradley.

What was Hegel's philosophy? Hegel argued that the universe is rational, working according to principles which are beyond the control of man. Although Hegel didn't believe in God, he did believe in a reality beyond the material world. According to Hegel, society progresses because opposing forces in the universe (which he termed thesis and antithesis) come together to form a new and better synthesis. Karl Marx later labelled Hegel's philosophy **idealist** because it looks beyond the real, material world in which we live.

In what ways did Bradley draw on Hegel's ideas? For Bradley the conflict between opposing forces becomes centred in the personality of the tragic protagonist. While the tragedy is confined to one individual, it also points to – or represents – a greater, but mysterious struggle beyond the understanding of man:

> 'What a piece of work is man,' we cry; 'so much more beautiful and so much more terrible than we knew! Why should he be so if this beauty and greatness only tortures itself and throws itself away?' We seem to have before us a type of the mystery of the whole world, the tragic fact which extends far beyond the limits of tragedy.
>
> *A.C. Bradley 1904: 38*

In this Bradley challenges Aristotle's 'rule' that tragedy should be formed from a single, self-contained episode.

MATERIALIST TRAGEDY

Man-made tragedy in the here and now

Marx applied Hegel's ideas to historical events which are totally explicable in the material 'real' world (rather than in a religious, spiritual or ideal realm) and so this philosophical approach is called **materialism**. Materialist philosophers argue that history is a process which can be explained by man's actions, and not, as Hegel and Bradley thought, by reference to an otherworldly or mysterious force. In Britain the critic who put Marxism most powerfully to use in explaining tragedy was Raymond Williams.

For Williams, talk of cosmic good and evil, as evident in Bradley's literary criticism, was a way of avoiding the truth that human suffering is caused by the avoidable actions of other humans. Williams' interest in the scope of tragic action was motivated by his belief in the material causes of events, and his refusal to explain suffering as a result of individual psychology or mysticism. Violence is not necessarily part of human nature but what people turn to in the particular circumstances in which they have to live. If we are to understand where tragic suffering comes from, and what drives people to the acts of cruelty and violence central to tragic drama, literary criticism must take account of the *whole* social and economic background depicted in the text.

According to this view, tragic criticism which places responsibility for events on 'fate' or 'the human condition', and does not show them to be the result of human agency, is blind and 'bankrupt', and written in the interests of those who have power now. Williams believed that to understand tragedy is to understand how we live our lives today. Those who deny the relevance of tragedy to life deceive themselves and those they address when they claim that:

> modern tragedy can be discussed without reference to the deep social crisis, of war and revolution, through which we have all been living. That kind of interest is commonly relegated to politics or ... sociology. Tragedy, we say, belongs to a deeper and closer experience, to man not society. [According to these critics] even the general disorders, which can hardly escape the most limited attention, which equally can hardly be said to involve only societies and not men, can be reduced to symptoms of the only kind of disorder we are prepared to recognise: the fault in the soul.
>
> *Raymond Williams 1979: 62*

In this view, modern tragedy comes from the fact that human suffering is caused by ordinary men and women, and can only be ended by our taking action against these men and women. The scope of tragedy lies in our common humanity, as real people who live and die in history, 'in the world which we prove real by dying in it', as another socialist writer, Edward Bond (1983: lxvi; **p.230**), puts it.

THE END OF A TRAGEDY

Catastrophe and catharsis

Catastrophe in Greek means a turning upside down. Since Aristotle's influential writing on tragedy, it has come to mean the conclusion of a tragedy.

The strange mixture of pleasure and sadness which the audience feel at the end of a tragedy is a distinctive feature of the art form. It is a complex experience which encourages us to reflect upon our response, and to think not only about our emotions but about wider moral, religious, philosophical and political matters.

The audience response

Central to Aristotle's discussion of tragedy is the response of the audience, as is evident from this frequently quoted and much debated extract from *The Poetics*:

> Tragedy, then, is a representation of an action that is worth serious attention, complete in itself, and of some amplitude ... presented in the form of action, not narration; by means of pity and fear bringing about the purgation of such emotions.

> *Aristotle c.330 BC: 38-9*

It seems reasonably clear that 'pity' refers to the sympathy we feel for the protagonist and others who are suffering on the stage. 'Fear' has been taken to mean a recognition that just such a disaster might also happen to us or those closest to us (Wallace 2007: 120). In the context of Greek tragedy, it has been argued that the fear the audience is encouraged to feel at the end of a tragedy is a response to seeing the power of the gods, or fate enacted on stage.

Catharsis and critical debate

For A.C. Bradley, writing about Shakespeare's tragedies in 1904 the complexity of our feelings at the end of tragedy is an insight into the nature of the universe itself. The death of the protagonist causes us sorrow, and a recognition of a sense of injustice. And yet, at the same time, we are aware of a greater sense of justice at work, as the universe strives to become a better place. Hamlet and Othello die, but they take with them the murderous usurper Claudius and the devilish deceiver Iago. Others (Polonius, Ophelia, Gertrude, Emilia) die too, and there is a great sense of waste. According to this view, despite the violence and sense of waste, we are uplifted by an inexplicable feeling that what happened was right and necessary. This is the experience of catharsis:

> Sometimes we are driven to cry out that these mighty or heavenly spirits who perish are too great for the little space in which they move, and

that they vanish not into nothingness but freedom. Sometimes from these sources and from others comes a presentiment, formless but haunting and even profound, that all the fury of conflict, with its waste and woe, is less than half the truth, even an illusion, 'such stuff as dreams are made on'. But these faint and scattered intimations that the tragic world, being but a fragment of the whole beyond our vision, must needs be a contradiction and no ultimate truth, avail nothing to interpret the mystery. We remain confronted with the inexplicable fact, or the no less inexplicable appearance, of a world travailing for perfection, but bringing to birth, together with glorious good, an evil which is able to overcome only by self-torture and self-waste. And this fact or appearance is tragedy.

A.C. Bradley 1904: 51

Bradley's ideas are Hegelian (**p.23**), but they are also Christian: for Christians, God became man and suffered on the cross in order to free man from original sin. The tragic mystery is the divine mystery, and is part of a world view that sees human progress as inevitable.

What is meant by catharsis?

Much critical debate has centred on Aristotle's use of the Greek word **catharsis** (which can be translated as purgation). By this term Aristotle could mean that tragedy allows us to experience these negative emotions vicariously, and thus we leave the theatre having expelled them:

the tragedy, having aroused powerful feelings in the spectator, has a therapeutic effect; after the storm and climax there comes a release from tension, of calm.

J.A. Cuddon 1976: 106

The audience's second-hand experience of suffering and death means that it remains unpolluted by such things, a notion which was important to ancient Greek society where contact with death would require ritual cleansing (Wiles 2000: 43). This interpretation of catharsis, however, makes tragedy an unreflective experience and a soothing, not a disturbing one, which forces the audience to 'confront feelings which typically have no solution' (Easterling 1997: 171). This politically neutral response is at odds with what we know about the status and role of tragedy in Greek society: for the ancient Greeks tragedy was always a politically engaged art form, as is suggested by the following extract from Euripides' *Women of Troy*. When, at the end of the play, having seen her family slaughtered in front of her, Queen Hecuba is dragged away from the burning ruins of Troy to be a slave in Greece, hard questions are asked about human cruelty and whether the gods have any care for mortals:

OEDIPUS   What more must I bear?

My country, my city burned.

Up, feet. Old woman, run.

Your city's dying.

Cherish it, say goodbye.

Troy! You breathed the breath of power, you ruled all Asia,

Now they steal your name away.

They burn you. They drag us,

Exiles, slaves. Oh gods!

Why call on the gods –

Did they hear when we called before?

Into the fire. Die now,

Die here in Troy.

Euripides: Women of Troy 415 BC: 6

Catharsis – an alternative view

Neo-classical critics (**p.62**) in the late 18th and 19th centuries, including the poet John Milton, took Aristotle to mean that our emotional faculties are 'cleaned up', refreshed, allowing us to leave the theatre better able to judge what is worthy of profound emotion and what is not. Tragedy teaches us to have some scale of proportion in our responses to the world, and to exercise properly a crucial part of our human state. The Marxist critic Terry Eagleton dismisses this interpretation of **catharsis**, since it makes tragedy something which seeks to control us, something sinister in the Athenian context of state-sponsored drama. In his book *Sweet Violence* Eagleton suggests that this reading of Aristotle makes tragedy:

> a kind of public therapy for those in the citizenry in danger of emotional flabbiness … tragedy hardens us against fear, as we grow accustomed to seeing those more eminent than ourselves coming to grief, as well as disciplining us to spare our pity for those who most deserve it … Tragedy is thus an instrument for regulating social feeling … a refuse dump for socially undesirable emotions, or at least a retraining programme.
>
> *Terry Eagleton 2003: 153-4*

Materialist critics such as Raymond Williams offer a further alternative interpretation of catharsis which presents the tragic drama as a far more radical, politically engaged art form. Williams reads Aristotle's 'pity' and 'terror' to be the condition in which we live now, in a world of suffering and injustice created not by God or fate but by human action – and which therefore is not inevitable. It is our tragedy – in the everyday sense – that the revolutionary activity required to end suffering involves more suffering for everyone concerned. The tragic sense:

is born in pity and terror: in the perception of a radical disorder in which the humanity of some men is denied and by the fact that the idea of humanity itself is denied. It is born in the actual suffering of real men thus exposed, and in the consequences of this suffering: degeneration, brutalisation, fear, hatred, envy. It is born in an experience of evil made more intolerable by the conviction that it is not inevitable, but the result of particular actions and choices.

And if it is tragic in its origins … it is equally tragic in its action, in that it is not against gods or inanimate things that its impulse struggles, nor against mere institutions or social forms, but against other men.

Raymond Williams 1979: 77

In the struggle to end injustice and suffering we acknowledge other people as human like us and so discover both our reason for struggling and our human sympathy for those whom we oppose. The tragic sense is not then mysterious, but rather a recognition that the suffering in the world is caused by humans, and can only be addressed by humans, and only through further human suffering.

Tragedy and the absurd – the influence of Nietzsche

But what if the ending of a tragedy reveals nothing more than the complete meaninglessness of life and human endeavour? That the universe is a hostile place and that our attempts to find purpose in human suffering are self-delusions?

The origins of such a view might be traced back to the German philosopher Friedrich Nietzsche (1844-1900). In his book *The End of Tragedy*, Nietzsche proposed that the pleasure we get from Greek tragedy comes from the breaking down of the rational, ordered front we put on the world – what he called the Apollonian, after the Greek god of art and culture. What is revealed in the **catastrophe** is the destruction of the rational individual and subsequent loss of self in what he called the Dionysiac, after Dionysus, the Greek god of ecstasy and theatre. Tragedy reveals the absurd horror of human existence. The only thing that gives delight is the art itself. Only creativity has value because it is this which gives shape to our understanding of the world.

In the 20th century the work of **absurdist** dramatists such as Samuel Beckett might be seen to owe something to such a view of the world. In the face of the horrors and alienation of the 20th century, Beckett's protagonists, such as Vladimir and Estragon in *Waiting for Godot* (1955; **p.180**) struggle to make any sense of their crazy, unexplained existence. Life is presented as purely theatrical, a brief show for an audience with no reality beyond the words and gestures of the performance. Art itself is the only meaning available to us. In *Waiting for Godot* the two tramp-like protagonists, Vladimir and Estragon, wait for Godot to arrive, on a bleak stage empty but for a tree. To pass the time they perform blackly comic routines which recall the comedy double acts of the music-hall (the popular theatrical variety entertainment of the late 19th and early 20th centuries). Godot (salvation? meaningfulness?) never arrives, but Vladimir and Estragon encounter the absurdity and cruelty of power in the form of Pozzo and his slave Lucky.

Beckett's hopeless and futile universe has been read as a denial of tragedy, but also as genuine tragedy in as much as it also presents the reality of human sympathy even in the most degraded modes of existence. In the interval between the play's two acts the apparently dead tree has sprouted some leaves. Even at the end of *Waiting for Godot*, Vladimir and Estragon still have hope that Godot will come and save them. Vladimir still looks for something unexpected, and cares for his friend's appearance:

> VLADIMIR   We'll hang ourselves tomorrow. (*Pause.*) Unless Godot comes.
>
> ESTRAGON   And if he comes?
>
> VLADIMIR   We'll be saved.
>
> *Vladimir takes off his hat (Lucky's), peers inside it, feels about inside it, shakes it, knocks on the crown, puts it on again.*
>
> ESTRAGON   Well? Shall we go?
>
> VLADIMIR   Pull on your trousers.
>
> ESTRAGON   What?
>
> VLADIMIR   Pull on your trousers.
>
> ESTRAGON   You want me to pull off my trousers?
>
> VLADIMIR   Pull ON your trousers.
>
> ESTRAGON   (*realizing his trousers are down*). True. *He pulls up his trousers.*

Samuel Beckett 1955: 88

At the turn of the 21st century, many people doubt whether common sympathy is enough to generate hope of human progress, as Bradley and Williams felt. But some notion of hope seems central to what we understand by the idea of the tragic catastrophe.

A TRAGEDY

TIMELINE

	BC	LITERATURE	SOCIAL, POLITICAL, CULTURAL CONTEXT
GREEK	533?		City Dionysia dramatic festival founded.
	458	Aeschylus: *Oresteia*	
	441?	Sophocles: *Antigone*	
	429?	Sophocles: *Oedipus Rex*	
	428	Euripides: *Hippolytus*	
	415	Euripides: *Women of Troy*	
	330	Aristotle: *The Poetics*	
	AD		
ROMAN	1		Birth of Christ.
	45?	Seneca: *Thyestes*	
MIDDLE AGES	1400	Chaucer: *The Monk's Tale*	
EARLY MODERN	1543		Copernicus's theory that the sun, not the earth, is at the centre of the universe.
	1561	Norton and Sackville: *Gorboduc*	
	1576		First theatre opens in London.
	1581	Sidney: *The Defense of Poesy*	
	1588	Kyd: *The Spanish Tragedy* Marlowe: *Dr Faustus*	Spanish Armada defeated.
	1591	Shakespeare: *Titus Andronicus*	
	1592	Marlowe: *Edward II*	
	1595	Shakespeare: *Richard II*	

EARLY MODERN	1597	Shakespeare: *The Merchant of Venice*	
	1601	Shakespeare: *Hamlet*	Essex rebellion.
	1603		Death of Elizabeth I. Accession of James I.
	1604	Shakespeare: *Othello*	
	1605	Shakespeare: *King Lear*	Gunpowder Plot.
	1606	Shakespeare: *Macbeth* Middleton: *The Revenger's Tragedy*	
	1607	Shakespeare: *Antony and Cleopatra*	
	1611	Jonson: *Catiline*	
	1612	Webster: *The White Devil*	
	1614	Webster: *The Duchess of Malfi*	
	1622	Middleton and Rowley: *The Changeling*	
	1623	Middleton: *Women Beware Women*	
	1625		Death of James I; accession of Charles I.
	1630?	Ford: *'Tis Pity She's A Whore*	
CIVIL WAR & RESTORATION	1642		Civil War begins. Closure of theatres.
	1649		Execution of Charles I.
	1660		Restoration of monarchy. Theatres re-opened.
	1677	Racine: *Phèdre*	
	1682	Otway: *Venice Preserved*	

ROMANTIC	1776		US Declaration of Independence.
	1789		French Revolution begins.
	1815		Defeat and final exile of Napoleon.
	1832	Goethe: *Faust*	
VICTORIAN	1837		Queen Victoria's accession.
	1867	Ibsen: *Peer Gynt*	
	1872	Nietzsche: *The Birth of Tragedy*	
	1879	Ibsen: *A Doll's House*	
	1890	Ibsen: *Hedda Gabler*	
	1895	Chekhov: *The Seagull*	
	1901	Chekhov: *Three Sisters*	Queen Victoria dies.
EDWARDIAN	1904	Bradley: *Shakespearean Tragedy* Chekhov: *The Cherry Orchard* Synge: *Riders to the Sea*	
	1908		Einstein's Theory of Special and General Relativity.
	1907	Synge: *Playboy of the Western World*	
WORLD WAR 1	1914		World War 1 begins.
	1916		Easter Rising in Ireland.
	1917		Communist revolution in Russia.
	1918		World War 1 ends.
INTERWAR	1919		18th Amendment bans alcohol in the US (Prohibition).
	1922		Irish Free State established.
	1923	O'Casey: *The Shadow of a Gunman*	
	1929		Wall Street Crash; Great Depression.

WORLD WAR 2	1939		World War 2 begins in Europe.
	1941	Brecht: *Mother Courage* O'Neill: *Long Day's Journey into Night*	German invasion of USSR. Japanese attack on Pearl Harbor
	1944	T. Williams: *The Glass Menagerie*	
	1945		WW2 ends with use of atomic weapon. Discovery of the concentration camps. Labour government elected in UK.
POST-WAR	1947	Miller: *All My Sons* T. Williams: *A Streetcar Named Desire*	
	1949	Miller: *Death of a Salesman*	
	1953	Miller: *The Crucible*	
	1955	Beckett: *Waiting for Godot* Miller: *A View From the Bridge* T. Williams: *Cat on a Hot Tin Roof*	Civil Rights movement in USA.
	1956		Suez Crisis.
	1958	Pinter: *The Birthday Party*	
	1960		Vietnam War begins.
	1962	Albee: *Who's Afraid of Virginia Woolf?*	Cuban Missile Crisis. Commonwealth Immigration Act.
	1963		Assassination of John F. Kennedy.
	1964		Harold Wilson elected Labour PM.
	1965	Bond: *Saved*	Capital punishment abolished in UK.
	1966	R. Williams: *Modern Tragedy*	
	1968		Abolition of stage censorship in the UK. Political unrest in France, Czechoslovakia and the USA.
	1970		Edward Heath elected Conservative PM.
	1971	Bond: *Lear*	
	1972		'Bloody Sunday'.

	1973	Bond: *Bingo*	Industrial unrest. '3 day week'. Oil crisis.
	1975		Vietnam War ends.
	1978	Hare: *Plenty* Shepard: *Buried Child*	
	1979		Margaret Thatcher becomes PM.
	1980	Friel: *Translations* Shepard: *True West*	
	1981		AIDS first recognised.
	1982	Churchill: *Top Girls*	Falklands War.
	1984		Miners strike begins. Ronald Reagan elected US President.
	1986		Chernobyl nuclear reactor accident.
	1988	Hare: *The Secret Rapture*	
	1989		Berlin Wall comes down.
	1990	Friel: *Dancing at Lughnasa*	Margaret Thatcher resigns. Germany reunited. Apartheid ends in South Africa.
	1991	Kushner: *Angels in America*	Collapse of the Soviet Union.
	1995	Hare: *Skylight*	
	1997		Tony Blair elected New Labour PM. Death of Princess Diana.
	1998		Good Friday Agreement brings an end to the Irish 'troubles'.
21ST CENTURY	2003	Eagleton: *Sweet Violence*	2nd Iraq War begins.
	2008		Barack Obama elected US President.

GREEK

TRAGEDY

OVERVIEW

The origins of tragedy as an art form lie in the performance of songs in praise of the god Dionysus in pre-classical Greece. Dionysus was the god of wine and theatre, the god of ecstasy or leaving behind one's normal identity, and the god of festivity and joy.

The 'classical' period in Greek culture was, roughly, the 5th and 4th centuries BC. During this period there were three great dramatists whose work has survived: Aeschylus, Sophocles and Euripides.

Festival performance

In democratic Athens tragedies were performed at festivals, principally that of Dionysus which took place in the spring each year. Attending the theatre was a civic duty for the citizens of Athens, because it was the place where issues of politics, morality and religion were presented; where conflicts were brought to the surface and where the audience, sitting in the political divisions in which they voted in the democratic assembly, were asked to respond.

Up to 16,000 citizens attended the festival, with the state paying the entry fee for those too poor to afford what was the equivalent of a day's wages for a manual labourer.

While all citizens were expected to attend, it is important to realise that citizenship was limited to free men (i.e. women, like slaves, did not enjoy the rights of citizenship), and there is no conclusive evidence that women were ever present.

The festival of the Great Dionysia normally lasted four days. Comedies were performed on the first day. On each of the next three days three tragedies were performed, by a different writer each day, followed by a **satyr play**, a short comic drama featuring the antics of a chorus of half-man half-goat figures sporting large erect phalluses. A jury of citizens selected by ballot decided which playwright should take the prize for that year. The prize was not financial, but glory for the playwright and actors – and prestige for the rich citizen who had paid for the winning playwright's production that year.

Actors and chorus

Greek tragedies were performed by three actors and a **chorus**, dressed in light and realistic-looking masks which covered the whole head, and brightly coloured 'Asiatic' looking costumes.

The three actors who played all the roles were professionals. The twelve or fifteen young men who danced the choruses were amateurs.

For the ancient Greek audience the chorus was the central part of the experience. Though the beauty of the singing and dancing was important in itself, the chorus had another more vital function. In the drama, the chorus is a body of people who watch the action unfold, offering comments to the characters and giving the audience its reflections on the action, from different perspectives. The chorus represents the voice of conventional common sense: elders of the city, for example. Its job is not to tell the story of the play, but to offer comments on it.

> The guidance offered by a tragic chorus may be quite elusive. The fact that a tragic chorus is a group of twelve to fifteen people and not a single figure gives its behaviour more scope to fluctuate with fluctuating circumstances: it does not have to be as consistent as a single individual, and it speaks of itself in the plural just as freely as the singular. Its job is to help the audience become involved in the process of responding, which may be a matter of dealing with profoundly contradictory issues and impulses.
>
> Often, indeed, the chorus combines witnessing with trying to understand, and its guidance is intellectual or even philosophical as well as emotional.
>
> *Pat Easterling 1997: 163-4*

Content

All but one of the extant (or surviving) Greek tragedies are set in the pre-democratic, epic past and deal with the lives of mythological heroes and gods. The exception is Aeschylus' *Persians*. Very few are set in Athens itself, but usually in foreign cities. The myths of the Trojan War and the story of Thebes form the basis of the stories, but the dramatists often adapt and re-characterise these narratives according to their own purposes.

> The heart of tragedy is ... disturbing, and affects its audience, ancient and modern, in a ... wrenching way ... The emotional and intellectual power of tragedy stems from the very difficulty of its examples. The figures of tragedy are not black-and-white villains and heroes, but complex characters locked into double binds of doubt and compulsion, wilfulness and loss ... Tragedy leads to self-questioning through the pain of others.
>
> This questioning has a powerful and disturbing effect on the inherited traditional tales of the city – the myths by which the world is navigated ... Tragedy depicts the hero not as a shining example for men to follow, but as a difficult, self-obsessed and dangerous figure for whom transcendence is only bought at the cost of transgression. The Greeks, as ever, had a word for it: *es meson*, which means 'put into the public domain to be contested'. Democracy prides itself on its openness to questioning. Tragedy is the institution which stages this openness in the most startling fashion.
>
> *Simon Goldhill 2004: 229*

Form

There are two types of writing found in all classical tragedies: the **choral ode** and the **episode**. They alternate. The choral ode is a song which is sung and danced by the chorus. The episode is a scene of dialogue between the characters in the play. Odes and episodes are written in different poetic metres. The episodes are usually in iambics. All tragedies follow the same structure as described here.

1. The prologos. An episode in which the action of the play is introduced. Three actors play all the roles in the drama, so there can never be more than three speaking characters in an episode, though there may also be 'mutes' who do not speak.

2. The parodos. A marching song sung by the chorus as they enter the 'orchestra', the circular dance floor in the middle of the tiered seating for the spectators. The chorus now remains on stage as observers and participants until the end of the play.

3. The first episode.

4. The first stasimon. A stasimon is a choral ode sung by the chorus when not leaving or arriving on stage. Episode and stasimon alternate.

5. The second episode.

6. The second stasimon.

7. The third episode.

8. The third stasimon.

9. The fourth episode.

10. The fourth stasimon.

11. The fifth episode – the **catastrophe** – when the action comes to a disastrous conclusion. A messenger arrives to describe the death or mutilation of the protagonist or another important character.

12. The exodos. A brief choral ode sung as the chorus leave the stage.

THE PLAYWRIGHTS

The plays of three Greek tragedians survive (often referred to as being extant). Writing between about 500 BC and 406 BC these playwrights dramatised the stories of the same families, offering different angles and perspectives on their fates.

AESCHYLUS (525-456 BC)

Aeschylus (seven plays extant) is the earliest tragedian whose work has survived. Most frequently performed today is his so-called *Oresteian Trilogy*, which tells the story of the murder of King Agamemnon on his return from the Trojan war by his wife Clytemnestra, and her subsequent murder by their son Orestes. The play raises challenging questions: if a man's sacred duty is to avenge his father's death, does this duty extend to matricide? Where should the cycle of revenge stop?

SOPHOCLES (496-406 BC)

Sophocles (seven plays extant) also wrote of the dilemma of Orestes in his powerful tragedy *Electra*, this time centring the tragedy on the daughter. He is best known today for his dramatisation of the myth of Oedipus (p.47) and for a play which dramatises the conflict between traditional religion and the power of the state, *Antigone* (p.43). Issues of loyalty and the limits of human suffering in warfare are explored in two of his Trojan plays, *Ajax* and *Philoctetes*. Sophocles' plays tend to suggest the importance of piety towards the powerful and inscrutable gods of Olympus.

EURIPIDES (484-406 BC)

Unlike Sophocles, Euripides (17, perhaps 18 extant) was famous for his scepticism about traditional belief. His gods are often selfish and destructive, as is Aphrodite in *Hippolytus* (p.52). The brutality and inhumanity of war is evident in his Trojan plays, especially *The Women of Troy* (p.55). Although some contemporaries thought his plays misogynist, his *Medea*, which tells of the savage revenge taken by a foreign princess when abandoned by her husband Jason, is today sometimes seen as a comment on the plight of women in a violent patriarchal society. In *The Bacchae* Euripides explores the power of ecstatic religion and the irrational. Euripides' later plays are often regarded as a form of tragicomedy since they conclude happily. In *Alcestis*, the wife of the eponymous king, sacrifices her life for her husband, but is rescued from Death by a drunken Hercules. Shakespeare's tragicomedy *The Winter's Tale* (1611) echoes this ending; both may be exploring the nature of theatrical fiction as well as, in Euripides' case, religious belief.

SOME KEY IDEAS TO CONSIDER

- The importance in Greek tragedy of the conflict between democracy and kingship.

- The role women play in the male-dominated world of the plays.

- How the plays examine and use persuasive language.

- How the plays work on stage as drama and spectacle.

- What the plays say about human suffering.

SOPHOCLES

OVERVIEW

Sophocles was the author of over 120 plays, of which seven survive. According to Aristotle, he claimed to portray people as they ought to be, whereas Euripides (p.53) depicted them as they are. Certainly, the surviving plays do not seem to contain the radical doubts and challenges of his younger contemporary.

Sophocles was the well-to-do son of an armour manufacturer. He was not politically active, but was twice elected as a general to lead part of the Athenian armed forces. He was also known to have been a priest. His plays tend to offer a conventional view of traditional religion. His long life corresponded with the height of Athens' power and prestige, but he survived to see the impending defeat of his city at the hands of the Spartans.

ANTIGONE (441? BC)

CREON   Take me away, I beg you, out of sight.

A rash, indiscriminate fool!

I murdered you, my son, against my will –

You too, my wife ...

Sophocles 441? BC: 127

SYNOPSIS

Oedipus's sons Polynices and Eteocles have killed each other in battle as Polynices was attempting to seize the city of Thebes from his brother. Thebes' new ruler, their uncle Creon, has decreed, against all religious custom, that the body of Polynices is not to be buried but left to the wild animals. Antigone is the dead brothers' sister. She takes it upon herself to bury Polynices, claiming that the will of the gods overrides the law of the city. She is arrested and sentenced to be walled up alive.

Creon's son Haemon, who is engaged to Antigone, attempts to persuade his father to pardon Antigone, especially as the people of Thebes are sympathetic to her. He is unsuccessful. After the blind prophet Tiresias has told Creon that the gods are angry with him, Creon is prompted by the chorus to rescind his decision. It is too late, however. A messenger reports to the chorus how Haemon found Antigone hanging in her prison and then killed himself. When Creon's wife Eurydice hears the news she too commits suicide, leaving Creon broken and despairing.

A polarised tragedy

Antigone remains one of the most performed and most controversial of all the surviving ancient plays. Critical opinion has often divided sharply between sympathy for Creon and sympathy for Antigone.

They both have claims to be regarded as the tragic protagonist. Creon is a firm leader who sees the necessity for national unity in the face of a crisis. He knows that without a strong state (*polis*), the individual household (*oikos*) with its rituals and traditions can be destroyed by the state's enemies:

> CREON   Remember this:
>
>   Our country is our safety.
>
>   Only while she voyages true on course
>
>   Can we establish friendships, truer than blood itself.

Sophocles 441? BC: 68

Equality before the law (*isonomia*) was the foundation of Athenian democracy. Despite his clear-headed leadership, Creon's judgement is faulty. In failing to reprieve Antigone not only does he fail to heed the will of the citizens, as expressed by his son Haemon and the chorus of Theban elders, he also fails to show respect to the gods.

Yet faced by a terrifying prophecy of his own fate he does relent, albeit too late to save his son and Antigone. The will of the gods is done and he is left distraught at the end. He has, however, realised his error and come to learn an important truth about excessive human pride (**hubris**) and its inevitable divine punishment. This **anagnorisis**, or moment of tragic recognition, gives a purpose to his suffering and conveys the idea that there is a divine justice at work in the universe, though this may at first be inscrutable to humans, and so a cause of human misery: it is only through suffering that we learn right conduct. This is, perhaps, a characteristically Sophoclean **catharsis**. The dramatist Aeschylus expressed this in the formula **pathe mathe**: through suffering comes understanding.

Antigone also has the noble qualities of the tragic protagonist. She shows great courage in defying Creon's edict against the burial of her brother, loyalty towards her family and both piety and duty towards the gods of the underworld until her very last lines in the play ('See what I suffer now/at the hands of what breed of men – all for reverence, my reverence of the gods!' [Sophocles, p.107]). But if the pious Antigone is the more tragic of the two, then the play would seem to be asking whether there really is any divine justice in the universe – a very challenging and radical question. This is the position of R.P. Winnington-Ingram:

If the play has been rightly interpreted, [Creon] is doubly found in opposition to the gods. He opposes the powers and rights of the dead ... and for this he is condemned, overtly by Tiresias and the Chorus. But he also opposes the force of a great power in the living world – the power of sexual passion. And it is characteristic that in each case he outrages human feeling and personal relationships: the feeling of a family for its dead, and the feeling of a lover for the beloved. He believes in gods, but identifies them with the interest of the state and, in the last analysis, the state with himself, his ambition and power ... [Antigone] upholds the ancient sanctities of the family and proves herself the better citizen thereby ... Yet if the gods avenge her, they do not save her. That a woman who, so far from breaking the divine law, had carried out a religious duty should die shamefully and under the imputation of impiety, if it justifies her indignant protest, might well cause poet and audience to reflect upon the kind of world in which such things happen.

R.P. Winnington-Ingram 1980: 147-9

The Homeric hero and the classical hero

One way of understanding the nature of the tragic predicament is to consider the position of the individual who is caught in the toils of historical change (for example, *Hamlet*, **p.87**, and *Othello*, **p.94**). Antigone's belief that the honour of the household and family have precedence over the claims of the city is a view characteristic of the heroes of Homer's great epics, the *Iliad* and *Odyssey*. The Greeks of Sophocles' time looked on these poems, which depict Greek society seven hundred years before, as core texts embodying the values and ideals of their civilisation. In Homer individual honour and loyalty to one's family and friendship group (*philia*) is primary: there is no expectation of loyalty to the tribe or city.

Yet by the 5th century BC, and especially in democratic Athens, citizenship had become the most treasured possession of a free Greek man. Loyalty to the state, rather than individual honour, was essential, especially in battle when citizens fought side by side in the tightly-packed phalanx. The ideal citizen, says Creon, will be:

staunch

in the storm of spears ... a loyal, unflinching comrade at your side

Sophocles 441? BC:94

In classical Athens, then, writes Simon Goldhill, there is an irreconcilable clash of values. The Homeric ideals to which Athenians subscribe, as represented in this play by Antigone, run into direct conflict with the duties of the citizen, as represented both by Creon (albeit that he is a king, not the voice of the citizen body), and Creon's sister Ismene who refuses to disobey the law:

> Antigone ... in her self-reliance behaves more like a Homeric hero. Moreover, the duty of care for the body of a dead relative is duty especially for female kin throughout the Greek world. ... [But] Antigone has to repress the fact that Polynices is an enemy of the city – and what the status of enemy implies in and for the city. Indeed Ismene, although she will come to admire her sister and claim a part in her deed, challenges Antigone's attitudes and plan from precisely such a different social perspective which includes a recognition of civic life and the dependent status of women. ... In the paradoxical tensions of this play where a brother can be an enemy, where the heroic past and contemporary world clash, the various attempts to find a univocal audience reaction or univocal reading seem merely to repeat one strand of the text.
>
> *Simon Goldhill 1986: 92*

There is not a single course of action that either Antigone or Creon could take which would not be ideologically contradictory in 5th-century Athens. Whatever they do, regardless of whether or not they do it for the right reason, will be wrong and likely to lead to disaster. They are therefore both tragic figures.

In this way the play radically challenges its audience, writes Goldhill:

> The possibility of the secure positioning of the individual within the conflicting claims of *polis* [city] and *oikos* [household] ideology is what this tragedy seems to put at risk. Antigone works through the logic of the conventional moralities of the terms to the point of destruction.
>
> *Simon Goldhill 1986: 105-6*

OEDIPUS REX (429? BC)

SYNOPSIS

Before the start of the play

Laius, the King of Thebes, learns from an oracle that he is fated to be killed by his son who, it is decreed, will go on to marry his own mother. Laius and his wife Jocasta decide to take action to avoid their fate, arranging to leave the baby Oedipus, with his feet bound together, on a mountainside outside Thebes. The shepherd who is given the task of abandoning the baby to starve decides to rescue it. Oedipus is taken by a messenger to the royal palace of Corinth where he grows up believing himself to be the son of the Corinthian king.

Years later, Oedipus is horrified to learn of an oracle which foretells he will murder his father and marry his mother. Desperate to avoid this fate, he leaves Corinth and the people he believes to be his parents.

On Oedipus's journey two significant events occur: he kills a man at a crossroads and solves the riddle of the Sphinx, so freeing the city of Thebes from its reign of terror. Oedipus is hailed as a hero by the people of Thebes and as a reward is given both the throne and the hand of Jocasta, the recently widowed queen. Oedipus is now King of Thebes and begins a wise and just rule of the city.

As the play opens

Once again Oedipus is desperately seeking to rescue the people of Thebes, this time from the plague which is decimating the city. His brother-in-law Creon reports from the oracle of Apollo that the plague will not end while the murderer of Laius remains in the city. Oedipus promises he will not rest until the murderer is found. Under pressure from Oedipus the prophet Tiresias reveals that Oedipus himself is the murderer. Oedipus at first refuses to believe this, maintaining that the accusation is part of a plot by Creon. However, when Oedipus mentions to Jocasta that he once killed a man outside Thebes, the possibility that the oracle is right is strengthened. Oedipus decides to send for the shepherd who is the only surviving witness to Laius's murder.

At this point a messenger arrives from Corinth with the news that the King and Queen are dead. Oedipus believes the prophecy is disproved and that he has escaped his fate. But the messenger recognises the shepherd. It is the very shepherd who rescued the baby Oedipus.

Realising the truth, Jocasta leaves the stage to hang herself. When Oedipus too understands that he has fulfilled the prophecy by killing his father and marrying his mother, he blinds himself, begging to be banished from the city. Creon takes power in Thebes, but will not let Oedipus leave the city until he receives guidance from the oracle of Apollo.

Although this play tells of an earlier episode in the story of the house of Oedipus, it was written after *Antigone* and should be regarded as a play in its own right.

Divine justice and the tragic hero

Sophocles' *Antigone* and the plays of Euripides (**p.51**) address a question central to Greek tragedy: is the universe indifferent to human suffering? The chorus in *Oedipus Rex* proclaims that in fact there are divine laws which will punish the tyrant and the unjust man; 'great laws', which 'tower above us, reared on high … within them lives a mighty god, the god does not grow old' (Sophocles 429? BC: 209). And indeed, if these laws are not seen to be executed, why should the chorus honour the gods; indeed, why should they dance in a tragedy in honour of Dionysus, god of wine and theatre: 'If all such violence goes with honour now/ why join the sacred dance?' (Sophocles, p.210).

Yet Oedipus is a man who does no wrong deliberately. He is a strong and resourceful leader, who has already saved the city once when he destroyed the Sphinx. Now he is straining every nerve to rid Thebes of the plague. The oracle has foretold that he will break two of the strongest taboos by killing his father and marrying his mother. He knows the prophecy and does everything he can to avoid its fulfilment. However, he cannot escape his fate, and must live with the knowledge of what he has done, and of the desperate future which awaits his children. How can a brave man who strives to be virtuous suffer so at the hands of the god Apollo? ('Apollo, friends, Apollo – /he ordained my agonies' [Sophocles, p.241]).

Some critics have attempted to explain this by imputing to Oedipus some crime which justifies divine retribution: his **hubris** in claiming he can answer his people's prayers (Sophocles, p.171); his angry dismissal of Tiresias (Sophocles, p.182) or his threats to torture the old shepherd to extract information from him (Sophocles, pp.229-30). But none of these are crimes proportionate to his punishment.

One answer might be that the play demonstrates that we live in a meaningless universe in which we cannot escape our fate. Such an answer would make the play similar to the later tragic vision of *Dr Faustus* (**p.67**) or *Waiting for Godot* (**p.28** and **p.180**), and such a response might well be part of the legacy of Greek tragedy. If the play is examined in its ancient context, however, perhaps the problem falls away. First of all, it was widely believed that divine foreknowledge of events did not constrain human action. The gods knew how Oedipus would choose to act, but it was still his free choice. Oedipus does indeed declare that it was Apollo who ordained his agonies, but in the next line he states:

> But the hand that struck my eyes was mine,
>
> Mine alone – no one else –
>
> I did it all myself.

> *Sophocles 441? BC: 241*

Furthermore, it has been argued that while pious Greeks in Sophocles' time did believe the gods were just, they also regarded their actions as incomprehensible to humans. E.R. Dodds writes that:

> Disbelief in divine justice as measured by human yardsticks can perfectly well be associated with deep religious feeling. 'Men', says [the philosopher] Heraclitus, 'find some things unjust, other things just; but in the eyes of God all things are beautiful and just'. I think that Sophocles would have agreed. For him, as for Heraclitus, there is an objective world-order which man must respect, but which he cannot hope fully to understand.
>
> *E.R. Dodds 1983: 187*

Oedipus's crimes strike so deeply against the norms of human behaviour, they are, in Greek terms, so 'polluting', that they cannot be overlooked or forgiven no matter how unintentional they are:

> Suppose a motorist runs down a man and kills him, I think he ought to feel that he has done a terrible thing, even if the accident is no fault of his: he has destroyed a human life, which nothing can restore. In the objective order it is acts that count, not intentions.
>
> *E.R. Dodds 1983: 183-4*

The function of tragedy here is to reveal a deeper moral truth than the forensic issue of culpability.

In an influential study which draws on the work of the Shakespeare critic A.C. Bradley (p.19), H.D.F. Kitto wrote that for Sophocles there is a rationality, a *logos* in the universe which 'shows itself ... as a balance, rhythm or pattern in human affairs' (Kitto 1966: 143). Intriguingly, for Kitto it was the elegance of the form of the play itself which suggests an intuitive harmony in the universe not apparent in the moral economy of the play itself. The injustice of Oedipus's fate might rankle, but the dramatic perfection of this play hints at some higher order, assuring us that there is an inscrutable justice in the universe. For mortals, an aesthetic harmony stands in for a sense of justice:

> The catharsis we are looking for is the ultimate illumination which shall turn a painful story into a profound and moving experience. ... The catharsis of plays like [*Oedipus Rex*] and *Macbeth* lies in the perfection of their form, which, by implication, represents the forces of righteousness and beneficence.
>
> *H.D.F. Kitto 1966: 142*

The tragic hero – the human desire to know at all costs

> OEDIPUS   And I'm at the edge of hearing horrors, yes, but I must hear!
>
> *Sophocles 441? BC: 230*

Oedipus Rex is perhaps the earliest expression in Western literature of the tragedy inherent in the human desire to know and to understand, and through the acquisition of knowledge to seek control over life. In recent years the triumph of science over our environment has led to great benefits for humanity but also to terrifying threats to our existence. Yet the refusal to want to know the truth about ourselves and our world would not be worthy of our capacities.

This paradox is at the heart of what makes Oedipus an archetypal tragic protagonist: his greatness lies in his honest searching after the truth at all costs, but it is that same honest searching that brings him down along with his whole family. In the play the paradox is expressed in the motif of blindness. When Oedipus has his sight, he is blind to the truth about himself. Only when he has lost his eyes does he see the truth of his condition. Dodds puts it like this:

> Certainly [*Oedipus Rex*] is a play about the blindness of man and the desperate insecurity of the human condition: in a sense every man must grope in the dark as Oedipus gropes, not knowing who he is or what he has to suffer; we all live in a world of appearance which hides from us who-knows-what dreadful reality. But surely [*Oedipus Rex*] is also a play about human greatness. Oedipus is great ... in virtue of his inner strength: strength to pursue the truth at whatever personal cost, and strength to endure it when found ... Oedipus is great because he accepts the responsibility for all his acts, including those which are objectively most horrible, though subjectively innocent ... Oedipus is a kind of symbol of the human intelligence which cannot rest until it has solved all the riddles – even the last riddle, to which the answer is that human happiness is built on an illusion.
>
> *E.R. Dodds 1983: 187*

SOME KEY IDEAS TO CONSIDER

- How the role of the unseen gods affects our response to Sophocles' tragedies.

- How the chorus operates to guide audience response in these plays.

- The notion of self-sacrifice in Sophocles' tragedies.

- The depiction of women and their role in the city as presented in these plays.

EURIPIDES

OVERVIEW

Euripides wrote over 80 plays, but fewer than twenty have survived into the modern world. In classical times his depiction of women in fiercely patriarchal Athens was controversial. Female characters are central to the two plays considered here. In *Hippolytus* sexuality is explored, and in *Women of Troy* the principal concern is the impact of war.

- Euripides was associated with a movement in the late 5th century BC sometimes known as the 'Greek Enlightenment'. Some philosophers and dramatists started to apply reason sceptically to conventional religious belief, and to the traditional moral and social conventions of Athens. Teachers of rhetoric known as sophists taught that all values are man-made, and not an integral part of human nature.

- For much of Euripides' career as a dramatist Athens was involved in a desperate struggle with the militaristic Spartans for dominance in Greece. Athens not only suffered terribly from plague before the final defeat in 404 BC, but, in an attempt to retain its dominance, the democratic city began carrying out atrocities. The year before *Women of Troy* was first performed the Athenians massacred all the men and enslaved all the women and children on the island of Melos because they wished to be neutral in the war, refusing to join the Athenian imperial 'alliance'.

HIPPOLYTUS (428 BC)

SYNOPSIS

When the play begins, Theseus, King of Athens, is staying for a year in the city of Trozen to purge his guilt for a murder. Aphrodite, the goddess of sexual love, opens the play by telling the audience that on this very day she will destroy Theseus' bastard son, Hippolytus. Hippolytus hates women and worships not Aphrodite, but Artemis, the virgin goddess of hunting. Aphrodite is offended and has made Theseus' wife Phaedra fall in love with Hippolytus. Ashamed at the dishonour of such an incestuous desire for her husband's son, Phaedra is not eating and is wasting away.

Phaedra's old nurse provokes her mistress into revealing the source of her distress. Unknown to the queen, the nurse tells Hippolytus of Phaedra's desire in the mistaken belief that he might become her lover and 'cure' her. Hippolytus is furious, but has sworn an oath not to reveal what the nurse has told him. The chorus too has sworn not to reveal what they know. In despair at what she takes to be her impending disgrace, Phaedra kills herself, leaving a suicide note accusing Hippolytus of rape. By incriminating him she hopes to ensure that her own sons will remain Theseus' heirs. Theseus finds her note and calls down a curse on Hippolytus, invoking the god Poseidon. Hippolytus is sent into exile by his father, but is killed, dragged along the ground, entangled in his chariot's reins after his horses are terrified by a monstrous bull sent by Poseidon, one of the gods and the father of Theseus. As Hippolytus lies dying, Artemis reveals the truth to the distraught Theseus. His son forgives him, and absolves him of blood-guilt for his death.

> **HIPPOLYTUS**   No god who uses the night to work her wonders
> finds favour with me.
>
> *Euripides 428 BC: 42*

Who is the tragic protagonist?

Hippolytus is a play in which all the main characters are potentially tragic according to Aristotle's definition: a man of high birth with **megalopsychia** or 'greatness of soul'. Hippolytus' single-minded devotion to Artemis, the 'purity' of his life and his capacity for forgiveness might make him appear noble although neither male chastity nor an unwillingness to take vengeance were regarded as manly or responsible attitudes in classical Athens. His **hamartia** or error of judgement is his refusal to break his oath of silence to the nurse. Phaedra is noble in her determination not to lose her honour and to protect her children's future, but she reveals her secret to the nurse and lies in her suicide note. Theseus is admirable and great-hearted in his love for his wife, but too quick to believe her and to curse his son without evidence. Critics have tended to take sides about who deserves sympathy as the tragic protagonist, but, as Sophie Mills explains, Hippolytus and Phaedra actually have much in common:

> Phaedra is excessively concerned with her reputation, whilst Hippolytus is obsessed with chastity and sense of his own rightness. Both are self-conscious and desire public affirmation of their goodness, but neither succeed, since their obsessions lead them to privilege appearance over reality, and their own narrow sphere of knowledge over broader considerations, thereby causing their own destruction ... Phaedra's feebleness [at her first entrance] is mirrored by Hippolytus' death scene, while there are frequent verbal echoes between the two.

Sophie Mills 2002: 101-20

Fate and the gods

Another dimension, the role of **fate** and the gods, affects the tragic potential of the protagonists. Aphrodite makes it clear in the play's opening speech that she has made Phaedra fall in love and that Hippolytus will not be able to escape his fate on this day. Poseidon allows his own son, Theseus, to use an infallible curse which he gave to him so that he can unwittingly destroy Hippolytus. Euripides' portrayal of the shallow, petty gods can make readers and audiences ask whether the play seeks to undermine orthodox piety. Furthermore, if no character can escape his or her fate, then they become automata, not genuinely human figures whose lives and deaths engage our tragic sympathy. Bernard Knox, however, points out that because the characters change their minds throughout the play we get a convincing idea of human freedom being apparently, but not actually, compatible with the divine purpose:

> As we watch the human beings of the drama, unconscious of the goddess's purpose, work out her will, we are struck by their apparent freedom ... the line of development of the characters' purposes is a zig-zag. Phaedra resolves to die without revealing her love, then makes a long speech about it to the chorus. The Nurse urges her to reveal it, regrets her action when she hears her mistress speak, and then returns to urge Phaedra on to further lengths of speech. And Hippolytus, when he learns of Phaedra's passion, first announces his intention to tell Theseus the truth and then changes his mind and keeps silent ... Phaedra chooses silence and then speech; the Nurse speech then silence, then speech, then silence; the chorus silence; and Theseus speech. The resultant pattern seems to represent an exhaustion of the possibilities of the human will ... And the context in which it is set demonstrates the non-existence of human free will, the futility of the moral choice.

Bernard Knox 1983: 312-3

Misreadings

A play in which characters frequently change their minds, in which the protagonists are more concerned with appearance than reality, has been read by Simon Goldhill as one which challenges its audience by making the normal sexual categories unstable:

> Hippolytus's rejection of sexuality is involved with his dislocation of [his] role in the *oikos* [Athenian household] … as his particular form of hunting-life seems to fit uneasily into the city's own model of its organisation. Phaedra, whose divinely inspired passion for her stepson stands to corrupt her role as chaste protector of the economic, sexual, spatial boundaries of the household unit, fights to maintain her values in the face of the dual onslaught of the attacks of Eros [sexual desire] on the one hand and the sophistic rhetoric of the nurse on the other … Each character distorts or is distorted by his or her relation to his or her sexual role.
>
> *Simon Goldhill 1986: 131*

Hippolytus is a disturbing play which does not allow its audience to settle into any easy judgements.

WOMEN OF TROY (415 BC)

SYNOPSIS

Troy has fallen after ten years of siege by the Greeks, as the sea-god Poseidon explains. The goddess Athena asks him to wreck the Greek fleet on its way home to punish the victors for the violation of her shrine: one of the Greek leaders, Ajax, snatched the prophetess Cassandra from an altar where she had sought sanctuary. Poseidon agrees to Athena's request.

Each episode of the play sees the surviving women of Troy's royal family suffer some new horror. First, Queen Hecuba sees her daughter Cassandra taken off to be the slave of the Greek commander Agamemnon. Cassandra raves about the future; she knows Agamemnon will be murdered when he returns home. Hecuba must next watch her baby grandson Astyanax taken from his mother's arms to be murdered: the Greeks will not let the son of their great adversary Hector live. In the next episode the baby's body is returned to his distraught mother Andromache.

Agamemnon's brother Menelaus now arrives to find his wife Helen, the woman whose abduction by the Trojan prince Paris began the conflict. He says he wishes to kill her in vengeance, and is encouraged in this resolution by Hecuba. But Helen, who says it was all the gods' doing, not hers, persuades her husband to spare her. The Greek herald, Talthybius, says that the women may bury Astyanax, but soon after they are all taken off to the Greek ships and into slavery. The remains of Troy are ordered to be flattened.

HECUBA	The gods planned this: my pain ...
	Why did they do this, uproot the world?
	To make a myth of us,
	Give poets a theme for plays?

Euripides 428 BC: 59

Tragic transcendence

Women of Troy is an unusual tragedy in that it does not seem to have what Aristotle called the **peripeteia**, the turning point when hopeful expectations are overturned (unless it is the grim hope that Helen will be killed by her husband Menelaus). Each scene deepens the desperate plight of the women, the only slight respite being the funeral rites they are allowed to perform for the slain baby Astyanax. Underlying the development of the narrative is the dramatic irony created by the play's prologue: the audience knows that Poseidon has agreed to the destruction of the Greek victors themselves once their fleet leaves the Trojan shores.

Hecuba, Queen of Troy, is the protagonist. She has seen her sons and husband killed, and now she watches her daughter taken off into slavery and her baby grandson slaughtered. Remarkably, however, Hecuba, in all her vengeful laments, acquires a profound tragic dignity. Even as she rages at the cruel gods, she surpasses them because she now cannot be hurt by them any more. The depths of her suffering, and all that she has endured, endow her with a mythical grandeur which will ensure that she is transfigured into a symbol of the suffering woman for future ages. She will not just be the 'theme' for this play, but also for *Hamlet* (2.2.443-59; 489-91, **p.87**) and Edward Bond's *The Woman* two thousand years later. According to D.J. Conacher, at the end of the play:

> As the smoke from the burning city rises in the background, we have reached the end of that rhythm which false and intermittent hopes has lent to the theme of suffering. Yet even here there is something more than mere desolation. It appears first in Hecuba's echo of that consolation suggested earlier by Cassandra: the recognition that, in a sense, Trojan greatness and future fame depend upon this utter ruin which the gods have sent. The stature which the ruined Hecuba acquires in these final scenes reminds us of the special kind of nobility which the ruined Oedipus possesses. ... This feeling for the nobility of an Oedipus, or a Hecuba, derives in part from the aura of superstitious awe with which the Greeks surround those necessarily great personages who have suffered the ultimate woe and yet endured. It derives in part, also, from the awareness which such strangely privileged beings have finally acquired of their real position in relation to the gods, or (in non-mythological terms) to the outside forces, merciless, because impersonal, which frame their destiny, and which can no longer hurt them more.

> *D.J. Conacher 1983: 339*

Timeless tragedy?

CHORUS   Ares the war-god

                   Bursts from that wooden womb,

                   Swaggers down every street ...

Euripides 428 BC: 28

It is sometimes thought that great works of art speak to all ages; that they sum up a truth about 'the human condition', which speaks to all times. *Women of Troy* has been very often performed in the last twenty years to express the suffering of women whose lives have been destroyed by the brutality of war today. We should, however, be cautious of making the arrogant assumption that other cultures and times were basically the same as ours. It may well have been the case, writes D. M. Carter, that Euripides wanted to express some outrage at Athenian conduct in the war with Sparta, and in particular the massacre at Melos (**p.51**). But this does not mean that the play's values are 'relevant' today:

> The first point is that the modern political doctrine of pacifism would have meant little to most ancient Greeks. Warfare was almost a fact of life in the ancient world; many or most Greek men would take part in armed conflict during the course of their lives ... In Homer's [epic poem the] *Iliad* the heroes can complain about the misery of war but also celebrate the glorious military deeds of themselves and others; the two views were quite compatible. (Similar views are expressed by Cassandra in *Trojan Women* [sometimes known as *Women of Troy*, Euripides, p.21]) ... The second, connected point is that the Greeks did not know the modern conventions of behaviour in war ... The idea of a war crime was unknown in the ancient world. On the other hand, there were rigorous standards of religious beliefs, to which warriors on both sides could be held ...
>
> The behaviour of the Greeks in *Trojan Women* would therefore have seemed shocking to an ancient audience, but not beyond the entitlement of victors. The only deed for which the Greeks will be punished is for a crime against the gods: the treatment of Cassandra by Ajax. The particular political tone of the drama is achieved by forcing the audience to see events almost entirely from the point of view of the conquered ... However, *Trojan Women* is not a drama of uninterrupted lamentation ... It is sometimes the very ordinariness of [the women's] manner, not withstanding their royal status and a Euripidean ability to argue and debate, that invites sympathy in the face of great suffering.
>
> *D.M. Carter 2007: 134-5*

The values of Greek tragedy may not be timeless, but they have been instrumental in shaping the values of European culture. 'Ordinariness' is not a heroic quality in the literature of classical Athens, but as the heirs of their democracy, it is a quality which may now belong to the tragic protagonists of our own time.

SOME KEY IDEAS TO CONSIDER

- To what extent Aristotle's ideas about the protagonist and catharsis apply in these plays of Euripides.

- Whether Euripides deserves his longstanding reputation as a misogynist.

- How the chorus operates to guide audience response in these plays.

ROMAN

TRAGEDY

SENECA AND HIS INFLUENCE

ROMAN TRAGEDY

Much of ancient Roman art and culture was developed in response to Greek models, and tragedy was no exception. The theatre in Rome did not play a central role in political and intellectual life as it had in democratic Athens. Rather, it was primarily a form of entertainment, with comedy being the dominant genre.

Tragedies based on Greek antecedents were performed. However, the writing of tragedies tended to take place as a literary exercise, not necessarily for production on stage, but for reading aloud to groups of friends. By the middle of the first century AD, when Seneca was writing, such tragedies as were performed tended to be opportunities for spectacle rather than drama.

Seneca, fate and bloodshed

Lucius Annaeus Seneca (c.4 BC to 65 AD) was a wealthy man who was a chief minister in the first part of the reign of the Emperor Nero. Seneca reworked the genre of Greek tragedy to produce plays which today seem static and lacking in dramatic tension, but often culminate in graphically described bloodshed.

A horrific incident is foretold at the play's opening. Characters doomed to tragic action struggle unsuccessfully to prevent their reason being overwhelmed by the desire to do evil. Towards the play's conclusion a messenger recounts a horrific catastrophe. In *Thyestes*, the eventual eating of his own sons by Thyestes is foretold both by the ghost of his grandfather Tantalus and by a Fury. Thyestes' vengeful brother Atreus murders his nephews and makes his unwitting brother eat his own children. The messenger in Act Four relates how Atreus:

> hacked the bodies
>
> Limb from limb – detached the outstretched arms
>
> Close to the shoulders – severed the ligaments
>
> That tie the elbow joints – stripped every part
>
> And roughly wrenched each separate bone away –
>
> All this he did himself; only the faces,
>
> And trusting suppliant hands, he left intact.
>
> And soon the meat is on the spits, the fat
>
> Drips over a slow fire ...

Seneca 45? AD: 79

In Act Five there is a characteristically ghoulish, heavy-handed moment at the climax of the tragedy as Atreus reveals to his brother what he has done. The earth shakes and the night darkens as the still ignorant Thyestes asks where his children are:

> What agitation in my stomach swells?
>
> What moves within me?

Atreus then suddenly displays their heads with the words:

> Embrace your children father! They are here
>
> Beside you.

Seneca 45? AD: 88-9

E.F. Watling writes that Seneca 'was not a constructor of tragic plots … he only recognises the power of evil to destroy good'. Furthermore, 'his tragedy is simply a disastrous event foretold and anticipated from the start, and pursued ruthlessly to its end. But nothing can be more horrifyingly final than the Senecan tragic climax' (Seneca, p.25). Jennifer Wallace observes that Seneca's plays:

> occur in a dark world, in which reason has departed and instinctual forces have been let loose … Everything is reduced to a nightmarish present, in which fate is predestined, the atrocity has already happened. The image of Thyestes feasting on his children, their body parts already in his stomach, figures precisely this hellish sense of enclosure, the literal absorption of past, present and future into the sickening compulsion of appetite

Jennifer Wallace 2007: 35

TRAGEDY AND STOICISM

ATREUS   **Am I a coward, sluggard, impotent**
And – what I count the worst of weaknesses
In a successful king – still unavenged?

Seneca 45? AD: 53

Seneca was also a philosopher who expounded the ideas of the Stoics. Stoicism, which had originated in Greece in the 4th century BC, taught that all history was predetermined, and was working itself out to a providential end which we cannot discern. Human beings are not in control of their fates, but they can learn to control their emotional response to events by realising that everything happens in accordance with nature. The wise person learns to be happy by not letting emotion overcome him or her, and instead applies reason to every situation.

As Jennifer Wallace suggests, Seneca's protagonists are figures who fail to control their ambitions and lusts, and thus stand as moral examples of how not to behave:

they 'abandon the lessons of philosophy' (Wallace 2006: 33). The drama is an internal struggle enacted in the minds of the characters and expressed in long set-piece speeches. Atreus knows he should not give in to vengeful desires, but cannot control himself. The outcome is tragic because reason loses the struggle. The Senecan **catharsis**, such as it is, combines horror with a clear philosophical message.

NEO-CLASSICAL TRAGEDY

France v England

Stoicism, with its emphasis on rationality and individualism, was also an influential philosophy in the Renaissance. Seneca's tragedies were taught in schools and universities. The Renaissance desire for elegance and decorum – the idea that every part of the work of art should be in keeping with the tone and style of the whole – found clear expression in his work. The **unities of time, place and action** are rigorously observed in Senecan tragedies. The belief that a play should depict the action of a single day, be set in one place and should only have one plot is found in Aristotle, but became an article of dogma for Renaissance literary theorists such as the Italian Ludovico Castelvetro (1505-71) who wrote a highly influential commentary on Aristotle's original text, *The Poetics*. Following Seneca's example, he decreed that there should be no comedy in tragedies, and that all the characters should be noble.

17th-century French tragedy adhered strictly to these rules, as can be seen in the work of Pierre Corneille (1606-84) and Jean Racine (1639-99). English tragedy never seriously adopted the framework of neo-classicism, and the London stage was consequently condemned in France as crude for its neglect of the teachings of the ancients. In 1747 the philosopher Voltaire described Shakespeare's *Hamlet* as 'a vulgar and barbarous drama, which would not be tolerated by the vilest population of France, or Italy' (cited in McEvoy 2006: 30). Even the most dedicated classicist among early modern English playwrights, Ben Jonson, did not feel constrained in practice by the unities when writing tragedy. His most neo-classical tragedy, the static and interminable *Catiline* (1611), flopped on stage. Jonson's other tragedy, the much under-rated *Sejanus* (1603), brilliantly reworks the conventions of classical tragedy to propound Jonson's own humanism, rather than follow the strictures of neo-classicism (see McEvoy 2008: 34-45).

Even after the restoration of the monarchy in 1660, when Charles II brought back many of the habits and tastes of the French court where he had been in exile during the Commonwealth, French influence was far from dominant. While it was true that in Restoration tragedy 'the princes of the English stage are stiff, noble figures' who would not, like Hamlet, 'trade quips and equivocations with a gravedigger' (Wheatley 2000: 70), there was nevertheless comedy intermixed with tragedy. One of the most successful and enduring tragedies of this period, Thomas Otway's *Venice Preserved* (1682), features an absurd scene where a Venetian senator impersonates a bull and a dog in front of his mistress (Otway, 3.1), and later seems to have some sort of fetishistic attachment to her foot (5.2.79-86).

SENECA AND ELIZABETHAN TRAGEDY

Seneca's influence in England was not particularly evident in the *form* of tragedies, but rather in their *content*. Tragedies written before the opening of the first, public commercial theatre in 1576 were performed by students at university or the Inns of Court. An example is Norton and Sackville's *Gorboduc* (1561), which preserves some of the reported bloodshed and grim movement towards general catastrophe typical of Senecan tragedy. The drama does, however, feature debate and argument rather than being dominated by internal agonising. The play's end is also impeccably Christian in its belief in God's Providence:

> yet must God in fine restore
>
> This noble crown unto the lawful heir:
>
> For right will always live, and rise at length,
>
> But wrong can never take deep root at last.
>
> *Gorboduc 5.2.276-9 (McIlwraith 1971:129)*

Even after the opening of the playhouses, successful dramas such as Thomas Kyd's *The Spanish Tragedy* (1588) retain both the Senecan ghost seeking vengeance and the themes of bloodshed and madness. Indeed, these features of Senecan tragedy survived into Shakespeare's *Hamlet* (1601; **p.87**) and appeared as late as Middleton and Rowley's *The Changeling* (1622; **p.138**). The Shakespeare play which features the elaborate rhetoric and violence of Seneca most strongly is *Titus Andronicus* (1594; **p.72**), although it is clear that other classical writers such as Ovid and contemporary plays such as *The Spanish Tragedy* are also among its sources.

SOME KEY IDEAS TO CONSIDER

- Whether order and symmetry make a tragedy more moving or in fact work to distance the audience from the action.

- Why it is that audiences find some violence appealing and other violence distasteful.

- The possible influence of Senecan tragedy on Shakespeare's tragedies.

- The way 'black' humour operates in our response to suffering both in works of art and in real life.

EARLY

MODERN

TRAGEDY &

SHAKESPEARE

WHAT WAS EARLY MODERN TRAGEDY?

The following quotations offer views on early modern tragedy ranging from the period to the present day.

Tragoedia: A tragedie being a loftie kind of poetrie, and representing personages of great estate, and matter of much trouble, a great broyle or stirre.

Thomas Thomas: Latin dictionary 1587

high and excellent Tragedy, that openeth the greatest wounds, and showeth forth the ulcers that are covered with tissue; that maketh kings fear to be tyrants, and tyrants to manifest their tyrannical humours; that with stirring the affects of admiration of commiseration, teacheth the uncertainty of this world, and upon how weak foundations gilden roofes are builded.

Sir Philip Sidney: The Defense of Poesy c.1581

Tragédia, a tragedie or moornefull play being a loftie kinde of poetrie, and representing personages of great state and matter of much trouble, a great broile or stirre: it beginneth prosperously and endeth unfortunatelie or sometimes doubtfullie, and is contrarie to a comedie.

John Florio: English-Italian Dictionary 1598

Tragedie, a solemne play, describing cruel murders and sorrowes.

Robert Cawdrey: A Table Alphabeticall of Hard Usual English Words 1604

Tragedie. A play or Historie ending with great sorrow and bloodshed.

John Bullokar: earliest English dictionary 1616

Shakespeare's plays are not in the rigorous and critical sense either tragedies or comedies, but compositions of the distinct kind; exhibiting the real state of sublunary nature, which partakes of good and evil, joy and sorrow, mingled wit endless variety of proportion and innumerable modes of combination.

Samuel Johnson: Preface to Shakespeare 1765

A tragedy is a story of exceptional calamity leading to the death of a man in high estate.

A.C. Bradley: Shakespearean Tragedy 1904

A story in which a noble protagonist's actions have disastrous consequences, for which they are not entirely to blame. Tragedy is the change from high to low state. Tragedy is about the punishment of tyrants, the turn of fortune's wheel. Tragedies act as a warning to people in positions of power not to abuse their power.

Actors at the RSC preparing to perform in Shakespeare's tragedies 2004

CHRISTOPHER MARLOWE

Who was Marlowe?

Marlowe was a young and provocative poet and playwright whose protagonists are tortured individualists motivated by a powerful desire to go beyond any boundaries set by morality and religion.

- Marlowe (1564-93) was a grammar school boy from Canterbury who studied at Cambridge before becoming a poet and playwright. His father was a shoemaker.

- It is believed that he was employed as a government spy, including a period spent at the seminary in France which was training English Catholic priests hostile to the Queen.

- He led a violent life and was murdered, probably for political reasons, at the age of 28.

- Marlowe was associated with Sir Walter Raleigh's 'School of Night', a small group of daringly sceptical thinkers. He was accused both of atheism and homosexual activity.

- Marlowe was born in the same year as Shakespeare but died just as Shakespeare's career as a dramatist began to blossom. He is the first of the important early modern tragedians.

DR FAUSTUS (1588-89)

FAUSTUS   Come, I think hell's a fable.
MEPHISTOPH Ay, think so still, till experience change thy mind.

V.128-129

SYNOPSIS

Faustus is a German scholar who is bored with all branches of learning. He uses his great knowledge to conjure up a devil, Mephistopheles, with whom he makes a pact: Mephistopheles will do Faustus's bidding for twenty-four years, 'letting him live in all voluptuousness', in return for his soul at the end of that time. Faustus makes poor use of the time. He sees a display of the seven deadly sins, travels to Rome where he strikes the Pope while invisible. Back in Germany, Faustus plays tricks on a horse salesman, and impresses the Emperor with some conjuring. He has sex with a diabolical spirit which he believes to be Helen of Troy. Faustus claims not really to believe in damnation, but at times almost repents and asks God for forgiveness. Eventually, however, Satan comes to claim his soul and he is dragged down to hell in terror.

As a tragic protagonist Faustus possesses enormous self-confidence and an overwhelming desire to know everything. He is driven to challenge all conventional beliefs, both in matters of religion and concerning the individual's place in the universe. Self-assertion is all to him. Marlowe creates a character to scandalise his Christian audience and at the same time win its admiration for his boldness, wit and energy. Faustus squanders his twenty-four years, but his foolishness both undermines his heroic status and yet conversely makes him a human, sympathetic figure. If Faustus is to have a 'paramour' it must be the most beautiful woman in history, but the audience can see that she is in reality a devilish apparition. The comic sub-plot scenes in which his servant Wagner apes his master's conjurings have the same dual impact.

Faustus is a distinctive kind of tragic hero. Nevertheless the powerful language of his final speech, where time itself speeds up as the final minutes of his life on earth race to their end, evokes both pity and wonder, in the conventional Aristotelian way (p.25). The beauty of Faustus's language is another means by which Marlowe persuades the audience to care for his protagonist:

> Ah, Faustus,
>
> Now hast thou but one bare hour to live,
>
> And then thou must be damn'd perpetually.
>
> Stand still, you ever moving spheres of heaven,
>
> That time may cease, and midnight never come;
>
> Fair nature's eye, rise, rise again, and make
>
> Perpetual day ...

XIX.133-9

The Romantic critic William Hazlitt was one of the first to recognise the 'sublime' nature of Faustus's awe-inspiring desire for knowledge and self-fulfilment:

> Marlowe is a name that stands high ... There is a lust of power in his writings, a hunger and thirst after unrighteousness, a glow of the imagination, unhallowed by any thing but its own energies. His thoughts burn within him like a furnace with bickering flames; or throwing out black smoke and mists, that hide the dawn of genius, or like a poisoned mineral, corrode the heart. His ... *Dr Faustus*, though an imperfect and unequal performance, is his greatest work. Faustus ... may be considered as a personification of the pride of will and eagerness of curiosity, sublimed beyond reach of fear and remorse.

William Hazlitt 1817: 27

Much of the play's drama however lies in Faustus's doubts about his bargain, and his fear that God has turned his back on him. This anxiety also ensures he remains a sympathetic, tragic figure and not merely an egoist monster.

> FAUSTUS   Ay, and Faustus will turn to God again.
>
> To God? He loves thee not;
>
> The god thou serv'st is thine own appetite

5.9-11

It is unclear in the text whether Faustus is really able to repent and accept God's mercy (which is offered him several times) or whether he was actually damned from the beginning, as was the conventional belief of Calvinist Protestants at the time. Calvinists, who were a powerful and influential voice in London at the time, believed that God had chosen who would be saved and who would be damned before mankind was created, and that the individual cannot alter his or her fate. But is it possible for there to be tragedy in a world of predestination, when goodness and wickedness are simply a character's unchosen lot?

Critic Lisa Hopkins' judgement is that Faustus seems always to have been damned and as such is not to be pitied – and, paradoxically at the same time worthy of pity and respect:

> When he achieves power, he does little that is evil – the horse courser was warned ... – and some things which the audience is likely to have approved of, such as gratifying a pregnant woman and humbling the Pope. Perhaps most troublingly, there are suggestions in the text that he did not really have any control over his own fate, if 'melting heavens conspired his overthrow' (Prologue, 22). In some ways, then, Doctor Faustus is both the most admirable and the most pitiable of Marlowe's heroes – and yet Marlowe, with typical perversity, apparently sets him up simply for us to condemn, calling into question the very concept of the tragic hero.

Lisa Hopkins 2008: 137

If there can be tragic heroes in the Calvinist universe, they are perhaps like Samuel Beckett's modernist protagonists, struggling to make sense of a hostile universe beyond human understanding. Transgressive self-assertion is the response of Marlowe's protagonists to such a plight.

EDWARD II (1592)

SYNOPSIS

Edward's promotion of his favourite, the French commoner Piers Gaveston, enrages the English nobility. They seem to resent his lack of aristocratic birth more than the love the King bears for Gaveston. Edward kisses him in public and creates him Lord High Chamberlain. After the King has assaulted the critical Bishop of Coventry, the Elder and Younger Mortimers, Lancaster, Warwick and the Archbishop of Canterbury force the King to exile Gaveston. The favourite is soon reprieved, however, when the Queen intervenes with the younger Mortimer, and later she begins an affair with the nobleman. Eventually the lords rise once more in rebellion, capture and kill Gaveston only to be defeated in turn by the King. Edward now has a new favourite, Spencer. The Queen and Mortimer lead another rebellion, which is successful, and the King is imprisoned in Berkeley Castle. Mortimer becomes Protector of England in the King's son's minority, but after the King is murdered, penetrated from behind by a 'hot spit', the new king Edward III seizes control, imprisons his mother and executes Mortimer.

> EDWARD   What, Gaveston! Welcome! Kiss not my hand;
>   Embrace me, Gaveston, as I do thee!
>
> *1.1.139-40*

Edward II is not a dynamic conqueror like Marlowe's Tamburlaine, nor a brilliant scholar like Faustus. But as with Shakespeare's Richard II, the protagonist's needy human qualities invest him with tragic status, despite his political ineptitude. Edward's love for male favourites does not antagonise his nobles in itself, but they are appalled by the gross misuse of his power as monarch in order to gratify his personal desires. The King promotes clearly unworthy, and in the case of Gaveston, unprincipled men to high office. Edward is self-absorbed, self-pitying and foolish. His melodramatic response when his ally Leicester is arrested by the victorious Mortimer's Welsh soldiers is typical of his emotional excess at many points in the play. The King is told there is a litter to take him to Kenilworth Castle:

> EDWARD   A litter hast thou? Lay me in a hearse,
>   And to the gates of hell convey me hence;
>   Let Pluto's bells ring out my fatal knell,
>   And hags howl for my death at Charon's shore,
>   For friends hath Edward none but these, and these,
>   And these must die under a tyrant's sword.
>
> *4.6.86-91*

Yet it is Edward's powerful emotions, his all-consuming need for love on a heroic scale, that somehow engage the audience's sympathy and render him tragic.

For Lisa Hopkins it is his transgression of conventional moral values which gives him unique status. Even one of the King's opponents admits that the great heroes Alexander the Great and Achilles had their 'minions':

> To have a male favourite, is, then no sign of wickedness, weakness of folly. In many ways, indeed, it is Mortimer who looks more like a flawed Marlovian hero [in] his meteoric rise ... and his contempt for those weaker or less cunning than himself ... Gaveston too has something of the superb contempt which characterises the Marlovian hero ... Marlowe's real dramatic energy finds itself gravitating to the most manipulative and contemptuous character onstage, even if he is not the official hero. In this as in so many other things, it is transgression which really fuels his plays.
>
> *Lisa Hopkins 2008: 139*

Edward's on-stage murder is one of the most savage on the early modern stage. Unlike Richard in Shakespeare's play, Edward acquires little self-insight or tragic dignity after his loss of the throne. The savage manner of his killing seems to be a moralistic comment on Edward's homosexuality, but its very cruelty compromises any member of the audience who might wish to be so judgemental. For Martin Wiggins and Robert Lindsey, the play's cathartic effect lies in its capacity to unsettle both the audience's emotions and their judgement; to challenge their sympathy for him, but also their condemnation. Edward's downfall may be deserved, but not his fate:

> the drama works not to make a compromise for its audience [between sympathy and judgement], but simply to compromise them, to give them an emotional commitment to both points of view. This is what makes it such an uncomfortable, challenging play: its persistent attention to both sides of the issue – gay and homophobic, public and private, moralistic and liberal.
>
> *Martin Wiggins and Robert Lindsey 1997: xxxvi-vii*

SOME KEY IDEAS TO CONSIDER

- How far protagonists like Faustus and Edward II undermine Aristotle's idea that the protagonist must be in some sense virtuous.

- How far the source of tragedy for Marlowe lies in the ideas by which society lives rather than in the personality of his protagonists.

TITUS ANDRONICUS (1591)

WILLIAM SHAKESPEARE

SYNOPSIS

The Roman general Titus Andronicus captures Tamora queen of the Goths, along with her sons and her lover, the moor Aaron. Titus sacrifices her eldest son in vengeance for his own sons killed in battle.

Rome is in the process of selecting a new emperor. Titus declines the throne when offered it by his brother, the tribune Marcus. Titus instead successfully nominates the nobleman Saturninus, who wishes to ally himself further to Titus by marrying the general's daughter Lavinia. She is already betrothed to Saturninus's rival Bassianus, and Saturninus marries the freed Tamora instead.

Tamora's sons Chiron and Demetrius avenge Titus' sacrifice of their brother by raping Lavinia, and then cutting off her hands and tongue so that she cannot accuse them. They also kill Bassianus. Aaron succeeds in falsely implicating two of Titus' sons who are executed for his murder.

Lavinia writes the names of her accusers in the soil with a stick held in her mouth. Titus, who had been tricked into cutting off his own hand to try to save his sons from execution, kills Chiron and Demetrius and serves their remains in a pie at a banquet for Tamora. Titus kills her, but is slain in turn by Saturninus. Titus' remaining son Lucius arrives with an army of Goths, kills Saturninus and becomes emperor himself. Aaron is sentenced to be buried up to his waist and starved to death.

MARCUS	Now farewell flattery, die Andronicus:
	Thou dost not slumber. See thy two sons' heads,
	Thy warlike hand, thy mangled daughter here ...
	Now is a time to storm. Why art thou still?
TITUS	Ha, ha, ha!

3.1.254-6; 264-5

| TITUS | Hark, villains, I will grind your bones to dust |
| | And with your blood and it I'll make a paste ... |

5.2.186-7

Shakespeare's classical models, where he followed them, were late Roman plays, not early Greek theatre or theorists; and two of his earliest plays, one comedy and one tragedy (*Comedy of Errors* and *Titus Andronicus*) show him openly imitating these ... great predecessors.

J. Dillon 2007: 8

The bloody and macabre events of *Titus Andronicus* did not endear it to critics in earlier centuries. Samuel Johnson could not believe that it was actually by Shakespeare, and wrote in 1765 that:

the barbarity of the spectacles and the general massacre which are here exhibited can scarcely be conceived tolerable to any audience.

Samuel Johnson 1765: 225

In 1927 T.S. Eliot thought, with a surely unintentional pun, that *Titus Andronicus* was:

one of the stupidest and most uninspired plays ever written, a play in which it is incredible that Shakespeare had any hand at all.

T.S. Eliot 1927: 82

Modern critics, however, do not doubt that Shakespeare wrote the play, and in the years since World War 2 the play has been frequently performed in a world where its extremes of brutality have found some resonance. Its protagonist, Titus, has been seen not as simply an insane ranter caught in an absurd and tasteless horror story, but a figure who achieves some tragic dignity in the form of the drama. In doing so he points to ways in which human beings can transcend the absurdity of suffering and cruelty in a hostile and irrational universe. This is not to say that Titus ever becomes a psychologically convincing and sympathetic tragic protagonist in the manner of Shakespeare's later plays, such as *Hamlet* (**p.87**) or *Othello* (**p.94**). Rather, the way that the older play is written has something to tell us about the power of the theatre itself to confront human suffering: the essence of tragedy as an art form.

Two different features of Elizabethan tragedy are at work here. The first is a direct descendant of Senecan tragedy: the elegant rhetoric of impassioned speech in classical tragedy, which even as it confronts the worst horrors asserts that human creativity can rise above pain and despair. Jonathan Bate writes that:

after Lavinia is brought to him, Titus stands 'as one upon a rock,/Environed with a wilderness of sea,' waiting to be swallowed by the water. After he cuts off his hand, there can be no rational restraint. Passion is bottomless and woe cannot be bound. Titus becomes the sea, the sighing Lavinia becomes the wind:

When heaven doth weep, doth not the earth o'erflow?

If the winds rage doth not the sea wax mad,

Threat'ning the welkin with his big-swoll'n face?

And wilt thou have a reason for this coil?

I am the sea. Hark how her sighs do blow!

She is the weeping welkin, I the earth:

Then must my sea be movèd with her sighs,

Then must my earth with her continual tears

Become a deluge overflowed and drowned … (*3.1.222-30*)

What is astonishing about these lines is the way in which, even as passion expresses itself through the overflowing imagery, reason restrains it through the controlled rhetoric, the balance of the lines, the doubling and the formal repetitions. Rhetorical tragedy proposes that humankind, even in the greatest extremity, is capable of something other than the howl of a wounded animal. The grief is expressed – pressed out – yet a dignity remains.

Jonathan Bate in Shakespeare 1995: 32

Self-conscious language, whether rhetorical description – or simply puns – and an inappropriate playfulness might seem crude to a Romantic critic, but both are part of Titus's response when confronted with horror. The serving of the grotesque banquet is the best example of this. Bate cites D.J. Palmer's suggestion that Titus's self-conscious performance of his grief is his means of coping with suffering:

Titus' passion is a continued struggle, not merely to endure the unendurable, but to express the inexpressible; he performs his woes out of the need to grasp what is all too real but virtually inconceivable in its enormity. The impulse to play, in other words, arises in Titus not as a retreat from the hideous world that confronts him, but as a means of registering its full significance.

D.J. Palmer 1972: 30

This is perhaps a commentary on the role theatrical tragedy plays in our lives.

Bate also identifies the structural role of black humour in the tragic effect of the play. Titus himself laughs when he realises his hand has been severed in vain:

At the end of the scene, he and Marcus carry off the heads; but, so as to be sure that Lavinia is not left out, he says 'Bear thou my hand, sweet wench, between thy teeth'. This is a visual joke, for it shows that she has become the handmaid of Revenge … If we laugh at Titus' line, as the audience in all three productions I have seen certainly did, we are sharing in Titus' experience. By laughing with him, we also participate in what he calls 'the sympathy of woe' … moments of laughter intensify rather than diminish the passionate fellow-feeling of tragedy.

Jonathan Bate in Shakespeare 1995: 12

Structure and tragic resolution

As Eugene M. Waith has observed, the two multi-faceted characters in the play are Titus and Aaron, whose roles complement each other as various reversals take place. After all his love for his sons, Titus commits deeds of great cruelty. After all his delight in his crimes, Aaron's defence of his baby son reveals his humanity. Waith writes that:

> Titus and Aaron are the poles of the contrast between civilization and barbarism which underlies the structure of the play. Titus is the noble Roman father for whom it is pleasing and proper to give up everything *pro patria* [for the fatherland], Aaron the barbarian to whom the exploitation of his environment comes as naturally as a tiger. Yet during the play Rome becomes 'a wilderness of tigers', and a savage ferocity latent in even the noblest of the characters leads them to commit the bloodiest of crimes performed on stage. Meanwhile, as Titus is being dehumanized by his commitment to revenge, another equally surprising transformation takes place as the barbaric Goths turn against their queen and Aaron and embrace the cause of the [noble Roman] Andronici [Titus's family].

> *Eugene M. Waith in Shakespeare 1984a: 65*

Tragedy here is a matter of regenerative transformation for Rome itself. The play ends with Rome under the hopeful rule of the noblest of Titus's sons.

John Kerrigan finds in the play's structure a series of witty parallels which climax in the final slaughter itself:

> Saturninus [kills] Titus on the words, 'Die, frantic wretch for this accursed deed!' 'Can the son's eye behold his father bleed?' Lucius responds: 'There's meed for meed, death for deadly deed' [5.3.64]. As 'meed' repays 'meed' (in phonetic revenge) and 'death' turns, via 'deadly' to a repeated rhyme, atrocity climaxes in syzygy [non-alliterative repetition of consonant sounds] of uttered 'deed' and the done. The stage is piled with corpses, yet the horrible dance of violence has a viciously playful beauty.

> *John Kerrigan 1996: 199-200*

It is the nature of revenge tragedy that its answering of like with like should produce an elegance of form, structure and event. This is part of the paradox of watching tragedy: it is both a painful and pleasant experience. Laughter and delight can be part of that pleasure.

SOME KEY IDEAS TO CONSIDER

- Whether the absurdity and playfulness works to accentuate or to undermine tragic sympathy in the play.

- The qualities that make Titus a tragic protagonist, if he is one.

- The way in which women, in particular, are depicted in this violent play.

TRAGICAL HISTORY AND TRAGICAL COMEDY

WILLIAM SHAKESPEARE

Although the first editors of Shakespeare's collected works ('The First Folio' of 1623) grouped the plays as tragedies, comedies and histories, writers for the early modern stage had a much more fluid attitude to genre:

> ... in 1623 ... 'comedy' and 'tragedy' had been terms denoting types of plays for only a century or so in England ... Samuel Johnson was of the opinion that neither Shakespeare nor 'the players, who in their edition divided our author's works into comedies, histories and tragedies, seem ... to have distinguished the three kinds by any very exact or definite ideas'; ... It was really from about the 1530s that 'comedy' and 'tragedy' began to be used more widely as a terms descriptive of dramatic genre ... But by about 1600, Shakespeare himself has Polonius describe the actors who come to Elsinore as 'the best actors in the world, either for tragedy, comedy, history, pastoral, pastoral-comical, historical-pastoral, tragical-historical, tragical-comical-historical-pastoral' (*Hamlet* 2.2.396-399). ... the joke tells us that categorisation according to genre was becoming an increasingly fashionable and complex matter.
>
> *J. Dillon 2007: 7-8*

Richard II and *The Merchant of Venice*, two of Shakespeare's non-tragic plays, are certainly worth considering from the point of view of tragic theory. *Richard III, Julius Caesar, Troilus and Cressida* and *The Winter's Tale* also include tragic content of various kinds and would be worth exploring through the lens of tragedy.

Shakespeare's account of the fall of King Richard II in the 1390s follows the chronicle sources to tell its story and is generally classified as a history play. Yet the first published 'quarto' versions of the play give it the title *The Tragedie of King Richard the Second* (Shakespeare 2002: 530-1). And, indeed, the story of the fall from power and murder of a king with a conflicted character clearly fits both early modern and contemporary notions of tragedy.

The Merchant of Venice is constructed around the principal conventions of romantic comedy: the father who blocks his daughter's path to true love, the disguised, cross-dressed heroine and the multiple marriages at the end, for example. But there may also be a genuinely tragic protagonist in the figure of Shylock, the enigmatic and vengeful Jewish merchant who loses his daughter and is forced to surrender both his fortune and his faith.

CITY AND ISLINGTON
SIXTH FORM COLLEGE
283 - 309 GOSWELL ROAD
LONDON

RICHARD II (1595)

Contexts

- Richard II was the last of the medieval English kings to inherit the throne without any taint of usurpation. His overthrow by Henry IV in 1399 was seen by some Tudor historians as an original sin which ushered in 85 years of civil war in punishment for the deposition of God's anointed monarch.

- The play depicts Richard attempting to rule as an absolute monarch, ignoring the ancient rights of the feudal nobility. In this Shakespeare's character Richard anticipates the actions of Elizabeth I herself.

- By the 1590s, Elizabeth's reign was coming to an end. Her government was not popular and comparisons were drawn between her and events 200 years before. She is reported to have remarked in 1601 'I am Richard II, know ye not that?' (Shakespeare 2002: 5).

RICHARD   **For within the hollow crown**
                         That rounds the mortal temples of a king
                         Keeps Death his court and there the antic sits,
                         Scoffing his state and grinning at his pomp …
                                                              3.2.155-8

SYNOPSIS

King Richard has to adjudicate between two of his nobles who accuse each other of treason: Henry Bullingbrook, son of John of Gaunt, Duke of Lancaster and one Thomas Mowbray. Shakespeare's audience would know that Richard had employed Mowbray to kill the King's uncle the Duke of Gloucester. They are about to settle their dispute through trial by combat, when the King intervenes. He exiles Mowbray for life, and Bullingbrook is sent abroad initially for ten years, a sentence which is rapidly commuted to six.

When John of Gaunt dies, Richard seizes all his property to pay for war in Ireland. Bullingbrook returns from exile to reclaim his inheritance. Richard, who has surrounded himself with favourites and taxed the people harshly, panics at Bullingbrook's invasion. His army melts from him. Bullingbrook claims that his only demands are his rightful title and property, but Richard abdicates and Bullingbrook ascends the throne. Richard's cousin Aumerle joins a conspiracy against the new King, but Henry IV pardons him despite the pleas of Aumerle's father, York, who demands that treason should be punished. Richard is imprisoned and here, having found some sort of self-knowledge and courage at last, is murdered by Exton, a nobleman hoping to win the new King's favour.

King Richard – tragic poet or bumbling tyrant?

The Victorian critic Walter Pater was the first to claim that Richard is a genuine tragic protagonist, arguing that, obsessed with his own poetic view of himself as a monarch, he is unable to survive in the real world of politics. The beauty of Shakespeare's language endows Richard with a nobility which invests his fall with tragedy. Even his rather fey invocation of the land, calling upon it to rise up against the invader Bullingbrook, has a poetic charm:

RICHARD   So, weeping, smiling, greet I thee, my earth,

And do thee favour with my royal hands.

Feed not thy sovereign's foe, my gentle earth,

Nor with thy sweets comfort his ravenous sense,

But let thy spiders, that suck up thy venom,

And heavy-gaited toads lie in their way,

Doing annoyance to the treacherous feet

Which with usurping steps do trample thee.

3.2.11-17

He ends the play with the tragic recognition that in the modern world of power politics which will follow his deposition, both monarchs and subjects will be forced to play a role, and thus will never be at ease with themselves. In his prison cell he imagines the different lives he might have led:

RICHARD   Thus play I in one prison many people,

And none contented. Sometimes am I king:

Then treason makes me wish myself a beggar,

And so I am ...

         But whate'er I am,

Nor I nor any man that but man is

With nothing shall be pleased, till he is eased

With being nothing.

5.5.31-4; 38-41

Andrew Gurr, however, argues that this interpretation of Richard as a tragic protagonist cannot be sustained throughout the whole play, for it:

projects sympathy for a dead king backwards ... it evokes a simple piety for the Richard of the mirror scene in 4.1 [where Richard calls for a mirror to examine his own image now he has lost the throne], and so allows

> us to overlook the fact that Richard calls for the mirror in order to evade
> Northumberland's insistence that he read the articles listing his misdeeds.
> It also invites a reading of 1.3 making Richard stop the duel merely out
> of histrionic self-regard, a desire to exercise arbitrary power and keep
> the centre-stage for himself. It thus ignores the essential point of the
> duel. Richard uses Mowbray to murder Gloucester. If Mowbray won the
> duel Richard would be open to Mowbray's blackmail ... The balance
> in *Richard II* is not between a medieval and out-of-date Richard and a
> modern, practical Bullingbrook. The man Richard has no more moral right
> to his office than Bullingbrook has legal right.

> *Andrew Gurr in Shakespeare 1990a: 22-3*

Furthermore, claiming Richard as tragic hero produces a distorted reading of the play, particularly in relation to Bullingbrook, who, as Richard's opponent, plays a central part both in the dramatic action and in its oppositional structure.

> RICHARD   Not all the water in the rough rude sea
>
>   Can wash the balm from an anointed king;
>
>   The breath of worldly men cannot depose
>
>   The deputy elected by the Lord.

> *3.2.49-52*

> RICHARD   Nay, if I turn mine eyes upon myself,
>
>   I find myself a traitor with the rest ...

> *4.1.242-3*

Nevertheless, an argument can be put forward for Richard as a genuinely tragic figure. In the first two acts he seems to lack wisdom and self-knowledge, provoking the feudal lords by imposing heavy taxes upon them, and joking about his visit to the dying John of Gaunt ('pray heaven we may make haste and come too late!' [2.163]). When he seizes Gaunt's lands and deprives Bullingbrook of his inheritance and title he undermines his own right to the throne, based as it is on being the eldest son of his father. Bullingbrook himself states that:

> If that my cousin king be king in England,
>
> It must be granted I am Duke of Lancaster

> *2.3.123-4*

Yet on his return from Ireland, when his army deserts him, he acquires an insight into himself and the nature of the kingdom which suggests he has the sympathy and intelligence to be a tragic figure, and furthermore one who understands the tragic conflict at the heart of kingship: that the king is only a man like his subjects, but has to behave, and is treated, as if he were some kind of god (the doctrine of 'the king's two bodies'). No man can live up to this role:

RICHARD   Throw away respect,

                  Tradition, form and ceremonious duty,

                  For you have but mistook me all this while.

                  I live with bread like you, feel want,

                  Taste grief, need friends. Subjected thus,

                  How can you say to me, I am a king?

3.2.167-72

In an alternative reading, Charles Forker writes that:

> as a monarch Richard never appears weaker, more self-absorbed or more in love with catastrophe than in this scene [3.2], which ends in his renouncing politics altogether: 'Discharge my followers. Let them hence away,/ From Richard's night to Bullingbrook's fair day' (3.2.214-5)

Bullingbrook remains an inscrutable figure, never revealing his intentions or even, particularly, his emotions to the audience. Forker continues:

> Clearly the scene functions to contrast the King's emotional instability with the icy and rigorous control of his adversary. Yet tragic sympathy for Richard begins to emerge with the challenge to his authority, and self-knowledge, though incomplete, begins to accompany self-pity. The brittle confidence, arrogant self-possession and careless indifference of the earlier Richard have melted to disclose a richer and more vulnerably complex personality … The new ingredient is Richard's own questioning of the integrity of the king's two bodies – a unity that he had heretofore shallowly assumed. Attack from without has sparked divisiveness within. And the result is a protagonist of greater capacity for self-understanding and emotional depth than has yet been disclosed. Meanwhile, Bullingbrook has remained a closed book – a figure whose inner self has been carefully screened from our gaze. Paradoxically, the ineffectual king appears to be a more interesting, interior and multifaceted human being than the figure who threatens him … Tragedy, even if its historical subject is a revolution, must concern itself as much with human beings as political theory.

Charles Forker in Shakespeare 2002: 31-2

The play suggests that the man who is an effective ruler able to unite the kingdom lacks human warmth and self-knowledge, whilst the man who is the 'fully sentient human being' (Forker in Shakespeare 2002: 46) is doomed to lose the throne and his life. This paradox makes *Richard II* a political, as well as a human, tragedy.

THE MERCHANT OF VENICE (1597)

SYNOPSIS

A young Venetian gentleman, Bassanio, asks his close friend the merchant Antonio to lend him money to furnish his attempt to win the hand of the rich heiress Portia of Belmont. All Antonio's wealth is invested in various trading expeditions, but he undertakes to obtain a loan from Shylock, the Jewish merchant whom he has previously slighted.

Shylock agrees to lend the money for a fixed term; with the condition that if it is not repaid on time Shylock will cut a pound of flesh from Antonio's body. Antonio is so certain that his ships will return loaded with wealth that he agrees.

Shylock's daughter Jessica elopes with Bassanio's friend Lorenzo, taking some of his wealth and intending to convert to Christianity. Shylock is distraught.

By the will of Portia's dead father, suitors looking to win her hand must choose which of three caskets – gold, silver and lead – contains her hidden picture. Two princes have already failed when Bassanio chooses the right casket, to the delight of Portia who had loved him when she had met him on an earlier occasion. Her servant Nerissa marries Bassanio's garrulous friend Gratiano. Their happiness is interrupted by the arrival of Lorenzo and Jessica with news that all of Antonio's ships have foundered with the loss of his fortune, and that Shylock is determined to enforce his bond.

Portia announces that she will not consummate her marriage until Bassanio tries to save his friend. Portia and Nerissa disguise themselves as a lawyer and lawyer's clerk and take upon themselves the task of defending Antonio in court. She cannot doubt the validity of the contract made between Antonio and Shylock, but wins the case by citing a law which states that, if any foreigner sheds a drop of Venetian blood, his property will be confiscated by the state and his life put at the state's mercy. Shylock concedes, and leaves the stage a broken man, his property to be given to Lorenzo and Jessica, and he himself forced to convert to Christianity on pain of death.

The disguised Portia and Nerissa demand the wedding rings given to Bassanio and Gratiano in payment for their services, which they grant. Back in Belmont, after some teasing riddling they reveal their true identities to their husbands. News comes that Antonio's ships are safe after all and his wealth is secure.

Contexts

- Venice was the Mediterranean's most wealthy trading city. Its citizens were noted for their ruthlessness and duplicity in business and in love.

- Jews in Venice were confined to living in the original 'ghetto' and forced to wear identifying clothing. In England Jews were rare, but anti-Semitism had been stirred up when the Queen's physician, a converted Portuguese Jew known as Dr Lopez, was falsely accused of trying to murder Elizabeth in 1593.

- Christians generally regarded lending money at interest ('usury') as sinful; when Jews fulfilled this economic need they were blamed for their greed.

Is Shylock a tragic figure?

> SHYLOCK   **I would my daughter were dead at my foot, and the jewels in her ear! Would she were hearsed at my foot, and the ducats in her coffin!**
>
> *3.1.59-61*

When the first printed version of the play was published in 1598, it was entitled 'The most excellent History of the Merchant of Venice. With the extreme cruelty of Shylock the Jew towards the said Merchant ...' (Shakespeare 2007: 413). It is apparent from this that Shylock's actions are to be interpreted as inhuman, which would, on the surface, deny him the possibility of tragic heroism. He might also be seen superficially as a two-dimensional character. When Shylock says that he would rather have back the jewels which his eloping daughter took from him than his daughter Jessica herself, he seems to conform to the worst anti-Semitic stereotype of the avaricious Jew. His strange and unyielding determination to have a pound of flesh cut from Antonio's body as forfeit for the bond, apart from its savagery, also accords with early modern Christian scare stories about 'the secret and unobserved (except in pictures and plays) bloody rituals of the Jews' (James Shapiro in Cerasano 2004: 93). In many productions Shylock has indeed been played as a man infused with the 'spirit', as Gratiano, says, of 'a wolf'. Cerasano also suggests that in the very first production Richard Burbage played him as 'an object of fun ... an extremely foolish man who deserves to be laughed at and mocked' (Cerasano 2004: 100).

It is in the theatre that Shylock's tragic dignity has emerged. Furthermore, Shylock's tragedy seems to be a larger one than his own personal situation: the character of Shylock seems to express a deeper tragedy about hatred and greed in Western capitalist society. William Hazlitt, inspired by Edmund Kean's performance in the role in 1814, was the first to offer a sympathetic appraisal of Shylock which took his treatment at the hands of Christian society into account:

If he carries his revenge too far, yet he has strong grounds for 'the lodged hate he bears Antonio' [4.1.61] which he explains with equal force of vehemence and reason. He seems the depository of the vengeance of his race; and though the long habit of brooding over daily insults and injuries have crusted over his temper with inveterate misanthropy, and hardened him against the contempt of mankind, this adds but little to the triumphant pretensions of his enemies … The desire of revenge is almost inseparable from the sense of wrong; and we can hardly help sympathising with the proud spirit, hid beneath his 'Jewish gaberdine' [1.3.103], stung to madness by repeated undeserved provocations … In all his answers and retorts upon his adversaries [in 4.1], he has the best not only of the argument but of the question, reasoning on their own principles and practice. They are so far from allowing any measure of equal dealing, of common justice or humanity between themselves and the Jew, that even when they come to ask a favour of him, Shylock reminds them that 'on such a day they spit upon him, another spurned him, another called him dog, and for these curtesies request he'll lend them so much monies' [a paraphrase of 1.3.116-9] – Antonio … threatens him with a repetition of the same treatment – 'I am as like to call thee so again,/To spit on thee again, to spurn thee too' [1.3.120-1].

William Hazlitt 1817: 206-7

Perhaps the most famously sympathetic rendering of a heroic Shylock on the stage was that of Henry Irving at the Lyceum in London (first performed in 1879). According to John Gross, a contemporary reviewer wrote that in the later scenes he was 'so impressive and austere, so much a figure from another, older world, that it was hard to think of him as a mere trader on the Rialto. The Christian characters, by comparison, were shallow and frivolous'. Indeed, to the reviewer he seemed, remarkably, almost a Christ-like figure 'as he stood with folded arms and bent head, the very image of exhaustion, a victim, entirely convinced of the justice of his cause …' (Gross 1992: 130).

SHYLOCK **Hath not a Jew eyes? Hath not a Jew hands, organs, dimensions, senses, affections, passions? Fed with the same food, hurt with the same weapons, subject to the same diseases, healed by the same means, warmed and cooled by the same winter and summer, as a Christian is? If you prick us, do we not bleed? If you tickle us, do we not laugh? If you poison us, do we not die? And if you wrong us, shall we not revenge?**

3.1.40-46

If Shylock is a tragic figure, his nobility and dignity rest in his calm, inflexible determination and in his pride and rigorous desire to see the law applied. This refusal to compromise to the crushing demands of society when they do not correspond to his own deep sense of racial and religious identity can be seen to make him a tragic figure. Equally, his vengeful determination could be seen to have been constructed by the prejudices and hatred of the society in which he lives ('And if you wrong us, shall we not revenge' [3.1.45]). He displays the conflicted understanding of the world created by the contradictions of an unjust society, a condition which has also been seen to be typical of the tragic protagonist.

Nevertheless, Shylock's determination is merciless. If indeed he is tragic, as Hazlitt suggests, it may well be crucial that he is 'the depository of all the vengeance of his race'; but perhaps his dignity might come from the fact that he stands for a wider principle. For Catherine Belsey, Shylock is invested with a 'tragic dignity' at the point where he argues for the common humanity of Christian and Jew:

> suddenly, we might after all be in the twenty-first century, acknowledging ethnic or cultural difference, while rejecting its association with inequality

Catherine Belsey 2007: 160

Belsey admits that the play itself displays prejudice, but also brings that prejudice into question. An audience cannot want Shylock to take his pound of flesh, but nor cannot it acquiesce in his final forced conversion:

> in ... stripping of his identification as a Jew a figure the play has invested with humanity, the Venetians effectively complete the process their persecution has inaugurated.

Catherine Belsey 2007: 167

For Belsey, Shylock approaches tragic status because he eloquently but problematically represents common humanity in the face of a racism which would deny him any identity at all. Kiernan Ryan argues that Shylock's fall gives us a political insight into Venetian capitalism:

> Shylock's bloodthirsty cruelty is not simply the result of the Venetians' abuse of him, but the deliberate mirror-image of their concealed real nature. The revenge is a bitter parody of the Christians' actual values, a calculated piercing of their hypocritical façade. The whole point of Shylock's demanding payment of 'a pound of flesh', and of Antonio's heart in particular (4.1.234), lies in its grotesque attempt to translate the heartlessness of Venice into reality. Venice is a world where the human heart is literally a quantifiable lump of meat ... The revenge uncovers the reality of a money-centred society, which has created Shylock in its own avaricious image in order to project upon him its guilty hatred of itself.

Kiernan Ryan 2002: 19

If tragedy is concerned with individuals who, trapped by powerful conflicting or self-contradictory forces, are destroyed in a manner which gives the audience powerful insights into human life and society, then – at least according to Belsey and Ryan – Shylock is certainly a tragic figure.

SOME KEY IDEAS TO CONSIDER

- The ways in which tragedy might be both a strand running through any kind of play and a genre in its own right.

- Whether there are other Shakespeare plays which, though not normally seen as tragedies, might also feature one or more tragic characters.

FOR RICHARD II

- How the imagery of *Richard II* contributes to, or contradicts, the notion of Richard as a tragic hero.

- The extent to which tragedy or history is the dominant mode (or genre).

FOR THE MERCHANT OF VENICE

- How Shylock's language might invest him with dignity despite his misanthropic and obsessive nature.

HAMLET (1601)

WILLIAM SHAKESPEARE

SYNOPSIS

Denmark has a new king. Claudius has just succeeded his brother Old Hamlet and married his queen, Gertrude. Old Hamlet's ghost appears to his distraught son, Hamlet, revealing that he was murdered by Claudius. He demands that revenge is carried out. Hamlet tells his friends that he will pretend to be mad and delays taking any action. A play is staged by the Prince re-enacting the ghost's account of the murder, which may or may not provoke a guilty reaction in the King. Hamlet kills the king's chief minister, Polonius, who is also the father of his love Ophelia. Ophelia goes mad and drowns. Hamlet is sent to England with covert orders for his own execution. He returns to fight a fencing bout with Polonius's son Laertes. The bout is a trap laid by the king and the vengeful Laertes to take Hamlet's life, but the plot backfires, and the play ends with the deaths of Gertrude, Laertes, Hamlet and, finally, Claudius at Hamlet's hands. Fortinbras, prince of Norway, whose father Old Hamlet killed in a duel many years ago, arrives at the crucial moment and takes the throne.

Contexts

- In *Hamlet* Shakespeare draws on and challenges the conventions of revenge tragedy (**p.126**).

- The issue of whether any subject ever had the right to kill the monarch was controversial. Those who believed the sovereign was God's appointed minister on earth argued that only God had the right to remove even the cruellest tyrant. Those who sympathised with the republican traditions of ancient Rome and modern Venice thought that a ruler who oppressed his people had forfeited his right to rule and must be removed.

- The ghost is clearly a Catholic figure from the medieval world, emerging from purgatory. Hamlet, who has been studying at a Protestant university, is torn between the demands of two conflicting historical worlds.

- Both the church and the government forbade revenge, even though it remained part of the aristocratic honour code.

- *Hamlet*, with its discussion of kingship, rights of succession and the Divine Right of Kings, is a political – and politically dangerous – play and further evidence that in the early modern period the potential of theatre to raise politically challenging ideas had been recognised.

HAMLET   The play's the thing
Wherein I'll catch the conscience of the king.

2.2.536-7

Probably the most performed tragedy in world history, the story of the Prince of Denmark has captivated audiences and challenged critics for four centuries.

The protagonist

Until the Romantic period (late 18th to early 19th century) the earliest critics had little sympathy with the Prince. Samuel Johnson expressed the following views:

> The conduct is perhaps not wholly secure against objections ... Of the feigned madness of Hamlet there appears no adequate cause, for he does nothing which he might not have done with the reputation of sanity. He plays the madman most when he treats Ophelia with so much rudeness, which seems to be useless and wanton cruelty ...
>
> Hamlet is, throughout the whole play, rather an instrument than an agent. After he has, by the stratagem of the play, convicted the King, he makes no attempt to punish him, and his death is at last effected by an incident which Hamlet has no part in producing.

Samuel Johnson 1765 in McEvoy 2006: 43-4

The Romantic critics saw in Hamlet someone much like themselves. They set out to find a psychological explanation for the Prince's inability to act on the Ghost's instructions. The poet and critic Samuel Taylor Coleridge thought Hamlet was a man for whom the world of the imagination had become more real than reality, and thus he could not commit himself to action:

> In *Hamlet* [Shakespeare] seems to have wished to exemplify the moral necessity of a due balance between our attention to the objects of our senses, and our meditation on the workings of our minds – an equilibrium between the real and the imaginary worlds. In *Hamlet* this balance is disturbed ... The effect of this overbalance of the imaginative power is beautifully illustrated in the everlasting brooding and superfluous activities of Hamlet's mind, which, unseated from its healthy relation, is constantly occupied with the world within, and abstracted from the world without, giving substance to shadows, and throwing a mist over all common place actualities ... Hence it is that the sense of sublimity [awe-inspiring ability to produce powerful emotion] arises.

Samuel Taylor Coleridge 1813 in McEvoy 2006: 45

Having been treated cruelly by him, Ophelia reflects upon Hamlet's apparent madness:

> OPHELIA   O, what a noble mind is here o'erthrown!
>
> The courtier's, soldier's, scholar's, eye, tongue, sword,
>
> Th'expectancy and rose of the fair state,
>
> The glass of fashion and the mould of form,
>
> Th'observed of all observers, quite, quite down!
>
> *3.1.148-52*

For Coleridge's contemporary William Hazlitt:

> He is the prince of philosophical speculators; and because he cannot have his revenge perfect, according to the most refined idea his wish can form, he declines it altogether.
>
> *William Hazlitt 1817 in McEvoy 2006: 46*

> **GERTRUDE**   **O Hamlet, thou hast cleft my heart in twain.**
>
> **HAMLET**   **O, throw away the worser part of it,**
>
> **And live the purer with the other half.**
>
> *3.4.161-3*

In the first part of the 20th century, the problem of Hamlet's psychology continued to exercise critics. But the founder of psychoanalysis, Sigmund Freud, claimed to have found the answer. The Romantics were wrong to claim that Hamlet is a man who cannot act: he kills Polonius and sends the King's spies, Rosencrantz and Guildenstern to their deaths. The only thing he cannot do is kill the man, Claudius, who has carried out the infant desires which Hamlet has never grown out of.

> What is it, then, that inhibits him in fulfilling the task set him by his father's ghost? The answer, once again, is that it is the peculiar nature of the task. Hamlet is able to do anything – except take vengeance on the man who did away with his father and took that father's place with the mother, the man who shows him the repressed wishes of his own childhood realized. Thus the loathing which should drive him on to revenge is replaced in him by self-reproaches, by scruples of conscience, which remind him that he himself is literally no better than the sinner whom he is to punish. Here I have translated into conscious terms what was bound to remain unconscious in Hamlet's mind; and if anyone is inclined to call him a hysteric, I can only accept the fact as one that is implied by my interpretation.
>
> *Sigmund Freud 1900 in McEvoy 2006: 49*

In 1904 the influential critic A.C. Bradley (**p.23**) thought the reasons for Hamlet's melancholy lie in his mother's immoral conduct, not his subconscious. Like Freud, he writes about the prince as if he were a real person, not a dramatic persona:

> Turn to the first words Hamlet utters when he is alone; turn, that is to say, to the place where the author is likely to indicate his meaning most plainly [1.2.129-37]. What do you hear? Here are a sickness of life, and even a longing for death, so intense that nothing stands between Hamlet and suicide except religious awe. And what has caused them? ... It was the moral shock of the sudden ghastly disclosure of his mother's true nature, falling on him when his heart was aching with love, and his body doubtless was weakened by sorrow. And it is essential, however disagreeable, to realise the nature of this shock.
>
> It matters little here whether Hamlet's age was twenty or thirty: in either case his mother was a matron of mature years. All his life he had believed in her, we may be sure, as such a son would. He had seen her not merely devoted to his father, but hanging on him like a newly wedded bride, ... [but] she married again, and married Hamlet's uncle, a man utterly contemptible and loathsome in his eyes; married him in what to Hamlet was incestuous wedlock; married him not for any reason of state, nor even out of old family affection, but in such a way that her son was forced to see in her action not only an astounding shallowness of feeling but an eruption of coarse sensuality, 'rank and gross,' [1.2.136] speeding post-haste to its horrible delight.
>
> Is it possible to conceive an experience more desolating to a man such as we have seen Hamlet to be; and is its result anything but perfectly natural? It brings bewildered horror, then loathing, then despair of human nature. His whole mind is poisoned. He can never see Ophelia in the same light again: she is a woman, and his mother is a woman.

> *A.C. Bradley 1904: 117*

The poet and critic T.S. Eliot also focused on the culpability of the female characters when he wrote that:

> Hamlet is up against the difficulty that his disgust is occasioned by his mother, but that his mother is not an adequate equivalent for it; his disgust envelops and exceeds her. It is thus a feeling which he cannot understand; he cannot objectify it, and it therefore remains to poison life and obstruct action. None of the possible actions can satisfy it; and nothing that Shakespeare can do with the plot can express Hamlet for him. ... To have heightened the criminality of Gertrude would have been to provide the formula for a totally different emotion in Hamlet; it is just because her character is so negative and insignificant that she arouses in Hamlet the feeling which she is incapable of representing.

> *T.S. Eliot 1919: 145-6*

In fact, for Eliot the play was an 'artistic failure' because its emotion had no adequate cause in the play; it lacked an 'objective correlative', by which he meant a certain situation in the drama crafted 'immediately' to produce the appropriate emotion. Eliot argues that the text of *Hamlet* does not produce the feelings which a drama should (but he does not consider the impact of the play in performance).

Society – interpreting Hamlet in the late 20th century

In the latter decades of the 20th century critics were more concerned with the forces in society which produce tragedy and our consciousness of it (**materialist criticism, p.24**).

The contemporary feminist critic Lisa Jardine's response to Freud and Eliot is direct and challenging:

> [Why does] Gertrude continue to carry the play's burden of guilt so recognisably – so convincingly – today? What is it in our contemporary version of the tragic which … requires a blameless hero – a hero whose tragic predicament derives from fatal flaws in others?
>
> I suggest that this critical shift mirrors, and perhaps takes its justification from, a prevailing political tendency to deny responsibility for the oppressed and disadvantaged of all races, genders and sexual preferences, and to transfer to them culpability for their own predicament.
>
> *Lisa Jardine 1996: 157*

Graham Holderness finds the tragic conflict in the play to be produced by changes in society in Shakespeare's own time:

> Hamlet also idealises the medieval world of his father, that strange chivalric realm in which kings could gamble with their territories in fighting heroic single combats [1.1.83-98]. The Denmark of the play is no longer ruled by such values, or by such a medieval warrior-king; when Claudius is confronted by the same kind of challenge from Norway, he settles it with a little summit negotiation [1.2.17-39; 2.2.54-89]. This may be an ignoble solution, but it is certainly a more modern one, and arguably more in the interests of the commonwealth than the heroic irresponsibility of Old Hamlet. Hamlet himself seems stranded between the two worlds, unable to emulate the heroic values of his father, unable to engage with the modern world of political diplomacy.
>
> *Graham Holderness 1989: 59*

In the 1980s critics were so keen to suggest that what we think and feel is entirely the product of society and its language that Hamlet was seen as a prime example of modern man who is a series of masks with no 'true' face behind any of them:

[Hamlet] spends most of his time eluding whatever social and sexual positions society offers him, whether as chivalric lover, obedient revenger or future king. As fluid as his father's ghost and as fast-talking as any Shakespearean clown, Hamlet riddles and bamboozles his way out of being definitively known, switching masks ... to protect his inner privacy of being against the power and knowledge of the court. This inner being, as he coldly informs Gertrude [1.2.77-86] [cannot be pinned down by any form of description] ... Hamlet has no 'essence' of being whatever, no inner sanctum to be safeguarded ... he is a hollow void which offers nothing determinate to be known.

Terry Eagleton 1986: 71-2

Today the play's politics are also seen to be intimately connected with its examination of the theatre itself:

Hamlet is a political drama as well as a play about the journey of an individual self ... it holds up a mirror to a world of royalty, courtiers, politicians and ambassadors, but also ordinary people: students, actors, gravediggers, even ... a 'rabble' who want Laertes to be king [4.4.105] ... In his melancholy, [Hamlet] ... points to the 'canopy' over the stage [2.2.281]. The self-conscious allusion to the architecture of the Globe theatre hints at how he finds his freedom: in play, first by pretending to be mad, then through theatre. It is the arrival of the actors that reinvigorates him. Hamlet loves plays and the players because he recognizes the power of acting to expose the feigning of public life, the fact that courtiership and rhetorical decorum are themselves but performances. He comes to the truth through 'a fiction' and 'a dream of passion' [2.2.483]. In this he can only be regarded as an apologist for the art of his creator.

Jonathan Bate in Shakespeare 2007: 1919-20

The play's most recent editors conclude that

Part of the fascination of this play is precisely its refusal to give us all the answers and its resistance to yield to any theory.

Ann Thompson and Neil Taylor in Shakespeare 2006: 135

SOME KEY IDEAS TO CONSIDER

- How women are depicted in the play.

- What kind of tragic protagonist Hamlet might be.

- Whether *Hamlet* could be interpreted as a political tragedy.

- Patterns of imagery in the play and what they depict.

- What the play is saying about the theatre itself.

- The use Shakespeare makes of the revenge tragedy genre in *Hamlet*.

OTHELLO (1604)

WILLIAM SHAKESPEARE

SYNOPSIS

Othello is a black North African Moor who is employed as a general in Venice. He elopes with, and marries, Desdemona, the daughter of Brabantio, a wealthy Venetian who complains to the Duke. The Duke, however, accepts the marriage since Othello is needed to lead an expedition against the Turks who are threatening the Venetian possession of Cyprus. A storm destroys the Turkish fleet but Desdemona, Othello and his officers arrive on the island safely. Iago, one of those officers, bitterly resents the promotion of Cassio to Othello's second-in-command and determines to destroy both by fabricating news of an affair between Cassio and Desdemona. With the aid of Desdemona's handkerchief, found by Iago's honest wife Emilia and placed in Cassio's possession by Iago, Othello is convinced of her guilt. At Othello's behest, Iago arranges the murder of Cassio but the killing, left to Desdemona's foolish suitor Rodorigo, is botched. Othello strangles his wife only for Emilia to reveal the truth about the handkerchief. Iago mortally wounds his wife and Othello kills himself. Iago is sentenced to torture and death and Cassio becomes Governor of Cyprus.

Contexts

- By making a Moor his protagonist Shakespeare was drawing on a tradition of Moors as violent, lustful barbarians, such as Aaron in *Titus Andronicus* (p.72). There is debate about the extent to which Shakespeare overturns these expectations in creating the character of Othello.

- There is some evidence to suggest that black people were regarded as unwelcome intruders in London, if Queen Elizabeth's ineffective 1601 edict for their expulsion has any weight:

  there are of late divers blackmoores brought into this realme, of which
  kinde of people there are already here too manie

  Iago tells Othello that Desdemona's love for him is unnatural:

  IAGO Ay, there's the point: as – to be bold with you –
       Not to affect many proposèd matches
       Of her own clime, complexion and degree,
       Whereto we see in all things nature tends –
       Foh, one may smell in such a will most rank,

  3.3.257-261

- The Moslem Turks were dangerous enemies of Christian Europe, with Venice the frontier state engaged in constant warfare against them, including the great naval victory of Lepanto in 1571. Nevertheless it is true that both the Moors and the Turks enjoyed good diplomatic relations with a Protestant England which was facing a common foe in Catholic Spain. Andrew Hadfield suggests that:

> Perhaps our understanding of the play would be altered if it were the case that [North African] Othello was represented on the Jacobean stage as similar to the Turks he was employed to fight rather than to what we think of as Africans.

> *Andrew Hadfield 2003: 10*

- Venice was regarded as a republic with a rational system of government which avoided much of the nepotism and favouritism of monarchies. Its status as a trading nation meant that it was relatively welcoming of foreigners. Despite this, Venetians were regarded as deceitful in trade, and their women as cunning and promiscuous. The elegant cortezani, high-class prostitutes and concubines, were an important part of Venetian social life for the upper classes.

> The visible legal and political processes of the [Venetian] republic, and especially the ways in which it deals with conflict and racial prejudice [1.3.52-236], stand in stark contrast to the sinister, untruthful and hidden methods of Iago, whose crimes are known only to the audience until near the end of the play. Iago's undoubted cleverness manifests itself only in cruelty and self-advancement, a common English view of the reality of Italian politics. If Venice shows Italian politics at their best, Iago, a scheming Machiavellian stage villain, demonstrates much about Italy that was feared and hated in 16th-century England.

> *Andrew Hadfield 2004: 169*

Othello is an intense domestic tragedy about a marriage which goes terribly wrong. Its political setting, focusing on the conflict between Christian and Turk, and upon the race of its protagonist, makes it also a play full of powerful resonances.

Characters – Iago

> OTHELLO   Will you, I pray, demand that demi-devil
>   Why he hath thus ensnared my soul and body?
> IAGO   Demand me nothing: what you know, you know:
>   From this time forth I never will speak word.
>
> *Iago's last words to Othello in the play's final moments,*
> *5.2.339-42*

The Romantic critic Coleridge found Iago's behaviour to be a result of his psychology: his passionless, single-minded pursuit of evil for its own sake make him seem to be a devil (or psychopath as he might be labelled today). Here Coleridge is writing about the concluding lines of Iago's corruption of Rodrigo at the end of I.3 (ll.342-72), when Iago persuades Rodrigo to pay Iago to help him to seduce Desdemona:

> Iago's passionless character, [is] all will in intellect; therefore the bold partisan here of a truth, but yet a truth converted into falsehood by absence of all the modifications by the frail nature of man. And the last sentiment – There lies the Iagoism of how many! And the repetition, 'Go make money!' (1.3.261) – a pride in it, of an anticipated dupe, stronger than the love of lucre.

> ['IAGO Go to, farewell, put money enough in your purse. Thus do I ever make my fool my purse.'] The triumph! Again, 'put money', after the effect has been fully produced. The last speech, [Iago's soliloquy, 1.3.371-93] the motive-hunting of motiveless malignity – how awful! in itself fiendish; while yet he was allowed to bear the divine image, too fiendish for his own steady view. A being next to devil, only not quite devil – and this Shakespeare has attempted – executed – without scandal!

> *Samuel Taylor Coleridge 1835 in Andrew Hadfield 2003: 49*

Othello – character, race and the outsider

Writing in 1952, F.R. Leavis, insisted on the 'simplicity' of Othello's character, seeing him solely as a 'man of action', who does not dramatise himself normally, and has learnt nothing through his suffering. He is, however, overcome with self-pity in his concluding speech. He snaps out of it to act out the very thing he is describing by stabbing himself:

> Contemplating the spectacle of himself, Othello is overcome with the pathos of it. But this is not the part to die in: drawing himself proudly up, he speaks his last words as the stern soldier who recalls, and re-enacts, his supreme moment of deliberate courage:
>
> > Set you down this.
> > And say besides, that in Aleppo once,
> > Where a malignant and turbaned Turk
> > Beat a Venetian and traduced the state,
> > I took by th'throat the circumcisèd dog
> > And smote him, thus.
> >
> > *Stabs himself.*
> >
> > 5.2.394-9
>
> It is a superb coup de théâtre.
>
> As, with that double force, a coup de théâtre, it is a particularly right ending to the tragedy of Othello. The theme of the tragedy is concentrated in it – concentrated in the final speech and action as it could not have been had Othello 'learnt through suffering'. That he should die acting his ideal part is all in the part: the part is manifested here in its rightness and solidity, and the actor as inseparably as a man of action. The final blow is as real as the blow it re-enacts, and the histrionic intent symbolically affirms the reality: Othello dies belonging to the world of action in which his true part lay.
>
> *F.R. Leavis 1952: 152 in Andrew Hadfield 2003: 63*

In recent decades the political situation rather than the character of the protagonist has been of more critical interest. It can be argued that Othello has power but no status (McEvoy 2006: 214-6). Venice is happy to employ mercenaries to lead its forces. Noble Italian birth is not a qualification in this modern situation; military proficiency is what matters. Yet Othello is black and foreign, so he cannot be accepted in the hierarchy of the Venetian state. Brabantio, Desdemona's father, cannot accept him as a suitable husband for his daughter because of his colour. Yet Othello does not come across, in either his language or his attitudes, as foreign. His foreignness and blackness are, however, emphasised by others. There is a certain grand pomposity to his language, but this is to do with Othello's vision of himself. He sees himself as a noble, almost legendary, warrior. The story of his life, which he tells to the duke and the senators, is a story of desperate adventures straight out of a 'romance' (a medieval story of the unlikely adventures that a wandering knight meets on his quest). It was the same story that he had told to Brabantio and which had made such an impression on Desdemona (1.3.142-84).

In the medieval romances a knight's feats of heroism win the lady's love. Chivalric prowess is actually inseparable from the love of the knight's lady who dignifies and sanctions his deeds. And it is for these very adventures that Desdemona loves Othello. He tells the duke and senators:

> She loved me for the dangers I had passed,
> And I loved her that she did pity them.

1.3.181-2

Desdemona's love for Othello is founded on his qualities as a warrior and his history of noble deeds. This is a love from the world of stories and legends, an idealised version of courtly love in feudal chivalry. It is completely at odds with imperialist, pragmatic, money-driven Venetian society.

Desdemona pleads to be allowed to accompany her new husband to Cyprus:

> I saw Othello's visage in his mind,
> And to his honours and his valiant parts
> Did I my soul and fortunes consecrate:
> So that, dear lords, if I be left behind
> A moth of peace, and he go to the war,
> The rites for why I love him are bereft me ...

1.3.267-72

Both lovers become dupes of the worldly Iago. Othello is an outsider in Venice and unsure of its ways. Desdemona is a young noblewoman who has been kept apart from male society and politics. Their love is not grounded in the reality of how their society operates, and so it founders when it comes into contact with that world in its most pure form: Iago.

Leavis's patronising reading of Othello caused a reaction. More recent critics have been very aware of the play's racial dynamics. In an important modern study, Karen Newman argues that Othello is caught in a contradiction where he is both the monstrous outsider who causes the errant, sexualised woman (Desdemona) to go against society's rules and, as a representative of Venetian male power, is also society's means of punishing her.

Desdemona's desire threatens the patriarchal privilege of disposing of daughters and in the play signals sexual duplicity and lust.

The irony, of course, is that Othello himself is the instrument of punishment, ... both confirming cultural prejudice by his monstrous murder of Desdemona and punishing her desire which transgresses the norms of the Elizabethan sex/race system. Both Othello and Desdemona deviate from the norms of the sex/race system in which they participate from the margins ... Women depend for their class status on their affiliation with men – fathers, husbands, sons – and Desdemona forfeits that status and the protection it offers when she marries outside the categories her culture allows ... The woman's desire is punished, and ultimately its monstrous inspiration as well. As the object of Desdemona's illegitimate passion, Othello both figures monstrosity and at the same time represents the white male norms the play encodes through Iago, Roderigo, Brabantio. Not surprisingly, Othello reveals at last a complicitous self-loathing, for blackness is as loathsome to him as ... any male character in the play, or ostensibly the audience ... Othello is both hero and outsider because he embodies not only the norms of male power and privilege represented by the white male hegemony which rules Venice, a world of prejudice, ambition, jealousy and the denial of difference, but also the threatening power of the alien.

Karen Newman 1987: 153 in Andrew Hadfield 2003: 76-7

Ewan Fernie argues ingeniously that what makes Othello heroic in his tragic suicide is that he fully acknowledges the shame of his conduct in a society where the whites merely transfer the shame they feel for their lives and actions onto the outsider:

Blackness in white Venice is invested with the shameful qualities of human existence: this is typical of Western culture generally ... An important lesson of *Othello* is that any hateful perception of other races, or women, or any other stigmatised individual or group, is like as not an indirect expression of shame. It is emblematic here that Othello begins to see Desdemona as black and blackened at the very point that he is possessed by a sense of his own hideous blackness. It is not so much that none should be shamed, which we often assume today, as that all should be ashamed: more or less equally, although beyond this they may compound their shame by shameful behaviour. The shame of stigmatised minorities is properly the shame of majorities too. But, as the one black in the play, Othello conspicuously, and more involuntarily than Hamlet, bears the shame of the world, though his wife temporarily and fatally has to bear his shame ... this is a saintly role. That Iago, Brabantio and Cassio are so precariously vulnerable to embarrassment and humiliation should instruct them that they are fallen – that they fall short – but they are not perceptive or courageous enough to accept this … Othello at the climax searingly sees that he is black, in a social context where blackness represents animalism, mortality and sinfulness. He sees this with an absoluteness the whites could not achieve, though in the same terms Iago especially is far, far blacker. Othello is morally degraded – we must never forget that he has killed his wife – but he is also a spiritual hero, one who shows up the cosseted and frightened self-deception of those who thrust off and misplace shame. He has been wicked, much more than Brabantio and Cassio, but there is a real sense in which only Othello is great enough for his climactic experience of shame in the worsening series of shames that has constituted the play.

Ewan Fernie 2002: 171-2

Fintan O'Toole, however, considers that the play's shifting contrasts between black and white, experience and innocence, malice and virtue is consonant with the close relationship between Iago and Othello. Iago is so involved with his superior that Othello cannot be considered a tragic hero separately from his ensign:

There is no Othello without Iago: it is Iago who draws out his inner fears and longings, who makes him the character that we see and hear. And the tragedy is not just Othello's, it is also Iago's. Iago is as much a tragic figure as any of Shakespeare's protagonists, as much caught between one world and another, one way of thinking and another … He has the soliloquies. He is the one who reveals himself to the audience. He is the most active character in the play. (Othello, for a hero, is strikingly passive … Othello suffers, kills and dies.) And Iago has the longest part, not merely the longest in *Othello* but the longest part in all of Shakespeare. To see the play as being about a tragic hero called Othello is absurd … And Othello, anyway, is not a tragic hero in any classical sense. In the first place, he is not a king or a prince or a ruler … And because of this, his personal tragedy does not involve the tearing apart of the state or the order of nature or the universe. On the contrary, he is a servant – a highly important servant, admittedly, but a servant nevertheless … The world will not be corrupted by his misdeeds and we, as an audience, do not feel that there is anything necessary or significant, never mind inevitable, about his death.

Fintan O'Toole 2002: 71-2

OTHELLO Speak of me as I am: nothing extenuate,
Nor set down aught in malice. Then must you speak
Of one that loved not wisely but too well:

5.2.385-7

Time

It has often been noted that there is a 'double time scheme' in the play. Given the compression of acts two to five, featuring the taut dialogues between Othello and Iago, it is impossible for Cassio to have had the time to have an affair with Desdemona. Fintan O'Toole takes this double time scheme and notes the play's concern with historical change, particularly the shift from the values of pre-scientific thinking and the static nature of feudal society to the emerging modern world (for a similar argument about *Hamlet* see **p.91**). This shifts the emphasis from a tragedy of individual weakness to one of an individual caught in a world of changing values.

> In this brilliant division of time into two different and at times competing logics, Shakespeare dramatises the core of the play. There is normal time in which the rest of the world and events unfold themselves in the usual way. But there is also the time of Iago and Othello. Both are out of synch with the times, Iago unable to reconcile himself with the new order, Othello ahead of the times as a man who has power but no status. This sense of the two men being out of their time becomes literal. We feel it and experience it as we watch the play, their fast, passionate time at odds with the unfolding of history.

> This bold breaking into two of time is possible because *Othello* is a play in which things in general are refusing to stand still, in which hitherto fixed things are turning into opposites. Most obviously, black and white, the clearest of distinctions, are melting together, both in the marriage of Othello and Desdemona and in the surrounding imagery of darkness and light. Othello himself as someone who is deeply ambiguous in his meaning for others is superbly dramatised in the opening scenes, where one group is seeking to apprehend him as a criminal and the other is seeking to appoint him a defender of the state ...

> In this, as in so much else, what happens in the play is caught in the middle of an old way of thinking and a new one ... If Othello were fully of the old way of thinking, he would stay within his 'clime, complexion and degree' (3.3.259). If he were of the new way of thinking, he would adopt the scientific way of looking at things, which is to move from the external to the internal, from outward evidence to inner conviction about what the evidence means. But he does neither of these things. He breaks with the old way of thinking by breaking out of his 'proper' position, but he doesn't adopt the new way. Instead of moving from external evidence to internal conviction, he moves from his inner conviction, his conviction that Desdemona must be unfaithful, to the 'evidence', the handkerchief and Desdemona's pleading for Cassio. He moves from conviction to evidence and not the other way round as a new humanist would do.

Fintan O'Toole 2002: 90-2

SOME KEY IDEAS TO CONSIDER

- How women are depicted in the play.

- How the play's imagery affects your understanding of the tragedy.

- Iago's relationship with the audience and its impact on the tragedy.

- The significance of race to the whole play.

- What the play is saying about violence and masculinity.

- To what extent Othello can be considered a tragic hero.

KING LEAR (1605)

WILLIAM SHAKESPEARE

SYNOPSIS

The tragedy is set in a mythical pre-Roman, pre-Christian Britain. The octogenarian Lear resolves to resign the throne and divide his kingdom between his three daughters. He asks each to declare how much they love him in order to receive a reciprocal portion of his lands. The eldest two, Goneril and Regan, offer grandiloquent and rhetorical statements of love, but the youngest, and his self-confessed favourite, Cordelia, refuses to join in the game of flattery. Lear disowns and curses her, but she is taken as wife by the King of France. The Earl of Kent, one of Lear's nobles, defends Cordelia but is exiled for his pains.

Lear intends to live alternately with Goneril and Regan accompanied by a troop of knights, but in the event neither will put up with his entourage or treat him with the respect he believes is due to him as a father or as a king. He ends up homeless on a heath in a thunderstorm. His only companions are his fool, Kent (who has disguised himself and been accepted back into his old master's employ) and a madman who calls himself 'Poor Tom'.

'Poor Tom' is in fact a nobleman named Edgar, the son of the Duke of Gloucester. Edgar's illegitimate brother, Edmund, has convinced their father that Edgar is plotting to kill him in order that he, Edgar the 'bastard', will inherit instead of his legitimate but disgraced half-brother. Edgar disguises himself as a half-naked madman ('Poor Tom') to evade pursuit.

Lear loses his reason on the heath but comes to see things about the world he could not grasp whilst a sane monarch. Gloucester attempts to help the king, but, betrayed by Edgar to Regan's cruel husband Cornwall, he is blinded and cast out on the heath himself. Gloucester is later rescued by the disguised Edgar, unaware until his dying moments that it is the son he disowned who has saved him. Regan's husband Cornwall is mortally wounded by a servant who rebels against his master's cruelty.

Cordelia returns with an invading army from France and is reunited at Dover with her father, who recovers some sanity. She is defeated by the forces of Goneril and Regan, both of whom have been scheming against each other for the love of Edmund. Edgar arrives in disguise and kills Edmund in single combat. Goneril poisons Regan and commits suicide following Edmund's death. Before dying Edmund admits that he had ordered the execution of the captured Cordelia and Lear. A messenger fails to prevent the death of Cordelia. Lear enters with her in his arms before dying himself.

Contexts

- The first recorded performance was before James I on December 26th 1606. James, the first king of both Scotland and England was attempting to unite the two kingdoms. Lear is also king of Britain, but he seeks to divide what James wanted to make a single kingdom. 'Britain' as a political concept dates from the precise moment when Shakespeare was writing.

- The play is based on the legend of Lear, told in the 'history' of Geoffrey of Monmouth, an 11th century historian and re-told in *The Chronicles of England, Scotlande, and Irelande* by Raphael Holinshed (1587).

- There was an earlier version of the play, *King Leir* (c.1594, but published 1605), in which Shakespeare may possibly have acted. In that play, which more faithfully follows the legend of Lear in the chronicles, Cordelia is victorious in battle and restores Lear to the throne at the end of the play (although in one source, the account by Geoffrey of Monmouth, she is overthrown after Lear's death by her nephews and commits suicide).

- The first version of the play, published in 1608, is different from the version published in the 1623 Folio of Shakespeare's collected plays. The later version is even bleaker and gives no indication that Britain is left with a ruler at all, unlike the 1608 version which suggests that Edgar will now take the throne.

A tragedy of state?

LEAR   O, I have ta'en
Too little care of this! Take physic, pomp.
Expose thyself to feel what wretches feel,
That thou mayst shake the superflux to them
And show the heavens more just.

3.4.34-9

King Lear is not only a family tragedy, but the story of a whole society which collapses into moral and political chaos following Lear's decision to divide the kingdom. In some ways Lear is a conventionally tragic figure, a noble king who makes an error of judgement which leads to disaster for himself and his kingdom. But Lear, before his fall, never seems to have been particularly noble of spirit or great as a ruler. His delight in his eldest daughters' obviously insincere rhetoric, and his violent, arrogant and precipitate rage against Cordelia and Kent ('come not between the dragon and his wrath' [1.1.116]) makes Regan's claim that her father 'hath ever but slenderly known himself' (1.1.299) sound most plausible.

CORDELIA	Nothing, my lord.
LEAR	Nothing?
CORDELIA	Nothing.
LEAR	Nothing will come of nothing: speak again.

1.1.79-82

Unlike most tragic protagonists, Lear's fall occurs early in the play, leaving him a long time to express what he has learned from the experience of losing both his daughters, his followers and his throne and of being reduced to destitution in a storm. Lear's recognition of his tragic plight, what the Greeks called **anagnorisis**, however, concerns political principles as much as his own life. Gloucester, whose error of judgement in believing Edmund's lies about the honest Edgar echoes Lear's own actions, suffers a similar awakening. As in Sophocles' *Oedipus Rex*, the tragedy is expressed in the fact that only when Gloucester is blind can he see the truth about the world and his life. Both Lear and Gloucester see that the violence and injustice which have erupted into their own lives were already present in the society which they ruled as wealthy aristocrats. Their tragedy was that their wealth and power rendered them unable to see this until they were made to suffer injustice and poverty themselves. Jonathan Dollimore argues that Gloucester, unlike Lear, realises that the sympathy that comes from shared experience with the deprived is not enough: wealth and power must be more equally shared if suffering is to be alleviated:

> Insofar as Lear identifies with suffering it is at the point where he is powerless to do anything about it. This is not accidental: the society of *Lear* is structured in such a way that to wait for shared experience to generate justice is to leave it too late. Justice, we might say, is too important to be trusted to empathy. Like Lear, Gloucester has to undergo intense suffering before he can identify with the deprived. When he does so he expresses more than compassion. He perceives, crucially, the limitation of a society that depends on empathy alone for its justice. Thus he equates his earlier self with the lust-dieted man '... *that will not see/Because he does not feel'* (4.1.69-71, my italics). Moreover he is led to a conception of social justice (albeit dubiously administered by the 'Heavens' (l.68) whereby 'distribution should undo excess,/And each man have enough' (4.1.72-3).
>
> *Jonathan Dollimore 1984; 2003 (3rd edition): 192*

Dollimore goes on to explain that *King Lear* is:

> a play about power, property and inheritance ... a catastrophic redistribution of power and property – and, eventually, a civil war – disclose the awful truth that these two things are somehow prior to the laws of human kindness and not vice-versa.
>
> *Jonathan Dollimore 1984; 2003 (3rd edition): 197*

Fintan O'Toole understands Lear's eventual realisation of the nature of power in a less materialist and more humanist way. O'Toole sees Lear's desire to quantify love and link it to property as being a modern, capitalist urge in tragic conflict with the feudal values of old Britain:

> Duty and bonds are the values of a feudal society, 'how much?' is the basic question of a capitalist one. Lear breaks the bonds, bringing his kingdom and all the fixed relationships within it tumbling down with the question 'Which of you shall we say doth love us most?' (1.1.42)
>
> *Fintan O'Toole 2002: 102*

Cordelia, who refuses to take part in the quantification of love in the opening scene, comes, as 'nothing', to stand for the most important value in the play, common humanity. She is a tragic figure because it is only through her death, her 'nothingness' that the play can validate human sympathy again:

> Her words 'Nothing my lord' in the first scene of the play made her nothing in Lear's eyes, but it is precisely as nothing, as an absence, that she is most powerful in the play. Lear has thought of her as a valuable piece of property, had seen her in monetary terms ('When she was dear to us we did hold her so;/ But now her price is fallen ...' [1.1.197-8]). When she is lost to him, as Edgar was lost to Gloucester, she becomes a human presence in his mind. When he stops thinking in terms of money and quantity and recognises that wealth and power have no real meaning, then he is able to find Cordelia again. Immediately after the scene in which Lear reveals, as much for himself as for his listeners, the true nature of authority [4.5.157-67], he does indeed find Cordelia again. But Cordelia has been so powerful an absence that she never really inhabits the stage a second time ... Alive she is a pale and colourless figure. She appears so fleetingly and with so little sense of personality that it is not surprising that Lear takes her at first for a spirit [4.6.46]. Dead, she becomes a powerful figure again, with the emotions to move both Lear and the audience to powerful emotions. As a dead nothing again, she is able to make something come of her nothingness: grief, anger, contempt for the power of the mighty, and, above all, a sense of our common humanity.
>
> *Fintan O'Toole 2002: 129-30*

But *King Lear* is not a play which puts forward any basis for how we might deal with power and property once the cataclysm inherent in Lear's society is unleashed. The fool speaks of an utopian time not even yet prophesied (3.2.84-94); the play offers us, as Kiernan Ryan says, only

> the understanding of why such tragedies happen, and anger at the price still paid in needless suffering to keep society divided.
>
> *Kiernan Ryan 2002: 101*

The tragedy of patriarchal families?

LEAR   Down from the waist

They are centaurs, though women all above:

But to the girdle do the gods inherit,

Beneath is all the fiends';

There's hell, there's darkness, there is the sulphurous pit: burning, scalding, stench, consumption. Fie, fie, fie! Pah, pah!

4.5.130-5

One of the notable features of the play is its absence of mothers. This has been read alongside the consistent misogyny of Lear in his speeches about his daughters, and in the play's (apparent) stereotyping of its three females into either lustful harridans or chaste and virtuous daughter. Kathleen McLuskie argues that the play is ultimately anti-feminist, and cannot but be read as an endorsement of the necessity for male power over the disruptive female desires which have brought about the tragedy:

> The deaths of Lear and Cordelia are contrasted with, and seem almost a result of the vindictiveness of the wicked sisters. Albany says of them: 'This judgement of the heavens, that makes us tremble,/Touches us not with pity' (5.3.233-4). The tragic victims, however, affect us quite differently. When Lear enters, bearing his dead daughter in his arms, we are presented with a contrasting emblem of the natural, animal assertion of family love, destroyed by the anarchic forces of lust and the 'undistinguished space of women's will' [4.5.272]. At this point in the play the most stony-hearted feminist could not withhold her pity even though it is called forth at the expense of her resistance to the patriarchal relations which it endorses.

> *Kathleen McLuskie 1985: 102*

But the absence of maternal values may well contribute to the tragedy in a manner which validates the importance of those values to a healthy society. Lear's denial of those values in a world without values might be seen as his tragic error of judgement. Coppélia Kahn writes that in *King Lear*:

> the only source of love, power and authority is the father – an awesome, demanding presence. But ... the play ... depicts ... the failure of that presence ... the failure of a father's power to command love in a patriarchal world and the emotional penalty he pays for wielding power ... When Lear begins to feel the loss of Cordelia, to be wounded by her sisters, and to recognise his own vulnerability, he calls his state of mind hysteria, 'the mother' [2.2.233], which I interpret as repressed identification with the mother. Women and the needs and traits associated with them are

supposed to stay in their element, as Lear says, 'below' [2.2.235] – denigrated, silenced, denied. In this patriarchal world, masculine identity depends upon repressing the vulnerability, dependency and capacity for feeling which are called 'feminine'.

Coppélia Kahn in Grace Ioppolo 2003: 63-4

Similarly, Kiernan Ryan, also argues that the play's tragedy exposes and challenges the dangers of a world where traditional male values are unchallenged:

Lear is at the centre ... of a group of male figures – Gloucester, Kent, Edgar, the Fool and Albany – who are, or who become, like Edgar, 'pregnant to good pity' (4.5.227), and who form an outcast community within the play of nurturing, tender-hearted men, in sharp contrast to Edmund, Cornwall, Goneril and Regan. Far from condoning patriarchal conceptions of gender, in other words, *King Lear* exposes their collusion in the tragedy, and portrays men moving beyond them.

Kiernan Ryan in Shakespeare 2005a: li

The ultimate catastrophe?

LEAR   **Why should a dog, a horse, a rat have life,**

And thou no breath at all? Thou'lt come no more,

Never, never, never, never, never!

5.3.323-5

In none of the narratives which Shakespeare used as sources for the play did Lear and Cordelia die after the battle against Regan and Goneril. The ending of the play, which seems to offer only death or despair to all the virtuous characters, is notoriously bleak. The apparently gratuitous death of Cordelia in particular continues to appal readers and audiences. In 1765, Samuel Johnson, wrote:

I was many years ago so shocked by Cordelia's death that I know not whether I ever endured to read again the last scenes of the play until I undertook to revise them as an editor.

Samuel Johnson 1765: 223

To this 18th-century rationalist, a tragedy stood condemned if it did not accord with our 'natural' idea that justice must be done, even if such an outcome is unrealistic:

A play in which the wicked prosper and the virtuous miscarry may doubtless be good, because it is a just representation of the common events of human life: but since all reasonable beings naturally love justice, I cannot easily be persuaded that the observation of justice makes a play worse.

Samuel Johnson 1765: 222

From 1681 until 1834 *King Lear* was only known on the stage in Nahum Tate's rewriting of Shakespeare's play. Tate's version ended with virtue rewarded, Lear back on the throne, and the marriage of Cordelia and Edgar.

In the late 19th and early 20th century critics found divine justice in *King Lear* by reinterpreting it as a Christian parable about the importance of renouncing the world in favour of patient suffering – the badge of salvation. Its tragedy consists in the proposition that man can only be saved by undergoing the trial of pain and death in this world, as Christ did. In 1904, A.C. Bradley wrote:

> I might almost say that the 'moral' of *King Lear* is presented in the irony of this collocation:
>
> ALBANY The gods defend her!
>
> *Enter Lear with Cordelia dead in his arms [5.3.263]*
>
> The 'gods', it seems, do not show their approval by 'defending' their own from adversity or death, or by giving them power and prosperity. These, on the contrary, are worthless, or worse; it is not on them, but on the renunciation of them, that the gods throw incense. They breed lust, pride, hardness of heart, the insolence of office, cruelty, scorn, hypocrisy, contention, war, murder, self-destruction. The whole story beats this indictment of prosperity into the brain. Lear's great speeches proclaim it ... But ... the poor and humble are, almost without exception, sound and sweet at heart, faithful and pitiful [in a footnote Bradley refers to the servants and the old man who helps Gloucester (4.1)]. And here adversity, blessed in spirit, is blessed. It is a fragrance from the crushed flower ... It purges the soul's sight by blinding that of the eyes: 'I stumbled when I saw,' says Gloucester [4.1.21] ... Let us renounce the world, hate it and lose it gladly. The only real thing in it is the soul, with its courage, patience devotion. And nothing outward can touch that.
>
> *A.C. Bradley 1904: 299-300*

In the post-1945 world which had witnessed the Nazi holocaust, and which lived with the threat of nuclear annihilation, a post-Christian interpretation of *King Lear* emerged which emphasised its vision of humanity posturing theatrically in a universe devoid of God or justice. In 1964 Jan Kott found *King Lear* to have much in common with the absurdist dramatist Samuel Beckett's view of the world (**p.178**). The function of Lear's Fool is to reveal the absurdity of the belief that there are any meaningful values in the world:

> Lear divided his kingdom and gave away his power, but wanted to remain a king. He believed that a king could not cease to be a king, just as the sun could not cease to shine ... In historical dramas royal majesty is deprived of its sacred character by a stab of the dagger, or by the brutal tearing off of the crown from a living king's head. In *King Lear* it is the Fool who

deprives majesty of its sacredness ... Only the Fool ... is looking from outside and does not follow any ideology. He rejects all appearances, of law, justice, moral order. He sees brute force, cruelty and lust. He has no illusions and does not seek consolation in the existence of natural or supernatural order, which provides for the punishment of evil and the reward of good. Lear, insisting on his fictitious majesty, seems ridiculous to him. All the more ridiculous because he does not see how ridiculous he is. But the Fool does not desert his ridiculous degraded king, but follows him to madness. The Fool knows that the only true madness is to regard this world as rational.

Jan Kott 1974: 166-7

Since such nihilist criticism, and the political criticism of the 1980s and 1990s (such as Dollimore and McLuskie), there has arisen a new approach which takes an ethical approach to literary criticism. Ewan Fernie has argued that:

true perception of the other [person], as this tragedy reveals, is the revolutionary move, the foundation of all ethical and political projects.

Ewan Fernie 2002: 206

It was often argued in the past that *King Lear* is distinctly humanist: it shows the heroic struggle of the flawed human individual against cosmic forces greater than itself. For Fernie the play is anti-humanist in that it reveals that if there is any kind of salvation, it lies not in the struggle of the individual but in the recognition that we live in and through others: the play shows that if there is hope for the future it is to be achieved through the denial of our own egos. For most of the play Lear feels shame because he has not acted as he feels a king should. But even when he realises in the storm scene that he could have ruled more justly (4.3.31-9), he still has not completed his tragic journey to ethical enlightenment: he still glorifies himself as a king. But a tragic king in this play must offend against all decorum and see that he is the same as all other humans. Lear sees this when he tries to be naked like poor Tom ('Off, off you lendings!' 3.4.89-90), and when he contemplates the blind, lost figure of Gloucester in Act 4 Scene 5. But even when captured after the battle he still wants Cordelia for himself (5.3.9-20). Only, finally, at her death does he painfully recognise her life to be separate and independent of his need of her, and thus achieves a state of knowledge and love. As Fernie puts it:

carrying his child, he at last becomes a father, instead of an aged dependent ... His unique distinction among tragic heroes is that he dies pointing away from himself, at someone else.

Ewan Fernie 2002: 206-7

Pray you undo this button: thank you, sir.
Do you see this? Look on her, look, her lips,
Look there, look there! [*He dies*]

5.3.326-8

The ending of *King Lear* may well represent the end of the world. But it might also be merely the 'image of that horror' (5.3.272), that is a dramatic representation which provokes the audience into thinking about our fundamental political and personal values and the ways in which these can survive in both the family and wider society. It is a powerfully cathartic conclusion.

SOME KEY IDEAS TO CONSIDER

- Whether Lear is in any way similar to other Shakespearean heroes such as Othello or Macbeth.

- If Kott and others are right, and there is no hint of a better future at the end of the play, should *King Lear* be considered a tragedy at all?

- Why blindness should be a symbolic motif which operates at several levels in the tragedy (as it does in Sophocles' *Oedipus Rex*).

- The meaning of so much on-stage violence and cruelty in *King Lear* (see also violence in plays in the Senecan tradition, **p.60**, and in the work of Edward Bond, **p.230**).

MACBETH (1606)

WILLIAM SHAKESPEARE

SYNOPSIS

In feudal Scotland King Duncan has just defeated a rebel army with the aid of two noble warriors, Macbeth and Banquo. Three witches appear and foretell to Macbeth that he will be king, and that Banquo's descendants will also be monarchs. When Duncan comes to stay at Macbeth's castle, emboldened by Lady Macbeth the host kills his guest and blames the murder on the King's grooms. Duncan's two sons flee, the elder, Malcolm, to England. Macbeth attempts to murder Banquo and his son, but only the father is slain. Banquo's ghost returns to haunt the king, who is becoming an increasingly cruel and ruthless tyrant. Macbeth kills Macduff's wife and children. Macbeth returns to the witches, who confirm Banquo's son will be father to a line of kings but assure Macbeth he will not be killed by man born of woman and will be safe until Birnam Wood marches upon his castle. Macbeth is confident he is invincible. Lady Macbeth, tormented by the blood on her hands, goes mad and kills herself. When Malcolm invades with the aid of an English army they disguise their numbers by cutting down the wood to use as camouflage. Macbeth's troops melt away and he is killed in battle by Macduff, a man 'ripped untimely from his mother's womb' – born by Caesarean. Malcolm becomes King of Scotland.

This short, bloody drama hurtles to its conclusion as the Scottish nobleman Macbeth, prompted by supernatural apparitions, murders first the king and then all those who oppose him. A play in which many scenes are set in the dark, *Macbeth* is a bleak and urgent study of the individual will to power and of the violence of feudal society; or, perhaps, of the loss of human reason and sympathy which can bring about appalling consequences.

It is widely believed that the text we have of this play was revised by the playwright Thomas Middleton some time after 1611.

Contexts

- King James VI of Scotland had become King James I of England in 1603. James claimed descent from Banquo, through whom he traced his line to the first King of Scotland. James does not, however, appear in the parade of Banquo's descendants shown as a vision to Macbeth by the witches (4.1.121-33).

- There had recently been an attempt on the king's life in the 1605 Gunpowder Plot. Anxiety about treason plots remained.

MACDUFF Confusion now hath made his masterpiece.
    Most sacrilegious murder hath broke ope
    The Lord's anointed temple, and stole thence
    The life o' th' building.
MACBETH What is't you say? The life?
LENNOX Mean you his majesty?

2.3.62-7

- King James wrote a treatise on witchcraft, *Of Demonology*. Not everyone believed in witches in 1606, but the King was convinced that there were women who were in league with the devil and used spells and rituals to harm men.

Why was King James so interested in witches? The main reason was that his ideology of kingship was closely bound to a cosmology of good and evil. He believed passionately in the idea that the monarch was God's representative on earth, the embodiment of virtue, blessed with the power to heal his people and restore cosmic harmony. The idea that the devil was active in the world through the dark agency of witchcraft was the necessary antithesis of this vision. The imagery of Shakespeare's play creates a pervasive sense of connection between the state and the cosmos: witness those signs of disruption in the order of nature reported by Lennox and Ross on the night of Duncan's murder [2.4.1-22].

Jonathan Bate in Shakespeare 2007: 1861

Only in Act 3 Scene 5 and the opening of Act 4 Scene 1, scenes which are now attributed to the playwright Thomas Middleton, are the 'weird sisters' referred to as 'witches'. Shakespeare's term ('weird sisters') highlights the role they seem to take in the play – classical apparitions speaking riddling oracles rather than women with demonic powers.

The conflicted protagonist

Macbeth is a feudal chieftain whose sense of self-worth stems from his capacities as a warrior. He kills not only his king but also his friend Banquo, and even the wife and children of his enemy Macduff. He does not possess, on the surface, those moral qualities which might engage the audience's normal identification with a tragic protagonist.

But William Hazlitt, writing in 1817, identified why it is that readers in particular find some sympathy and pity for this play's brutal main character. In the first place:

> What he represents is brought home to the bosom as part of our experience, implanted in the memory as if we had known the places, persons and things of which he treats ... It has the rugged severity of an old chronicle with all that the imagination of the poet can engraft upon traditional belief. The castle of Macbeth, round which 'the air smells wooingly,' [1.6.5] and where 'the temple-haunting martlet builds,' [1.6.7] has a real subsistence in the mind; the Weird Sisters meet us in person on the 'blasted heath' [1.3.79]; the 'air-drawn dagger' [3.4.72] moves slowly before our eyes ... the workings of passion, the spells of magic, are brought before us with the same absolute truth and vividness.
>
> *William Hazlitt 1817: 12-13*

Hazlitt argues that Macbeth has a humanity which sets him apart from Shakespeare's other famous usurper, Richard III. As critics have often done in former times, he also blames his wife for leading him into temptation:

> Both are tyrants, usurpers, murderers, both aspiring and ambitious, both courageous, cruel, treacherous. But Richard is cruel from nature and constitution. Macbeth becomes so from accidental circumstances. Richard is from his birth deformed in body and mind, and is naturally incapable of good. Macbeth is full of 'the milk of human kindness' [1.5.12], is frank, sociable and generous. He is tempted to the commission of guilt by golden opportunities, by the instigation of his wife, by prophetic warnings. Fate and metaphysical aid conspire against his virtue and loyalty ... Macbeth is full of horror at the thought of the murder of Duncan, which he is with difficulty prevailed on to commit, and of remorse after its perpetration ... Macbeth is not destitute of feelings of sympathy, is accessible to pity, is even made in some measure the dupe of his uxoriousness, ranks the loss of friends, of the cordial loss of his followers, and of his good name, among the causes which have made him weary of life.
>
> *William Hazlitt 1817: 20-1*

LADY MACBETH   yet I do fear thy nature:
                      It is too full o'th'milk of human kindness
                      To catch the nearest way. Thou wouldst be great,
                      Art not without ambition, but without
                      The illness should attend it.

1.5.12-15

A 21st-century critic, Tony Nuttall, similarly finds in the character of Macbeth a tragic quality which supports his idea that action in Shakespeare's plays is not a product of social and political factors:

> The gradual diminution of the intelligence of the protagonist need not imply a failure in the tragedy taken as a whole. The ferocity of the ending has overwhelming dramatic strength, though there is a problem, linked to the reduction of intelligence, in the tragic status of Macbeth himself. 'This dead butcher' (5.7.114) cannot, some feel, command the pity and fear common to both Greek and early modern tragedy. A nasty piece of work who gets what he deserves is not tragic, and Macbeth at the end of the play is close to this ... [But] the slow diminution of intelligence started with the babble of the Weird Sisters ... trigger[s] a pre-existing tendency in Macbeth's mind. They are telling a man to do something he had already considered doing, something he partly wants to do in any case ... the 'trigger' in Macbeth belongs to the darkened, primitive world I have set in opposition to the dwindling light of reason in the protagonist ... It is now as if Shakespeare has become interested in how small a thing, how simple a thing could impinge from outside and radically transform the sequence of events ... What the Weird Sisters do to Macbeth is oddly like what a practised hypnotist can do to a subject, using post-hypnotic suggestion ... The voice at the ear of Macbeth is immemorial, pre-academic, pre-intellectual. *Macbeth* is after all the play of darkness, fog and blood.

Tony Nuttall 2007: 288-90

Social and political criticism

MACBETH   Bring forth men-children only,
                 For thy undaunted mettle should compose
                 Nothing but males.

1.7.79-81

Feminist and other critics interested in gender have found the representation of the female in *Macbeth* interesting. Writing in the 1980s, Marilyn French finds Macbeth not only to be dominated by male violence, but also asserts that what she calls the 'female principle' of love, nurture and caring is lacking in the play:

At the conclusion of the tragedy, we accept without demur the conclusion that Macbeth is a butcher. In fact, however, he is no more a butcher at the end than he is at the beginning. Macbeth lives in a culture that values butchery. Throughout the play manhood is equated with the ability to kill. Power is the highest value in Scotland, and in Scottish culture, power is military prowess. Macbeth's crime is not that he is a murderer. His crime is a failure to make the distinction his culture expects among the objects of his slaughter.

A world that maintains itself by violence must, for the sake of sanity, fence off some segment – family, the block, the neighbourhood, the state – within which violence is not the proper mode of conduct. In this 'civilised' segment of the world, law, custom, hierarchy and tradition are supposed to supersede the right of might ... [this] inner world is one which harmonises the two gender principles. Ruled by law ... the inner world also demands a degree of subordination in all its members ... [but] the laws bind by themselves ... If the laws of the inner world must be enforced, that world becomes identical with the outer one ... Macbeth chooses to break the rules.

The factor responsible for Macbeth's doing so is Lady Macbeth ... and within the feminine/masculine polarity of morals and roles in Shakespeare's division of experience, it is Lady Macbeth's function to dissuade him. But Lady Macbeth, a powerful person, is drawn to the role in which worldly power resides ... In Shakespeare's eyes, Macbeth has violated moral law; Lady Macbeth has violated natural law ... she is seen as supernaturally evil. Her crime is heinous because it violates her social role, which has been erected into a principle of experience; she fails to uphold the feminine principle.

Marilyn French 1992: 15-17

The feudal society Shakespeare depicts in Scotland contains a crucial contradiction which, it could be argued, produces Macbeth's tragedy. Acts of valour and daring are what make a man worthy in this society. A real man, as Lady Macbeth successfully argues, keeps his word and is not afraid even to murder the king (1.7 37-58). The most worthy man is he who will challenge the strongest authority in the country: the king. Yet the king is the very man in whose interest Macbeth is supposed to use violence, the person to whom he owes ultimate loyalty. This contradiction within feudal society is what divides and destroys Macbeth. Macbeth cannot avoid living on the line of division running through his society; his fate is therefore tragic.

Macbeth's feudal loyalty to Duncan can also be seen to be in conflict with an emergent kind of masculinity. According to Kiernan Ryan:

Macbeth is the tragedy of a man driven, despite the resistance of a new kind of self-awakening within him, to become a savage individualist, whose defiant creed is 'For mine own good/All causes shall give way' (3.4.156-7). The play affords an unflinching demonstration of the cost of that creed, with whose less eloquent, latter-day slogans ('me first', 'look out for number one', 'every man for himself') most of us are all too familiar.

Kiernan Ryan 2002: 90

The play shows that the result of this modern, ruthless individualism is that by the end of the play Macbeth is isolated, hated and hopeless, his life, as he says:

> a tale
> Told by an idiot, full of sound and fury,
> Signifying nothing.

5.5.26-8

The play presents, to the audience, in its feudal context, a 'new kind of awakening' that 'the individual's true interests and those of the human community are ultimately identical' (Ryan 2002: 94). For Macbeth's wife fears that he may be 'too full o'th'milk of human kindness' (1.5.12) to stoop to murder. Before the assassination, it is pity, figured as a 'naked new born babe' (1.7.21) which is the most powerfully imagined, clinching factor which makes him temporarily lose his resolve to kill the king, not the sin of regicide (1.7.13). This realisation, of the moral claims of our common humanity, looks forward to a possible better future where individualism is revealed to be as cruel and empty a way of living as feudalism is now realised to be.

Patterns of imagery

This is a tragedy where the state of mind of the troubled, self-analytical protagonist is subject to a great deal of attention, especially in the soliloquies where Macbeth shares his doubts and fears with the audience. Ideas and desires which are hidden inside a treacherous mind, or dreads which are unacknowledged by those that own them, emerge in the tropes of the play's language.

It is also a tragedy where appearances deceive. The witches proclaim that 'foul is fair and fair is foul' (1.1.12); King Duncan, betrayed by Cawdor, declares that 'there's no art/To find the mind's construction in the face' (1.4.12-13). The apparitions' prophecies to Macbeth in Act 4 turn out to have an equivocating double meaning (4.1.85-101): Macbeth's nemesis Macduff was not 'of woman born' (4.1.86) in the conventional sense. That key ideas should be embedded to the point almost of concealment in the texture of the language should be no surprise.

And indeed Macbeth displays an intricate pattern of imagery first identified by Caroline Spurgeon in the 1930s:

> Few simple things – harmless in themselves – have such a curiously humiliating and degrading effect as the spectacle of a small, ignoble man enveloped in a coat far too big for him ... and it is by this homely picture that Shakespeare shows us his imaginative view of the hero ... the idea constantly recurs that Macbeth's new honours sit ill upon him, like a loose and badly fitting garment belonging to someone else [1.3.113-4; 1.3.156-7; 5.2.7-18; 5.2.23-4] ... This imaginative picture ... should be put against the view emphasized by some critics (notably Coleridge and Bradley) of the likeness between Macbeth and Milton's Satan in grandeur and sublimity ...
>
> Another image or idea which runs through Macbeth is the reverberation of sound echoing over vast regions ... [which] is used to emphasize in the most highly imaginative and impressive way ... the boundless effects of evil in the nature of one man [1.7.21-4; 4.3.5-9; 4.3.219-21].
>
> Another constant idea in the play arises out of the symbolism that light stands for life, virtue, goodness; and darkness for evil and death. This is, of course, very obvious, but out of it develops the further thought which is assumed throughout, that the evil which is being done is so horrible that it would blast the sight to look on it, so darkness or partial blindness is necessary to carry it out [1.4.55-6; 1.5.48-9; 2.2.63-5; 2.3.68-9; 3.2.51-8] ...
>
> The images of animals also, [are] nearly all predatory, unpleasant, or fierce ... such as a nest of scorpions [3.2.40], a venomous serpent [1.5.67; 3.4.31] and a snake [3.2.15], a 'hell-kite' eating chickens [4.3.250], a devouring vulture [4.3.84], a swarm of insects [1.2.14], a tiger [3.4.177], a rhinoceros [3.4.117], and bear [3.4.116], the tiny wren fighting the Owl for the life of her young [4.2.10-13] ... and the bear tied to the stake fighting savagely to the end [5.7.2].
>
> *Caroline Spurgeon 1936: 34-43*

Macbeth is a strange tragedy; taut, disturbing and containing some lurking element of gross inhumanity.

SOME KEY IDEAS TO CONSIDER

- How the supernatural is depicted in the play and how it impacts on the idea of the protagonist's free will.

- The kind of tragic protagonist Macbeth is.

- Whether *Macbeth* can be interpreted as a political tragedy.

- What the play is saying about violence and masculinity.

- How Christian a play *Macbeth* is.

- How the Macduff subplot relates to the tragic main plot.

ANTONY AND CLEOPATRA (1606-7)

WILLIAM SHAKESPEARE

SYNOPSIS

At the play's opening the Roman empire is jointly ruled by three men: Octavius Caesar, Lepidus and Mark Antony. Antony is in Egypt where he is having an affair with Queen Cleopatra. Reluctantly he is drawn back to Rome to resolve wars which are being waged against Caesar by Pompey and, until her death, by Antony's own wife Fulvia.

Antony swallows his pride and makes peace with Caesar to form an alliance against Pompey. To cement that alliance he agrees to marry Caesar's sister Octavia. Cleopatra is outraged. Meanwhile, faced with a united Antony and Caesar, Pompey makes peace.

Antony goes to Athens to live with Octavia but he cannot bring himself to stay away from Cleopatra. When Caesar imprisons Lepidus and breaks the truce with Pompey, Antony abandons Octavia and war breaks out between Antony and Caesar. Antony and Cleopatra are defeated in a sea battle at Actium. Cleopatra is interrupted by Antony as she is apparently making her peace with Caesar's ambassador Thidias, but he forgives her. Antony's faithful lieutenant Enobarbus, in despair at his conduct, leaves him, only to die broken-hearted when he later repents his decision.

Antony and Cleopatra retreat to Egypt. After some brief military success for Antony, a second battle takes place at sea, and the Egyptian navy refuses to fight against Caesar. Antony thinks Cleopatra has betrayed him. Cleopatra, fearing that Antony seeks her life, sends a messenger to tell him that she is dead. Antony, believing the report to be true, tries to kill himself and is left mortally wounded. A messenger then brings word that Cleopatra is in fact still alive, and in her 'monument', her family's ceremonial tomb. The wounded Antony is brought to her, where he dies in her arms.

Caesar hears news of Antony's death and weeps. One of the Roman officers guarding the Queen is charmed into revealing that Caesar wishes to parade her in disgrace through the streets of Rome as a captive. This makes Cleopatra resolve on suicide. Caesar appears and falsely promises clemency. Caesar leaves, but before he can return again Cleopatra and her two maids, Charmian and Iras, have killed themselves.

Antony and Cleopatra, a play in which the question of heroism is raised, is unusual in having two protagonists. The audience is left wondering whether either (or both) of the central figures has reached the status of a tragic hero.

Contexts

- The historical Octavius Caesar went on to become Augustus, Rome's first emperor (27BC-14AD). He ushered in a long period of peace in which Christ was born. King James I, who came to the throne in 1603 and made Shakespeare's company the King's Men, also saw himself as a peacemaker for ending the long war with Spain.

- Many plays written in the years 1604-8 presented female monarchs in a poor light. James had succeeded Queen Elizabeth I, the last years of whose reign had been neither prosperous nor placid.

- Elizabeth, however, had put down an abortive revolt by her favourite, the military adventurer the Earl of Essex, in 1601. Like Essex, Antony is a 'sworder', a man whose identity and prowess depends upon his fading skill on the battlefield. Such qualities were no longer needed in the political leaders of early modern Europe.

Antony as tragic hero

CLEOPATRA   Though he be painted one way like a Gorgon,

　　　　　　　The other way's a Mars.

2.5.139-40

Antony's behaviour is contradictory and vacillating. The conflicting sides of his character dramatise the conflict between opposing attitudes and values. In the opening scene of the play he celebrates his love for Cleopatra with a public embrace, and the cry 'the nobleness of life/Is to do thus' (1.1.37-8). Yet in the following scene he declares to the audience that 'I must from this enchanting queen break off' to avoid 'ten thousand harms' (1.2.124-5). He marries Caesar's sister Octavia, and then returns to Cleopatra, precipitating war with Caesar. Antony forgives Cleopatra's apparent treachery with Caesar's messenger Thidias, but blames her when, later, the Egyptian fleet will not fight. He wants to kill her, but loves her again even when dying from the wound he gave himself after she sent false news of her own death.

Antony is torn between his duty as joint ruler of the Roman empire and as a man of honour, and his passion for the infuriating but all-consuming Cleopatra (the imagery of food permeates this play). Enobarbus explains her allure for Antony:

Age cannot wither her, nor custom stale

Her infinite variety: other women cloy

The appetites they feed, but she makes hungry

Where most she satisfies.

2.2.271-4

If Antony's tragedy lies in the fact that he is a noble (or once noble?) figure caught in an irreconcilable contradiction, it might also reflect a tragic contradiction in the lives of the audience, a contradiction which the play itself identifies so well. David Bevington writes that when we watch the play:

> we should all experience divided responses. Those responses seem structured into the play itself in its many antitheses: Egypt and Rome, the contrary attractions of pleasure and of political or military ambition, and the like. Such polarities are inherent in the life of every individual to a greater or lesser extent ... The quest for synthesis thus becomes intensely relevant: are the oppositions dramatised in this play assimilable into a whole view of the human personality? Is the love portrayed an attempt at wholeness or is it polarised into extremes of lust and chaste marital responsibility? The fact of Antony's tragic fall seems to argue that the task of reconciliation is impossible because the goals are too inherently contradictory, but the dreams of Antony and Cleopatra persuade us that life cannot be sustained without the hope at least of transcendent wholeness.
>
> *David Bevington 2005: 15*

Antony may also be tragic in a more mundane but still significant sense. From the play's very first speech the other Roman officers comment on how Antony is no longer the man he once was. In the past, according to Caesar, the heroic Antony would put up with the most extreme privation (1.4.61-76); but now:

> he fishes, drinks and wastes
> The lamps of night in revel. Is not more manlike
> Than Cleopatra ...
>
> *1.4.4-6*

Antony himself recognises his decline, and at his death asks Cleopatra to remember 'my former fortunes/Wherein I lived, the greatest prince o'th'world' (4.15.61-2) and asks her to recall not how he is now, but how he once was.

Yet Antony's values, past and present, are now shown to be outdated in a world where the ways of the cunning politician Octavius Caesar rule supreme. Antony is first and foremost a warrior and swordsman, not a politician. His crucial tactical error of taking on Caesar at sea, not on land, appears to be a childish response to a challenge to his sense of self-worth. When asked, why, against all advice, he will fight at sea, his response is 'for that he dares us to't' (3.7.38). After his defeat, absurdly, he challenges Caesar to single combat to resolve their dispute. Both Enobarbus (3.13.30-33) and Cleopatra, subtly, (4.6.45-7) recognise the foolishness of this act, which is scorned by Caesar (4.1.4-6). Single combat was the ancient feudal means of settling disputes (as in the case of Old Hamlet and Old Fortinbras in *Hamlet* [1.1.90-105]). Antony is the Earl of Essex figure in 17th-century England: he lives by an outdated feudal system of honour, noble and heroic, but irrelevant to a changed world.

Jonathan Dollimore writes that Antony still believes that his identity as a leader depends upon his individual heroism and valour. But the world has changed, and identity is produced by the possession of political power. Antony's tragedy is evident in the dissolution of his own identity as the play progresses:

> As effective power slips from Antony he becomes obsessed with reasserting his sense of himself as (in his dying words); 'the greatest prince o' th' world,/The noblest' (4.15.62-3). The contradiction inherent in this is clear … Antony's conception of his omnipotence narrows in proportion to his obsessiveness to reassert it; eventually it centres on the sexual anxiety – an assertion of sexual prowess – which has characterised his relationship with both Caesar and Cleopatra from the outset … [there is] an obsessive attempt on the part of an ageing warrior (the 'old ruffian' 4.1.4) to reassert his virility, not only to Cleopatra but also to Caesar, his principal male competitor … When servants refuse to obey him he remarks 'Authority melts from me' – but insists nevertheless 'I am/Antony yet' (3.12.113-4); even as he is attempting to deny it Antony is acknowledging that identity is crucially dependent upon power … it is only when the last vestiges of his power are gone that the myth of heroic omnipotence exhausts itself, even for him … in place of … 'the firm Roman' (1.5.50) … Antony now experiences himself in extreme dissolution:

> That which is now a horse, even with a thought

> The rack dislimns, and makes it indistinct

> As water is in water …

> Eros, now thy captain is

> Even such a body: here I am Antony,

> Yet cannot hold this visible shape … (4.14.11-17)
>
> *Jonathan Dollimore 1984; 2003 (3rd edition): 210-11*

It has been claimed that Antony is too foolish in his conduct to be convincing as a tragic hero. Even his suicide (4.14.90ff.) is bungled, and can generate laughter on stage. The playwright George Bernard Shaw wrote that:

> You can't feel any sympathy with Antony after he runs away disgracefully after the battle of Actium because Cleopatra did … If you knew anyone who did that you'd spit in his face. All Shakespear[e]'s rhetoric and pathos cannot reinstate Antony after that, or leave us with a single good word for his woman.
>
> *George Bernard Shaw 1927 in Shakespeare 2005: 13*

But it can also be argued that it is precisely Cleopatra's vision of Antony, especially as expressed after his death, that invests his old-fashioned, ineffective valour with heroism. In her language she creates for the audience not Antony the insecure competitive male womaniser, as Dollimore suggests, but something much grander and potentially tragic:

> CLEOPATRA   His legs bestrid the ocean, his reared arm
> Crested the world: his voice was propertied
> As all the tunèd spheres, and that to friends:
> But when he meant to quail and shake the orb,
> He was as rattling thunder. For his bounty,
> There was no winter in't: an autumn it was
> That grew the more by reaping.
>
> *5.2.100-6*

Cleopatra as tragic heroine

Cleopatra's character is puzzling. She is not trustworthy: she appears about to betray Antony with Caesar's messenger Thidias; her pretended death, which causes Antony's suicide, seems to be a ruse to observe the effect it will have on Antony (4.13.9-12), but she is also mesmerising, with a grandeur and at times a dignity which elevates her above the ordinary. Her suicide, in full regalia, is moving and impressive. Theatricality and pretence are central to her character, both in regard to how she sees herself and how she sees Antony. Cleopatra's dignity and nobility come from her role as the representation of art itself: she makes us want to believe in her dramatised vision of the world, though both she and we know it is an illusion. David Bevington writes that:

> Cleopatra is thus the play's best spokesman for the transforming power of art, but she is also, with Antony, a tragic protagonist. The consolations of art that she applies to her own last scene of immolation atone for, but do not deny her own suffering.
>
> *David Bevington in Shakespeare 2005: 28-9*

Cleopatra gains sympathy from the audience and ironically, perhaps, tragic nobility, at moments where the artifice crumbles and she presents herself more simply – 'no more than e'en a woman' – a 'lass unparallelled' (4.15.85; 5.2.357). The theatricality of her death, as performed on stage, gives substance and weight to the illusions of her life. Death, like art can escape the changeable nature of human life, as she says:

> and it is great
> To do that thing that ends all other deeds,
> Which shackles accidents and bolts up change
>
> *5.2.4-6*

Tragic deaths, like the art form of tragedy itself, transcend the moment of suffering. Cleopatra's role as tragic protagonist is also given greater credence by the fact that Shakespeare chooses to end the play not with Antony's death but with that of Cleopatra. Act 5 is devoted to the re-assertion of her grandeur, heroic status and renewed dignity.

Finally, to deny Cleopatra tragic status may well be to relegate art and love to second place behind the male realms of war and power politics. It is also to deny the complexity of the play's presentation of two conflicting elements in human life.

SOME KEY IDEAS TO CONSIDER

- How the dominant image patterns of the play (for example, the four elements, architectural grandeur and eating), convey the tragic conflict at the heart of the play.

- The extent to which not only Enobarbus, but other minor characters such as Eros, Charmian, Iras and Pompey might also be seen as tragic figures.

- What the play might have to say about the tragedy inherent in all love which seeks to deny or defy the realities of the material world.

- Whether the play demonstrates that tragic protagonists can be foolish people.

- Whether this is a play about the private tragedy of two individuals or the political tragedy of an empire.

REVENGE TRAGEDY –
AN INTRODUCTION

Revenge is a central idea in many tragedies from the Greeks onwards. It is, however, a genre particularly associated with Renaissance (or early modern) drama, flourishing in England from the 1570s right through until the 1620s.

- The protagonist of these dramas is typically a noble character driven to deceit and cunning in order to avenge a terrible wrong done to him.

- The setting is never in England: since revenge tragedy presents corrupt rulers, it was safer if these scandalous narratives were set in allegedly more hot-tempered locations.

- Noble characters often behave in ways quite inappropriate for their social station, and can mix with characters from the lower orders.

- Comedy intertwines with tragedy, not only in certain characters and dialogue, but at moments of high seriousness when the plays seem to teeter on the edge of black comedy. Revenge tragedy thus challenges and undermines the classical notion of 'decorum' (the idea that language, action and character should all be appropriate to each another).

- Revenge tragedy dramatises a moral code in which personal vengeance rules and a cycle of violent reprisal continues until all the principals have been slaughtered. This can be interpreted either as a challenge to a society which forbids taking justice into one's hands, or an endorsement of the rule of law.

- The final act often features some masque or entertainment which conceals a murderous plot, and which concludes with the deaths of the main characters.

  'Revenge is a kind of wild justice; which the more man's nature runs to, the more ought law to weed it out. For as for the first wrong, it doth but offend the law; but the revenge of that wrong putteth the law out of office. Certainly, in taking revenge, a man is but even with his enemy; but in passing it over, he is superior; for it is a prince's part to pardon.' (Francis Bacon)

Bacon's words point to the anxiety about moral and political authority at the heart of any tragic plot shaped by revenge. The revenger who can be seen as the figure of the playwright, attempts to wrest control of the action from the corrupt authorities, usually with the result that the revenger becomes contaminated by the violence he or she abhors.

The flourishing of revenge tragedy in early modern England is a symptom of a society in transition, where traditional forms of authority and the nature of law were being questioned.

Rebecca Bushnell 2008: 66

The logic of revenge is at once impeccable and intolerable. To those wholly caught up in its structure, the duty of retaliation is self-evident, the guilt of the victim is patent, the justification of the avengers – even if they must sacrifice their own lives – absolute. This is not tragic for them. They can exult in death, both their own and others. But to those outside its structure, or anyone less than wholly absorbed in it, the logic of revenge is a nightmare whose only issue is death and more death. Is there not some other way forward, that would break free of the past, leaving it dead and truly buried?

Adrian Poole 2005: 36

Seneca's plays focus upon the depiction of physical violence and went on to influence the sensational excesses of Jacobean revenge tragedy, including plays such as Shakespeare's *Titus Andronicus* or Tourneur's *Revenger's Tragedy*.

Jennifer Wallace 2007: 31

Here are the final lines of Middleton's *Women Beware Women* (1623), where the ambitious and beautiful Bianca joins the other corpses strewn around the stage after the concluding masque which acted as a cover for vengeful slaughter. Thomas Middleton's play is typical of the revenge tragedy genre in its presentation of a corrupt ruler, its complex sexual intrigue and its violent conclusion:

LORD	See, my Lord,
	What shift sh'as made to be her own destruction.
BIANCA	Pride, greatness, honours, beauty, youth, ambition,
	You must all down together, there's no help for't:
	Yet this my gladness is that I remove,
	Tasting the same death in a cup of love. [*Dies*]
CARDINAL	Sin, what thou art, these ruins show too piteously.
	Two kings on one throne cannot sit together,
	But one must needs down, for his title's wrong;
	So where lust reigns, that prince cannot reign long.

5.2.213-22

Some key revenge tragedies

George Chapman, *Bussy D' Ambois* (1604)
Thomas Kyd, *The Spanish Tragedy* (1592)
Thomas Middleton, *Women Beware Women* (1623)

THE REVENGER'S TRAGEDY (1606)

THOMAS MIDDLETON

For many years this play, published anonymously in 1606, was thought to be by Cyril Tourneur, the author of *The Atheist's Tragedy*. Many scholars today regard Thomas Middleton as the most likely author.

My fault being sport, let me but die in jest.

1.2.66

SYNOPSIS

The action takes place in a nameless Italian city. The fiancée of Vindice ('The Avenger') has been murdered by the corrupt Duke because she would not submit to his advances. His brother Hippolito, a courtier, is sent to find someone to act as a pimp for Lussurioso, the Duke's son and heir. Vindice, in disguise, applies for, and is given, this job in order to effect his revenge. The Duchess's youngest son by a previous marriage, meanwhile, is found guilty of rape, but sentence is deferred by the Duke. The Duchess is outraged that her son has not been pardoned, and begins an affair with the Duke's illegitimate son Spurio, who is himself plotting to kill the Duke's legitimate stepsons and become the heir.

A series of macabre intrigues and events follow. The disguised Vindice is employed to persuade his own sister Castiza to become Lussurioso's mistress. Vindice is delighted when she refuses, but appalled when their mother agrees to persuade her to take the offer up. The mother later repents.

Vindice and Hippolito tempt the Duke into a secret assignation where they murder the ruler by making him kiss the poisoned skull of Vindice's fiancée. As he dies the Duke watches his wife embracing his bastard son Spurio.

The Duke's stepsons plot to have Lussurioso executed for treason, but their bungling only leads to the beheading of their rapist brother.

A group of discontented nobles led by Antonio, whose wife was the victim of the rape, plot with Vindice and Hippolito to kill the ruling family whilst taking the role of dancers in a masque. The coup succeeds, and Antonio becomes Duke. Vindice admits his guilt in killing the previous Duke, but Antonio orders his execution together with Hippolito: 'You that would murder him would murder me!' (5.3.105)

Contexts

- The noble families of Italy were popularly regarded as lustful, deceitful and unprincipled. Their Catholicism and exotic foreignness also deflected any possible accusation that such plays as this were covert 'applications' (depictions) of events at James I's own court, itself not noted for moral rectitude.

- The play contains many of the features of the revenge tragedy genre (**p.126**). There is a clear allusion to *Hamlet* as the play opens with Vindice holding a skull, in this case of his dead fiancée.

A 'black farce'?

The Revenger's Tragedy boasts a plot of such grotesque events, and so many episodes of black farce, that critics have not been sure what to make of it. Often it seems a ludicrous parody of the genre. In other revenge tragedies such as Kyd's *The Spanish Tragedy* (1588) the final act of vengeance takes place under cover of a masque or performance (or, in *Hamlet*, a fencing match). Here there are, absurdly, two masques of disguised murderers. The second set of dancers, comprising the Duke's stepsons and Spurio, arrive on stage to see their target, the new Duke Lussurioso, already slain by Vindice and the first set. They immediately fall upon each other, each becoming Duke for a second before being struck down by his brother:

AMBITIOSO	(*aside*) Here's a labour saved:
	I thought to have sped him. 'Sblood – how came this?
SUPERVACUO	Then I proclaim myself. Now I am Duke.
AMBITIOSO	Thou Duke! Brother thou liest. (*stabs Supervacuo*)
SPURIO	Slave! So dost thou. (*stabs Ambitioso*)
4th LORD	Base villain, hast thou slain my lord and master? (*stabs Spurio*)

5.3.51-5

As the corpses pile up on stage, this comic business can surely only be a parody of the conventional revenge tragedy ending such as that of *Hamlet*. Throughout the play there are plenty of asides to the audience, often sending up the drama through sheer inappropriateness. When the duke intervenes in his son's trial for rape, the indignant Spurio splutters to the audience 'Pox on't,/What makes my dad speak now?' (1.2.82-3). When Vindice is hired by the Duke's heir Lussurioso to kill the pimp whom he himself was impersonating, he calls to the heavens for thunder as a sign of vengeance. Immediately, and comically, it is heard ('There it goes!' [4.2. 202]), as if the actor were giving the cue for the effect.

All these, and many other effects, can be seen to prevent the play's egregious violence and suffering from being taken seriously. The self-conscious theatricality of the drama sends up the conventions of revenge tragedy in a very entertaining way. One result of this is to make us aware of a key paradox of tragedy: how we get pleasure and excitement from watching the extreme pain and suffering of the characters on stage.

The names of the play's characters (Lussurioso: 'lustful'; Castiza; 'chaste'; Spurio: 'of doubtful origin') might seem to echo the practice of the old morality plays of the 14th century and earlier. Jonathan Dollimore, however, suggests that the play's parodic self-consciousness of itself as theatre is used to undermine the old fashioned moralism of those plays, and especially the idea that God's providence is at work in the play, punishing the wicked and rewarding the virtuous. He argues that *The Revenger's Tragedy* is:

> sophisticated and self-conscious, at once mannered and chameleon; it celebrates the artificial and the delinquent; it delights in a play full of innuendo, perversity and subversion; by mimicking and misappropriating their glibness it exposes the hypocrisy and deception of the pious; through parody it declares itself radically sceptical of ideological policing.

> *Jonathan Dollimore 1984; 2003 (3rd edition): 149*

Dollimore proclaims that the mocking tone of the play, which takes sarcastic delight in perverted pleasures, is a way of refusing any attempt by the powerful to impose conventional morality upon society.

A whole society corrupted

DUKE   It well becomes that judge to nod at crimes
        That does commit greater himself and lives.

2.3.124-5

The protagonist, Vindice, is barely presented as a psychologically credible character. Contemporary actors, such Anthony Sher who played the role in 1987, have had to find a bizarre motivation to play the role in a modern way:

> what finally released the part was the realisation that Vindice must have some kind of joy in it all, otherwise it's too ghastly to contemplate.

> *M.R. Mulryne and M. Shewring 1989: 121*

If the play really is a tragedy, it may be because it depicts a society so corrupted by the wickedness of its rulers that it can only be redeemed by violence as excessive as the crimes of those in power. Michelle O'Callaghan writes that:

> The tyrant is a tragic character type that allows the dramatist to explore the interdependence of power and desire, sex and politics. By giving

free rein to his lust and perverse appetites, the tyrant is enslaved by his own passions ... In revenge tragedies, the violence of desire resonates across the dramatis personae; it is not simply confined to the tyrant, but infects all involved in court politics, including those who seek to redress its injustices. The distinction between the all-consuming sensual appetites of the tyrant and the all-consuming retributive justice of the revenger is frequently blurred – both are driven to excesses and become terrifying machines of annihilation ... The [original crime] in *[The] Revenger's Tragedy* is the Duke's poisoning of Vindice's betrothed, Gloriana:

Because thy purer part would not consent

Unto his palsy lust; for old men lustful

Do show like young men – angry, eager, violent,

Outbid their limited performances. (1.1.33-6)

The sense of the moribund state of the royal court under his rule is conveyed by this image of 'his palsy lust'. Decrepitude and illness pervert sexual desire which, in such a sick state, can only be expressed through the violent destruction of youth, beauty, and virtue.

Michelle O'Callaghan 2009: 109-10

If this is tragedy, it is reminiscent of Raymond Williams' modern notion of tragedy (p.24); a tragic situation which is inherent in all societies where only the cruelty and suffering of revolution can address the facts of injustice.

SOME KEY IDEAS TO CONSIDER

- The way in which men fight for control over women's bodies in the play.

- The connections between lust and violence in the play.

- Whether the dark laughter prevents the play from being a tragedy at all.

- The presentation of revenge and what this reveals to the audience about man's need for personal vengeance.

- The presentation of power and its corruption.

THE DUCHESS OF MALFI (1614)

JOHN WEBSTER

BOSOLA   We are merely the stars' tennis balls, struck and
                                         bandied

Which way please them.

5.4.53-4

SYNOPSIS

The Duchess is the twin sister of Ferdinand, Duke of Calabria, and younger sister to the Cardinal of Aragon. She is young, recently widowed and a fine prize for another man. Ferdinand employs Bosola as Master of the Horse in his sister's court, setting him to spy on her actions. Unbeknownst to Ferdinand, the Duchess is in love with her steward Antonio. After she reveals her feelings to him, they make a verbal contract to each other in the presence of the Duchess's maid Cariola, going on to be married and have children – both in secret. Bosola discovers the children, but cannot find out who the father is.

Her twin brother, enraged with what seems an incestuous jealousy, is secretly admitted by Bosola into her chamber where he overhears his sister talk of her love. He swears he will kill her husband and declares that he will never see her again. The Duchess, in order to divert suspicion, denounces Antonio as a thief and dismisses him from her service, having already planned to meet him later at the shrine of the Virgin Mary in Ancona. Not knowing that Bosola is in the employ of her brother, she unwisely reveals her husband's identity to him. Banished from Ancona at the Duke's orders, she is separated from Antonio and arrested by Bosola.

Antonio still hopes that a reconciliation can be made, but the increasingly deranged Ferdinand seeks revenge. He torments his sister by offering her a dead man's hand to kiss in the dark, and then shows her a wax tableau of Antonio and her children dead. After a masque of madmen perform in front of her, Bosola, in disguise, supervises the strangling of the Duchess and her children. Her heroism moves Bosola to repentance and he resolves to protect Antonio and become her avenger.

Bosola, having heard his own death purposed by the Cardinal, stabs Antonio in the dark, believing him to be his enemy. Bosola kills the Cardinal and then Ferdinand, who believes himself to have become a wolf. In the scuffle Bosola himself is mortally wounded. At the conclusion a surviving son of Antonio is declared the Duchess's heir.

Webster's two surviving plays both feature a strong woman trapped in a web of male conspiracy in Renaissance Italy. The protagonist of *The White Devil* (1612), Vittoria Corombona, is the married object of desire, sought after by competing and conniving aristocrats. Although Vittoria is a brave individual, and a victim of an active misogyny, she perhaps lacks the virtue and honesty to render her a genuinely tragic figure. The unnamed but eponymous protagonist of *The Duchess of Malfi*, however, beset as she is with macabre cruelty and male intrigue of a striking and disturbing kind, achieves a tragic dignity which also throws the conflicted nature of her society into relief.

A tragic heroine of female virtues?

> DUCHESS   I pray thee look thou giv'st my little boy
>
>   Some syrup for his cold, and let the girl
>
>   Say her prayers, ere she sleep.

4.2.195-7

The play's ending is bloody and chaotic, and the arrival of the scarcely mentioned son, to provide some sort of conventional hope, fails to convince. Because of the lack of any obvious workings of divine **providence** in the play, traditional critics have found it to be rather nihilistic: it fails to provide some of the moral or religious uplift which such critics felt a tragedy should have. Sandra Clark, after citing the early 20th-century poet Rupert Brooke's belief that Webster's characters are 'writhing grubs in an immense night', expresses the view that 'the sense of moral anarchy in the play is great, perhaps even overwhelming' (Clark 1987: 124). The world of the play, though 'convincing', is 'mysterious and irrational',

> in which the wills of those in power, emancipated from all normal considerations of ethics and morality, reign supreme ... Good or evil are irrelevant in those supreme moments of horror or agony when the human spirit is put to the test, when for example the Duchess is able to invite her executioners to end her life.

Clark 1987: 125

In fact the Duchess's heroic noble speech has a political point to make. Salvation is for the godly, not the powerful:

> DUCHESS   Pull, and pull strongly, for your able strength
>
>   Must pull down heaven upon me.
>
>   Yet stay; heaven gates are not so highly arched
>
>   As princes' palaces; they that enter there
>
>   Must go upon their knees [*Kneels*].

4.2.222-6

The values which make the Duchess tragic are not such pure abstractions as 'goodness'. Seventeenth-century audiences may perhaps have condemned her conduct for giving way to desire for her own steward, or for her slighting of religion by using a visit to a shrine to cover a secret. William Empson, however, memorably suggested that:

> the moral of this play, driven home as with the sledge-hammer of Dickens
> I should have thought, is not that the Duchess was wanton but that her
> brothers were sinfully proud

> *William Empson 1969: 297*

Nevertheless, the Duchess has been seen by modern critics to stand for emancipatory and nurturing values in the face of aristocratic male class-hatred.

In the midst of the moral anarchy, the domestic love of the Duchess for Antonio and her family depicted in Act 3 Scene 2 stands out for its sanity and warmth. Catherine Belsey points out that:

> The text valorizes women's equality to the point where the Duchess woos
> Antonio, repudiating the hierarchy of birth in favour of individual virtue;
> it also celebrates the family, identifying it as a private realm of warmth
> and fruitfulness separate from the turbulent world of politics, though
> vulnerable to it. Act 3 Scene 2 shows the Duchess alone with Antonio and
> Cariola ... Their exchanges are intimate, affectionate and playful. Indeed,
> it is the spirit of play which causes Cariola and Antonio to steal out of the
> room while the Duchess brushes her hair, and which is brutally dissipated
> by the entry of Ferdinand, the personification of patriarchal absolutism.

> *Catherine Belsey 1985: 197-8*

The Duchess might be seen as embodying female values of love and nurture which cannot survive in the brutal power politics of the play, and to look forward to an age when women can choose their partners without patriarchal or class prejudice constraining their desire. This might make the Duchess tragic because she embodies noble qualities, prefiguring the possibility of a more just society, yet remains fatally trapped in her own times.

This is not the conclusion Belsey draws, however. In valorizing domestic life as no concern of politics – indeed, in showing politics to be a threat to the family – the play works to:

> suppress recognition of the power relations which structure the family,
> and by this means liberalism opens a gap for the accommodation of an
> uncontested, because unidentified, patriarchy

> *Catherine Belsey 1985: 199*

To put family life outside 'politics' is to refuse to analyse its own power relations which are drawn up in favour of men. Belsey does not remark, however, that it is in fact the woman who holds power in this scene.

For some feminist critics, it is a patronising gesture to ascribe tragic dignity to the Duchess as a substitute for the loss of political power. In the play the widowed Duchess only holds her lands and authority conditional upon her conduct, a status similar to the 'dowager' in contemporary England. When the Pope takes the Dukedom of Malfi away from her because of her 'looseness' (3.4.31), she no longer has any political power but is, according to Lisa Jardine:

> reduced to the safe composite stereotype of penitent whore, Virgin majestic in grief, serving mother, patient and true turtle-dove mourning her one love. Strength of purpose is eroded into strength of character in adversity.
>
> *Lisa Jardine 1983: 91*

Tragic female figures are affecting spectacles to men, but no threat to their power.

The role of the tragic malcontent

> BOSOLA   What's my place?
> The provisorship o' th' horse? Say then my
>   corruption
> Grew out of horse-dung. I am your creature.
>
> *1.1.276-8*

The Duchess dies in Act 4. The play continues to examine how Bosola, struck by her virtue, seeks to avenge the deed which he himself carried out. The focus is as much on the society which brought about the destruction of the Duchess and her children as it is on the protagonist herself. Christina Luckyj has argued that only when the play examines the human qualities of her destroyers in the final act do we see that she has not been the victim of some Satanic force, but wickedness which is the result of 'simple frail humanity' (Luckyj 1989: 101). The Cardinal, just after he has killed his mistress Julia, feels haunted by his sister's ghost and wishes for penitence (5.2.39-43); his conscience stings him in his final scenes (5.4.25, 5.5.4, 53). Ferdinand's lycanthropy is his subconscious acknowledgment that he has excised his own humanity in his treatment of his sister. At her death he cannot bear to look upon her face ('Cover her face: mine eyes dazzle: she died young' [4.2.256]).

But, as René Weis demonstrates:

> it is Bosola particularly who epitomizes 'frail humanity' in collusion with evil ... As a student in Padua he studied hard 'to gain the name

of a speculative man' (3.3.346), but became subsequently disenchanted because service performed by him for the Cardinal went unrewarded. His use of the pitiful image of the disabled soldier, who takes swings on 'crutches, from hospital to hospital' (1.161-2), to express his sense of wrong, indicates that Bosola's moral being has not entirely been twisted by circumstances. But his malice can be savage, as in his gruesome exposition to the midwife of her [cosmetic] 'closet' (2.1.32-40), and his Hamlet-like 'meditation' about what it is 'in this outward form of man/To be beloved?' (2.1.41-2) is acerbically dismissive of any form of idealistic aspiration. But when Ferdinand asks how his sister bears up in prison, Bosola describes her behaviour as 'so noble/As gives a majesty to adversity' (4.1.5-6). He repeatedly urges Ferdinand to show some pity ('Faith, end here,/And go no further in your cruelty': 4.1.117-8), and professes regret and sorrow about the strangled children, but these sentiments do not sway his better self enough to refrain from overseeing the torture of the Duchess in 4.1. and 4.2, or from crudely dismissing Cariola's desperate pleas to be spared.

René Weis 1996: xxii

The conflicted malcontent such as Bosola is a familiar figure in revenge tragedy (consider also Vindice in *The Revenger's Tragedy* **p.128**, Alsemero in *The Changeling* **p.138** or even *Hamlet* **p.87**). While not conventional tragic protagonists in themselves, they nevertheless come to stand as statements for the contradictions in their society. Lacking the 'self-sufficiency' of the conventional tragic hero, according to Jonathan Dollimore:

> they internalise rather than transcend the violence of their society, being incapable of surviving its alienating effects except by re-engaging with it … as terrorist-revengers … [they are] satirical and vengeful; at once agent and victim of social corruption, condemning yet simultaneously contaminated by it; made up of inconsistencies and contradictions which, because they cannot be understood in terms of individuality alone, constantly pressure attention outwards to the social conditions of existence.

Jonathan Dollimore 1984; 2003 (3rd edition): 49-50

The figure of the tragic malcontent such as Bosola lays bare the origins of violence and cruelty in the political arrangements of the state, and at the same time demonstrates a desire for justice in a world where divine providence is shown to have no purchase.

SOME KEY IDEAS TO CONSIDER

- The moral and political world of Webster and how far it is like and unlike that of Shakespeare's tragedies.

- Whether the use Webster makes of the spectacle of violence adds to, or detracts from the tragic intensity.

- How Bosola, through his colourful language and audience contact, affects the way the audience sees the main action of the play.

- Whether the play delights in, or attacks, the misogyny of its male characters.

THE CHANGELING (1622)

THOMAS MIDDLETON AND WILLIAM ROWLEY

The Changeling, a play with a female protagonist, is a claustrophobic and disturbing tragedy of irrational lusts and thwarted passions. Yet it also possesses a darkly comic aspect.

> **DE FLORES**   Y'are the deed's creature ...
>
> *3.4.137*

SYNOPSIS

The action takes place in Alicante, mostly in the castle of Count Vermandero. The Spanish noblewoman Beatrice-Joanna, finding herself engaged to Alonzo de Piracquo but in love with Alsemero, arranges the murder of Alonzo. One of her father's servants is the ugly De Flores, whom she has hitherto despised. De Flores secretly loves her and is keen to become the assassin, supposedly for gold.

However, once the crime is committed De Flores will not accept gold as payment: only the taking of Beatrice-Joanna's virginity will prevent him from publicly revealing their conspiracy. Beatrice-Joanna becomes increasingly dependent upon her new lover, and connives with him to murder her servant Diaphanta, who knows of the murder, having taken Beatrice-Joanna's place in Alsemero's dark bridal chamber in order to prevent her mistress's own unchaste condition being revealed to her new husband.

Beatrice-Joanna's secret is discovered by Alsemero's friend Jasperino, who was Diaphanta's lover. Beatrice-Joanna admits her crimes, and De Flores is exposed too. He stabs his lover, and then himself.

The play's sub-plot, most probably written by William Rowley, parodies but inverts the main plot. It is set in a lunatic asylum whose inmates are being trained to present a dance at Beatrice-Joanna's wedding. The keeper's wife Isabella is sought by two suitors disguised as madmen. The servant Lollio tries to blackmail her into allowing him to sleep with her, but unlike Beatrice-Joanna she resists all advances. Virtue is thus found in a madhouse, not a noble castle, although there is ample deception and counterfeiting in both.

Contexts

- Thomas Middleton wrote for Shakespeare's company, the King's men. He is thought to have been responsible for editing the existing texts of *Macbeth* and *Measure for Measure*. He is now thought by many to be the author of *The Revenger's Tragedy*.

- By 1622 the fashion for revenge tragedies (**p.126**) was still strong, but they had become more macabre and sinister (for example, Webster's *The Duchess of Malfi* **p.132**), perhaps as a reflection of the intrigues which were associated with the court of James I.

The tragedy of 'the irresponsible and undeveloped nature'

Beatrice-Joanna is a young woman full of life and energy, who loves Alsemero and hates De Flores with equal passion. She does not appear naïve or wicked, but in possession of an authentic love which is being stifled by the conventions of her society. She is not an unsympathetic figure. Yet she easily slips into commissioning murder, and is appalled to find a hidden lust for De Flores arising out of their common complicity. She discovers that her birth and wealth, the very factors which threatened to trap her in an unwanted marriage, are powerless in the face of De Flores' hold over her once she has employed him to kill Alonzo. She is 'the deed's creature' because the murder takes control of her life, rather than freeing her, and because she is a woman for whom sexual desire is the shaping force of her destiny.

T.S. Eliot felt that under the conventions of the revenge tragedy genre (**p.126**) there was in this play:

> a stratum of truth permanent in human nature. The tragedy of *The Changeling* is an eternal tragedy, as permanent as *Oedipus* or *Antony and Cleopatra*; it is the tragedy of the not naturally bad but irresponsible and undeveloped nature, caught in the consequences of its own action. In every age and in every civilisation there are instances of the same things: the unmoral nature, suddenly trapped in the inexorable toil of morality – of morality not made by man but by Nature – and forced to take the consequences of an act which it had planned light-heartedly. Beatrice-Joanna is not a moral creature; she becomes moral only by becoming damned. Our conventions are not the same as those which Middleton assumed for his play. But the possibility of the frightful possibility of morality remained permanent.

> *T.S. Eliot 1927: 163*

Eliot sees Beatrice-Joanna's tragedy as the discovery that there is a moral order in the universe which she had lacked the foresight to understand in her youth and energy. That is why she is a tragic, not an evil protagonist.

Predestination and the tragic woman

DE FLORES   Your eye shall instantly instruct you, lady.

1.1.93

Middleton, who is believed to have written the main plot scenes, is noted for his Calvinist views in other plays. As with Marlowe's *Dr Faustus* (**p.67**), Calvinist belief is not easily compatible with tragedy. Calvinists, who were a powerful and influential voice in London at the time, believed that God had chosen who would be saved and who would be damned even before mankind was created, and, as a result, the individual could not alter his or her fate. But is it possible for there to be tragedy in a world of predestination, when goodness and wickedness are simply a character's unchosen lot?

Michelle O'Callaghan points out that the sin which caused God to damn mankind was committed by a woman, Eve. For the Calvinist, all women are the descendents of Eve and so are marked out as sinful. Some may be saved by God's grace, but Beatrice-Joanna is not one of those, as her actions demonstrate. From the Calvinist perspective, Beatrice-Joanna is doomed from the very beginning of the play.

> If Beatrice-Joanna is irredeemably fallen, then she is comparable to Eve only in the misogynist sense that she will bring sin and death into this world. This reading makes sense of the recurrent association of De Flores with the serpent, most tellingly when Beatrice-Joanna is brought to the awareness of her predestined fallenness by De Flores: 'Was my creation in the womb so cursed,/It must engender with a viper first?' (3.4.165-6). 'Calvinist psychology' brings a different cluster of keywords relating to sight and judgement to the fore. These keywords are established in the first scene when the question of eyesight is particularly prominent. Beatrice-Joanna warns Alsemero:
>
> Be better advised, sir:
>
> Our eyes are sentinels unto our judgements,
>
> And should give certain judgements what they see;
>
> But they are rash sometimes, and tell us wonders
>
> Of common things, which when our judgements find,
>
> They can check the eyes, and call them blind. (1.1.71-6)
>
> Both Alsemero and Beatrice-Joanna have problems with their eyesight. Yet it is only Beatrice-Joanna's eye that is darkened in the scriptural sense: 'But if thine eye be evil, thy whole body shall be full of darkness' (Matthew vi:23). Her blindness derives from self-ignorance. It is important to point out that both Alsemero and Beatrice-Joanna mistake physical beauty for spiritual worth, and we need to consider why it is Beatrice-Joanna that is marked out as damned in the play. Part of the reason lies in the misogyny driving this Calvinist psychology that genders fallen nature feminine.

Michelle O'Callaghan 2009: 145-6

Beatrice-Joanna's own ignorance of the moral consequences of her desires, in this reading, is merely part of her doomed, fallen nature. The play is set in a castle and a madhouse, places where escape is precluded, and Beatrice-Joanna meets her death in a locked closet. Yet the part of Beatrice-Joanna does not seem to be written as a study in irredeemable evil. She has a vivacity and energy which make her more than a misogynistic embodiment of the fallen woman. The play is either an unsuccessful tragedy or an unsuccessful Calvinist text. T.S. Eliot, at least, thought that it 'stands above every tragic play of its time, except those of Shakespeare' (Eliot 1951: 165).

The tragic consequences of male language about women

> BEATRICE Forgive me, Alsemero, all forgive;
> 'Tis time to die when 'tis a shame to live.
>
> *5.3.178-9*

In the drama, but especially the poetry, of early modern England, women are often described in contradictory ways. On the one hand, they were the idealised beauties of courtly love poetry, creatures of holy purity. Alsemero's first sight of Beatrice-Joanna was 'in the temple'; he loves 'her beauties to the holy purpose' (1.1.1, 6); her voice is 'music', and his love is such that he lacks 'more words to express me further' (1.1.66, 69). On the other hand, women were the untrustworthy and lustful descendants of Eve, a condition to which all women were born; they are 'snares of beauty' (1.1.38) as Alsemero's friend Jasperino puts it. This is the way she is seen by De Flores, who believes that women will lust after even ugly men, such is their insatiable and irrational nature:

> there's daily precedents of bad faces
> Belov'd beyond all reason ... I ha' seen
> Women have chid themselves abed to men
>
> *2.1.83-4; 87-8*

A woman is so insatiable that if she is unfaithful once:

> she spreads and mounts then like arithmetic,
> One, ten, a hundred, a thousand, ten thousand ...
>
> *2.2.62-3*

Sara Eaton identifies this contradiction in the very language men use about women, and women about themselves in the play. This discourse places Beatrice-Joanna in a tragic situation, where she has no autonomy over her actions:

> Throughout *The Changeling*, Beatrice-Joanna succeeds all too well in her attempts to be as she is perceived. On the one side of Courtly Love's polarities, she portrays Alsemero's idealization of her. On the other side,

she personifies De Flores's view of self-degradation. Her rhetoric merely reproducing theirs, Beatrice-Joanna becomes an apparently harmonious representation of their conflicting desires. As a woman capable of seeming to be as they perceive her, she comes to perceive herself as an image of both idealized and degraded femininity – as a fallen Eve. Not autonomous in her actions, Beatrice-Joanna internalizes and reflects the inherent contradictions in male perceptions of women, especially as couched in the rhetoric of Courtly Love.

Sara Eaton 1991: 275-6

To be the subject of the 'inherent contradictions' of a powerful ideology is a tragic condition according to the **materialist** critics of the 20th century (**p.24**). This argument would also explain the sympathy which her character can engender in modern productions.

A comic catharsis? Involving the audience

BEATRICE   [*aside*] He's bold, and I am blam'd for it!

3.4.97

The Changeling, like all the great early modern plays, asks fundamental questions about the basis of what it means for each of us to be an 'individual' in a society where appearance stands for substance. It poses questions about the connections between our emotions and our sense of morality, and about love, sex and social class. It also constantly involves its audience in its action through a wide range of soliloquies and asides. The effect of this audience involvement is not necessarily to deepen the audience's emotional involvement in the tragedy, but often to induce black and ironic laughter. This humour operates to make us reflect upon the nature and the causes of the suffering in the play, and its connection with our own lives, perhaps: it has a **cathartic** function. Performance itself is the central means by which theatre can explore complex and conflicted – tragic – lives as they are lived.

Throughout the play Beatrice-Joanna and De Flores acknowledge the audience's presence and seek its understanding. A significant proportion of their lines are directed to the audience. This is particularly so in the most dramatic moments. For example, when De Flores makes clear the price of the murder to Beatrice (3.4.63-104), she speaks to the audience eight times in forty lines. If we read these asides as being some kind of internal monologue we miss the point. On stage De Flores must stand upstage of (behind) Beatrice as she confides her feelings to us, initially smugly ('What will content him? I would fain be rid of him' [line 72]), but ultimately disingenuously protesting her innocence ('He's bold, and I am blam'd for't! [line 97]). The actor playing De Flores is not inert during all this. He has already confided to the audience what his intentions are (2.2.146-53), and his expression must convey his feelings to them from behind her back.

This particular kind of dramatic irony, in which the audience shares knowledge with one on-stage character and not another, is typical of the play, and implicates us in De Flores's actions, especially if the actor's expression shares his undiscerned intention – almost, indeed, the joke – with us. For the covert communication of characters' feelings directly to the audience, asking for their approval, and the sharing of secrets, can certainly produce humour, albeit of a very dark kind. Even the murder of Alonzo plays upon this dynamic. De Flores' aside (3.2.4) acknowledges the audience's presence as witnesses to the act. Alonzo stands downstage, looking out, gazing through a window, but we can see his murderer approaching from behind. De Flores has already made several ambiguous remarks about Alonzo's fate whose meaning is hidden to his victim, but which we understand (3.2.1, 5, 13-14, 15). The grim humour here echoes the play's frequent use of more light-hearted but often very explicit sexual double entendre, both in the main and sub-plots, where the audience is invited to laugh knowingly at what characters may understand but cannot politely acknowledge (for example 1.1.136-52).

At crucial points in this play characters are helpless on stage for both our pathos and amusement. As the clock indicates the blatantly unreal passing of an hour in ten lines (5.1.1-10), Beatrice's frustration at Diaphanta's reluctance to leave Alsemero's arms is a very funny moment. But just as the murder scene concluded with the grizzly severing of Alonzo's bejewelled finger, the sudden appearance of his ghost at the moment when Beatrice and De Flores have agreed Diaphanta's death chills the mood again. When, in the final scene, Alsemero puts his wife and her lover into his closet to 'rehearse again/Your scene of lust' (5.3.114-5), and then twenty lines later she calls 'Oh, oh, oh!', we are again invited to think for an instant that we are overhearing off-stage sex just as Beatrice did earlier (when it is, of course, her mortal wounding which we hear).

The Changeling in performance is a troubling play because its tragedy succeeds in being extreme and implausible; yet it powerfully engages with the thoughts and emotions of the audience at the same time.

SOME KEY IDEAS TO CONSIDER

- The use of the imagery of sight in the play.

- The connections the play makes between sex and death.

- The impact of dark humour upon tragic sentiment.

- To what extent De Flores can be seen as a tragic figure.

EUROPEAN TRAGEDY IN THE LATE 19TH CENTURY

OVERVIEW

> Because they are modern characters, living in a period of transition more feverish than its predecessor at least, I have drawn my figures vacillating, disintegrated, a blend of old and new.
>
> *August Strindberg, outlining the principles of Naturalism, 1888*

All tragedy has an element of the unspeakable about it. Whether it be in Greek tragedy with Medea sacrificing her children, Hamlet harbouring strange Oedipal desires, or Brick Pollitt in *Cat on a Hot Tin Roof* quietly drinking himself into sexual denial, tragedies have always engaged with those aspects of contemporary society which either cannot, or will not, be articulated in everyday life. As theatrical fashions and styles have developed and evolved, the roots and causes of tragedy have changed and altered accordingly. When the food of the stage is war, kings, battles and politics, so the tragedies it produces reflect upon flawed soldiers and misguided leaders of men. When the stage turns inwards however, as it did towards the end of the 19th century, the tragedies become smaller also, but never relinquishing their power to shock, to outrage and to provoke in equal measure.

A spectacular pursuit

In the mid-19th century, theatre was becoming an increasingly grand, genteel pursuit. Thousands would attend huge theatres to watch performances of plays designed to give the best possible sense of a 'real' world. These spectacles, under threat from the rising popularity of the moving image, would use new tricks of staging to entertain audiences with their theatricality and illusion. Acting, meanwhile, was a simple process of declamation, and the concept of plot revolved mainly around the need to finish the show with a 'moral' conclusion and a bang. Great actors and companies ruled the stage – Edmund Kean, Henry Irving, David Garrick and others became successful 'actor-managers', the first impresarios – and often the great plays of the past were re-written or re-staged so as to make them more palatable to Victorian audiences. The emotional complexity of tragedy was increasingly marginalised as audiences looked, above all, to be entertained and to have the social order of their world reinforced and maintained, rather than torn down.

Reality bites back

In response to this gradual neutering of tragedy and its innate power, a new strand of drama sprang up aiming to 'force the theatre into sparing some room for intelligent discussion of recent developments in contemporary thought,' as Glynn Wickham puts it (Wickham 1992: 214). In this new theatre realistic, detailed situations were still produced, yet now with explicitly social or political comment as the writer's aim. The new style incorporated and influenced the teachings of Konstantin Stanislavski, who expounded a highly **naturalistic** style of theatre, presented as if the audience did not exist behind the 'fourth wall'. Writers from around Northern Europe – Henrik Ibsen and August Strindberg in Scandinavia, Anton Chekhov and Maxim Gorki in Russia – began to create detailed, realistic and contemporary theatre. They adopted many of the forms of tragedy and created works in which real lives are lived realistically, in all their ugly glory. These quiet tragedies would frequently deal with taboo topics, yet in an implicit way. Often the most shocking concerns of these works – sexual disease, infidelity, female liberation, social injustice – would never be fully articulated. Instead the lives of the characters on stage were displayed as realistically as possible, as if they existed in a kind of muted prison; eternal and inescapable, yet mundane and real.

Quiet tragedies

In these plays there is no great, final battle or brave sacrifice. Rather they end simply: sometimes with a small act of defiance or an implied decision which is never presented, sometimes with a return to stasis and halt. The tragedy in plays like Chekhov's *The Cherry Orchard* and *Three Sisters* is never fully realised; rather the traditional tragic form is inverted as shattered lives must simply go on. In works such as Strindberg's *Miss Julie* or Ibsen's *A Doll's House*, the conclusion is more definite, yet subtle, a moment or an action left to linger incomplete. Sometimes a play ends with a definitive act – Ibsen's Hedda Gabler leaving the room to commit suicide, or Chekhov's Konstantin shooting himself offstage in *The Seagull* – yet the moment is always one of quiet, fatalistic resolution, rather than gory, embattled comeuppance.

At the time of their first productions many – if not all – of these plays were met with only limited critical praise at best and open hostility at worst. That they were bringing the difficulties, the complexities and the pain of tragedy into the normal, social sphere was radical in the extreme. Audiences were not used to seeing dilemmas such as they might face themselves played out on stage, without any certainty of a happy outcome. Consequently the resistance to these works was, for a great many years, entrenched and firm. Yet these playwrights, and the **Naturalism** movement that formed around them, paved the way for the kind of theatre we know today – founded on principles of realism and presented often without recourse to happy endings or easy solutions. According to Martin Esslin, these works:

> contained the seeds of developments that would in due course bring about great changes in theatrical practice as well as a revaluation of the role of theatre in society.
>
> *Martin Esslin in John Russell Brown (ed.) 1997: 341*

LATE 19TH-CENTURY EUROPEAN TRAGEDY – OVERVIEW

These playwrights revived tragedy as an artistic tool and made it both explicitly political and uncomfortably real. By putting ordinary people in tragic situations, the theatre of the late 19th century directly made possible the powerful, grand and often explicitly angry works of writers such as Tennessee Williams, Samuel Beckett, John Osborne, Harold Pinter, Arthur Miller, Edward Bond and many more. Writers like Chekhov, Ibsen and Strindberg formed the vanguard of a new movement towards psychological realism in European theatre and, in so doing, they were also among the first to move tragedy from the realms of the untouchable and into the very tiny details of normality which create tragedians of us all. In embracing the unspoken and the unjust, these writers battled quietly but forcefully to pull tragedy down from the gods and the clouds and push it behind the fourth wall, out into the audience.

HENRIK IBSEN

OVERVIEW

It takes quite a leap of faith to be able to imagine how much of a sea change Henrik Ibsen and his style of theatre brought about in the late 19th century. Into an age of spectacle, scale and eternal morality, Ibsen was at the forefront of a movement that thrust complexity, psychology and a strong sense of social justice onto the stage. His was a moment at which theatre was emerging from an era of black-and-white issues, of good triumphing over evil, and beginning to explore the possibility of the grey area – those problematic margins in which no issue is necessarily as clear cut as it may seem. The style and thinking of the Moscow Art Theatre, under the auspices of Konstantin Stanislavski and his school, was spreading rapidly across Europe, and a new wave of progressive thinking artists were looking to challenge and reject traditional Victorian values and move into a modern era of greater liberty, equality and thought.

A long legacy

Throughout his plays, including his later, more psychologically involved works such as *The Wild Duck* (1884), *Hedda Gabler* (1890) and *Little Eyolf* (1894), Ibsen strove to present the unspeakable to audiences and to challenge their preconceptions and beliefs. His plays are tragedies in the sense that during the action a central character always comes through great difficulty to a point of realisation. The turmoil in these lives is almost always something Victorian society would have preferred to hide and yet, in his insistence on a true **naturalism**, Ibsen creates vividly real, persuasive characters within what Michael Booth refers to as:

> rooms where the family, under external and internal pressure, begins to disintegrate.
>
> *Michael Booth in John Russell Brown (ed.) 1997: 327*

These tragedies, however, differ from the classical model by being the first to touch on the lives of people just like those in the audience. In bringing tragedy down from the realms of gods and kings, Ibsen instigated a massive shift in drama, moving the stage away from mere spectacle and putting it right back at the centre of attempts to understand and explore the human condition – an avowed aim of tragedy right back to the time of the classical Greeks.

Early years

Ibsen grew up in a wealthy family that had fallen on hard times, always wanting to write. He worked for many years in Norway's major theatres as producer, stage-manager and director, but none of his own plays was ever produced. Having grown disenchanted he left Norway and finally found success, almost by accident, with two rough, sprawling, allegorical dramas about the difficulties facing man in his quest to be morally good. Neither *Brand* (1865) nor *Peer Gynt* (1867) were intended to be staged, yet their success allowed Ibsen the freedom to write the more socially concerned plays for which he was to become highly revered. His move toward a drama that would challenge and critique society inevitably meant a move towards tragedy and into an engagement with contemporary tragedies of real-life, those dramas in which good decisions are not always rewarded and good intentions do not always succeed.

The social play

The critic Martin Esslin has described these plays, from *Pillars of Society* in 1877 onwards, as being vital in pioneering the new theatre of **Naturalism**:

> No longer was the drama merely to make people feel good, it should become a branch of scientific inquiry, an experimental laboratory to explore human relations presenting images of the world as it really was, with all its ugliness, all its blemishes.
>
> *Martin Esslin in John Russell Brown (ed.) 1997: 342*

This meant that in all of Ibsen's naturalistic dramas he was breaking more radically with previously accepted dramatic conventions whereby morality and order were always seen to be restored. Instead, in plays such as *A Doll's House* (1879), *Ghosts* (1881) and *An Enemy of the People* (1882) the conclusions are almost universally complicated. Nora, in *A Doll's House*, decides to leave her husband in an era where female equality was still considered to be a shocking ideal. *Ghosts* concludes with a mother debating whether or not she should kill her syphilitic son who is slowly descending into a madness brought about by the philandering of his supposedly morally-upright father. Again, the mere mention of venereal disease onstage was unheard of in this era. Meanwhile Dr Thomas Stockmann, the eponymous *Enemy of the People*, stands forcefully for the idea that one individual can be proven correct even if the will of an entire community is against him. 'The strongest man in the world is the man who stands most alone,' Stockmann claims, firmly at odds with the Victorian notion of the community as a sacred institution.

In each of these plays Ibsen strove to explore the reasons why people must sometimes make hard decisions even in the face of social or cultural thinking to the contrary. In taking on the tired, outdated mores of his culture head on, Ibsen created memorably tragic figures, misunderstood by all around them, outnumbered and outfought, yet still able to make their influence felt long after the curtain had fallen on their demise.

A DOLL'S HOUSE (1879)

NORA	Sit down and play for me Torvald dear; criticize me, and show me where I'm wrong, the way you always do.
HELMER	I'd like to do that, if that's what you want.

A Doll's House 1879: 203

SYNOPSIS

Nora Helmer seemingly leads a contented life as a wife and mother, looked after by her husband Torvald, who treats her like a foolish child. Over the course of a few days either side of Christmas, the cosy married life of the Helmers falls apart catastrophically. Nora's husband, Torvald, has just been made manager of the local bank, but with new financial security comes a major worry for Nora, who has a secret from her husband – years ago she forged her father's signature in order to borrow money from Nils Krogstad. This money paid for a holiday vital to Torvald's health, but her actions were illegal. Now Krogstad, an employee at the Bank, visits Nora to plead for his job. When she ignores his pleas he threatens to reveal Nora's secret and shame both her and her husband unless she ensures that he keep his job.

Nora's friend, Christine Linde, agrees to try and convince Krogstad – her former lover – to relent. She persuades him by agreeing to rekindle their romance, but Krogstad has already posted a letter to Helmer and can do nothing to stop it being read.

Nora, in desperation, tries to distract her husband, but fails. Having read the letter, Helmer turns on Nora. He refuses to protect her, until word reaches him that Krogstad will relent. He then forgives his wife, but Nora by now realises she no longer loves him or her life. After a long debate about the nature of marriage, Nora leaves the house, and her family, for good.

Can you imagine a play causing a riot, a play with a subject so unspeakably horrific that it could spark an audience to violence? Imagine a star actress point-blank refusing to perform a role unless the dramatist re-writes the ending to make it more palatable. What could such a play possibly be about? If this were to have happened today, we might suggest religious or racial hatred, child abuse or gross depravity, perhaps. But in 1879 all it took was the sound of a front door closing.

Shockingly real

A Doll's House is arguably Henrik Ibsen's most famous play and certainly his most studied. It is also, on the surface at least, one of his simplest. To our modern palates it is the relatively prosaic tale of a marital breakdown, wrought under the pressure of circumstances including blackmail, guilt and excessive pride. Yet, during his lifetime, Ibsen's plays – and none more so than *A Doll's House* – were almost routinely greeted with disgust and incomprehension, the playwright receiving support only from limited, intellectual quarters. So why should this be? And what does the playwright's insistence on incorporating the tragic form tell us about the power of the genre to present challenging issues on the stage?

Ibsen was part of a new movement in European theatre which sought to create **naturalistic** plays: works in which characters react with psychological realism to situations as complex and demanding as real-life often throws up. As a result, the action of *A Doll's House* is set in one detailed and life-like room, lending a sense of real-life being observed to the audience's experience; the action unfolds over the course of a few days and involves only a few characters in a tale of marital breakdown. In this respect, Ibsen creates a 19th-century tragedy which follows, in formal respects, the parameters set out by Aristotle in his **unities of time, place and action**. Unlike classical Greek tragedy, however, this is a subtle play whose power comes from allusion and familiarity rather than spectacle and might. To appreciate the true power and tragedy inherent in what has often been described as the first ever 'feminist' play, we need to consider it within the context in which it was originally performed.

An ordered society

Almost from the very beginning of the play the audience is made aware of a powerful set of routines and strictures governing the lives and the specific roles of the characters on stage. It is this order that Ibsen was seeking to criticise and demolish. The sense of a formalised and hierarchical relationship between husband and wife is created in the very first scene as Nora Helmer, the central figure in the drama, tries to hide her illicit nibbling of macaroons from husband Torvald. 'Didn't Little Sweet-Tooth just look in at the confectioner's?' asks Torvald. Nora replies with multiple denials, before assuring her husband 'I wouldn't do anything that you don't like' (Ibsen, p.151). From this short piece of interaction, through the pet-name-calling and the deference of Nora, we infer that this is a marriage based on order, duty and ownership. Nora's lie further creates a sense that beneath this surface lies deception, not trust and affection. In subtly revealing the tensions in the Helmer household, Ibsen is dramatising a situation and set of relationships which was far from uncommon in Victorian society. Indeed the established order of Torvald's household – in which the children are raised largely by a nanny, Helmer works privately in his study and Nora is left largely alone to maintain the prettiness of both the household and herself – was the accepted norm. That the play goes on radically to challenge the old order is tantamount to a shocking declaration of dissatisfaction with the established patterns of society.

Attacking the sacred order of marriage was a radical act in Ibsen's time. Throughout the action it becomes clear that Nora is trapped in a marriage which is simply a convenient social façade, and little else. In her constant playing up for Torvald, the trilling, the role-playing, the all-too-hearty insistence that it is 'wonderful to be alive and happy' (Ibsen, p.163) we see her desperation to attain affection. Yet all these actions also point unmistakably towards a deep and inexpressible unhappiness in the character. Driven to breaking point by Krogstad's threats, Dr Rank's declaration of unending love and the thought of bringing shame and ruin upon her husband, Nora ends Act Two with a startling dance, made all the more grim for its gaiety at a moment of crisis.

Describing what he calls 'The Function of Tragedy', Aristotle states that 'through pity and terror [tragedy] effects the purgation of these emotions' (McLeish, ed., Aristotle, p.8). He is referring to the effect made upon the spectator yet, also, the same notion could easily be applied to Nora's frantic Tarantella. In trying to distract Torvald from reading his mail, Nora desperately offers to practise her dance for the party that evening. She goes on to do so, as Helmer observes, 'as if your life depended on it!' (Ibsen, p.204). The release of emotion, stress and anger that is implicit in this wild and frantic act is used quite brilliantly by Ibsen to point toward a watershed in Nora's thinking. Here, at the conclusion of this crazy dance, having visibly purged her emotions and her sense of social decorum, Nora finally seems to come to some sort of realisation. She has experienced the **catharsis** that Aristotle believed to be brought about by tragedy, and tells Mrs Linde that it is 'a wonderful thing to be waiting for a miracle' (Ibsen, p.206). In the final act, just as predicted, the miracle arrives – much to the shock of Ibsen's Victorian audience.

Ibsen's view of contemporary tragedy

Of course, such a shocked response is exactly what Ibsen hoped to achieve with this play, and with those that followed it. To challenge ingrained attitudes was his stated aim and in setting out to write A Doll's House he made initial plans under the telling heading 'Notes for the contemporary tragedy'. According to Hanssen:

> Ibsen's project in this play is to apply the classical form of tragedy to a modern body of material. On the formal level Ibsen does not engage in radical experimentation in A Doll's House. For example the three classical unities are maintained, the unities of time, space and action. What is new is the modern material of conflict, the topicality of what is taking place on the stage.
>
> J.M. Hanssen: 'Ibsen and Realism' 2003: www.ibsen.net

To bring the matter of his tragedy down to the level of ordinary people would give it greater power to shock and, crucially, to influence the thinking of people who may be in the same type of predicament. As a result we see, over the course of the play's three acts, the reality of the pressure upon the Helmers' marriage, the rigid social strictures to which the marriage must nevertheless adhere and, crucially, the inexpressible conclusion to which this strain finally leads.

The final twist

In giving Nora her famous and triumphant moment of recognition, Ibsen wrought a terrific trick on his audience. At just the point at which a Victorian audience would expect the play to move into the realms of the cosy, morally-resolved melodrama, Ibsen reasserts the principles of tragedy to emphatic effect:

TORVALD	Nora! Wait, I must read it again… Yes, it's true; I'm saved! Nora, I'm saved!
NORA	And I?
TORVALD	You too, of course. We're both saved – both you and I.

A Doll's House 1879: 222

With her simple question, Nora begins to articulate the sense of **anagnorisis**, or realisation, at which the true tragic hero must finally arrive. 'I have another duty…,' she announces, 'My duty to myself' (Ibsen, p.227, 228), before going on to challenge Helmer's commitment to their marriage and, finally, to slam the door on their relationship (potentially) forever.

The play truly was a 'contemporary tragedy', with Ibsen placing a woman in the role of tragic hero. Nora is brought low by mistakes and flaws, certainly, but it could be argued that none of her personal flaws are more than simple mistakes of judgement. Rather the flaws which truly bring about her defeat are not, for Ibsen, within herself – they are ingrained within the institution of marriage and within the very society in which both she and the audience lived. Her final departure is both the defeat to which the tragic hero must succumb – she loses, after all, her children, her security and her respect in such a harshly moral society – and a deliberate act of defiance. In turning her back on her marriage and her perceived duty, Ibsen makes a hero of Nora, whilst simultaneously challenging his stunned audience to deny that they would ever even think of doing the same.

SOME KEY IDEAS TO CONSIDER

- Whether you interpret Nora's final departure as permanent or temporary, and the difference each interpretation makes to the play's tragic status.

- Why Nora seems finally to find clarity in the final act.

- What Ibsen means when he refers to the 'greatest miracle of all'. Is this a reflection of his opinion on Victorian society?

- Whether Krogstad, too, could be considered a tragic hero in the light of his final act.

- Why the play caused such controversy in its day.

- How the play changes and subverts aspects of classical tragedy.

ANTON CHEKHOV

> In life there are no clear-cut consequences or reasons; in it everything is mixed up together; the important and the paltry, the great and the base, the tragic and ridiculous. One is hypnotised and enslaved by routine and cannot manage to break away from it. What are needed are new forms, new ones.
>
> *Anton Chekhov in Vera Gottlieb and Paul Allain (eds) 2000: 60*

OVERVIEW

Anton Chekhov was not a revolutionary playwright in the typical sense. His plays are not angry or violent or overtly political. They are largely well-made, domestic and concern the upper classes and educated professionals. He wrote very few full-length plays and certainly never considered himself a playwright any more than he considered himself an author or, indeed, a doctor. Yet his legacy – arguably as much as any playwright since Shakespeare – is enormous. What Chekhov created, against all fashion at the time, was a new way of treating drama, of using his characters, of creating and advancing plot. From old forms he created new ones, and from classical tragedy he created a modern, flexible template for the 20th century.

Chekhov's dramatic output is, comparatively, very small. Alongside a number of one act plays – mostly considered by their author to be farces and vaudevilles not worthy of serious consideration – there exist only six full-length plays, of which two, *Platonov* and *Ivanov*, are considered to be minor works, either unfinished or lacking in the clear, precise dramatic vision of his later work. The four remaining plays, however, represent an amazingly strong canon of work: *The Seagull* (1896), *Uncle Vanya* (1899), *Three Sisters* (1901) and *The Cherry Orchard* (1904) form a powerful quartet, each play distinctively different from the next and yet linked by a richness of detail and a difficulty of performance that has become known as 'Chekhovian'. The theatre director Trevor Nunn sums up this difficulty:

> These are plays that one could work on for the whole of one's life and never exhaust them.
>
> *Trevor Nunn in Vera Gottlieb and Paul Allain (eds) 2000: 108*

Theatre of disappointment

All of Chekhov's great plays are characterised by an absence, a lack of progression, a sense of things remaining the same for better or for worse. This does not mean, however, that nothing happens. Indeed there is a curious contradiction in Chekhov's major plays: there are large casts of characters, multiple plots and many actions unfolding, yet still the impression the audience is left with is one of lack – what we are not shown, what is not said and what does not change. What happens in these plays is driven by character and by psychology, and is often only suggested in the text and what we see and hear on stage. Ingrained in this sense of stillness is a kind of stoic acceptance of fate and circumstances which often comes across as both brave and strange. Vera Gottlieb sums this idea up when she observes that Chekhov deliberately alternates 'the serious' with 'the trivial'. She goes on to remark that:

> it is one of the most important characteristics of his style and intent: his concern, often expressed, was with the banalities and trivialities of everyday life – and yet time passes, life slips by, opportunities are lost, and unhappiness and disappointment are poured out over a glass of tea.
>
> *Vera Gottlieb 2000: 59-60*

Chekhov's characters so often seem to accept their fate that in his plays there can be found a rich seam of the tragic that is often never expressed or presented, but is instead merely implied or ignored.

Unlike the tragedies of the classical authors, his plays are not grand or triumphal; nor are they controversial or startling like those of his contemporaries Ibsen, Strindberg or Gorky. Chekhov's is a theatre of disappointment, exploring what he called 'the sad comicality of everyday life'. He takes the banalities, the trivial and the mundane moments of life and elevates them to great and touching dramatic heights. He explores those tiny disappointments that affect us all, and he explores in great detail the tragic and the heroic that can often be found in people's reactions to them. As Gottlieb observes:

> When people are really unhappy, Chekhov said, they just whistle.
>
> *Vera Gottlieb 2000: 60*

THE SEAGULL (1896)

Of the four major plays, *The Seagull* stands somewhat apart in that it does feature a definite, violent and tragic climax, although even this is subtly presented. The young writer Konstantin, depressed, suicidal and rejected by those around him, shoots himself, having realised the damage he has done to the young, beautiful Nina. However, the act itself happens offstage and is conveyed to the audience in a genteel, reserved way as Dr. Dorn brings the famed writer Trigorin to one side and whispers the news that Konstantin has shot himself – the last words of the play. This conclusion may seem to be very definite, but even here Chekhov was creating a new, more subtle form. This is seen best in the preceding scene in which Konstantin: 'for two whole minutes... silently tears up all his manuscripts and throws them under the desk' (Chekhov, p.140), a brave dramatic move signalling utter, yet very quiet desperation. This scene is a greater representation of the quiet, symbolic tragedy to which the writer would later return.

UNCLE VANYA (1899)

Uncle Vanya is infused by a strong sense of quiet, noble sadness. The sense of lost opportunity and wasted potential which permeates proceedings is typical of Chekhov's later style. His plays rely heavily on the unsaid and on subtext and, in this, they offer an ideal form of what Aristotle called *mimesis* – they are a true representation of real life. 'The arts imitate people doing things', Aristotle declared, adding that 'tragic characters idealise those of real life, comic ones parody them' (McLeish, ed. 1998: 13). Chekhov's plays are all about people doing things, and doing them in a recognizable yet idealised way. An audience is asked to see the predicaments of the characters and their decisions as being the result of many complex forces, not as simple questions of right or wrong.

In *Uncle Vanya* many characters sacrifice themselves for reasons that may never be made entirely clear. Wives stay with awkward husbands, dreamers sacrifice themselves for the communal good and Vanya himself, who believes he could have been the next Dostoevsky but for his own selflessness, turns away from thoughts of suicide and murder, choosing not the grand tragic gesture, but an acceptance of the status quo. It's a conclusion which powerfully highlights for the audience both his own tragedy and the redemptive nature of his (and mankind's) situation. The play's closing speech, given by Vanya's niece Sonia, is an apt distillation of the tragic power of good faith, stoicism and patience. 'What can we do?' she asks her Uncle.

> We've got to live! (*A pause*) We shall live, Uncle Vanya. We shall live out many, many days and long evenings; we shall patiently bear the trials fate sends us... and when our time comes, we shall meekly die, and there beyond the grave, we shall say that we suffered, that we wept, that we were sorrowful and God will have pity on us.

> *Anton Chekhov 1899: 200*

The play closes with Sonia announcing that, when that time comes, 'We shall rest' (Chekhov, p.140). To bear up and face real life is not easy, to deny oneself opportunity is hard, but this is real life as Chekhov saw it and in this, mankind's tragic state, he tells us we must find hope and solace from the trials of others.

THREE SISTERS (1901)

Chekhov's last two plays – *Three Sisters* and *The Cherry Orchard* – both expand upon this idea of tragic and powerful acceptance. At the heart of *Three Sisters* lies the ideal of Moscow, the city for which the sisters of the title yearn but to which they will never move. The play is infused with both the possibility and, ultimately, *impossibility* of escape as, finally, each sister must settle for her lot: Olga, her reluctant position as headmistress in the local school; Masha, her unhappy marriage, having been swept away by the soldier Vershinin; and Irina, her dreams and aspirations, after a duel between her two suitors results in the death of the Baron Tusenbach. Again, the conclusion reached is that to continue is the only way to survive – and this realisation is one of both tragedy and redemption. In this case it is Irina, the youngest sister, who declares that:

> A time will come and everyone will know the reason for all this, all this suffering, there will be no secrets, but for the time being we must live ... we must work, just work!

> *Anton Chekhov 1901: 279*

THE CHERRY ORCHARD (1904)

In *Three Sisters*, the women find that to remain is to survive; in *The Cherry Orchard* the opposite is the case. Probably the most subtextual and delicate of all the plays, *The Cherry Orchard* is a masterclass in the theatre of evasion and sadness. It contains no single main plot, no great romance, no death and, as Chekhov boasted, not even one gunshot. As Edward Braun notes, during the course of the action:

> it becomes clear that everyone is at the mercy of a process of change beyond their control and comprehension.

> *Edward Braun in Vera Gottlieb and Paul Allain (eds) 2000: 116*

It is a play in which the tragic and the comic are blended, as a wealthy, land owning family come to realise that change is inevitable and that to admit defeat is also to display bravery. As the family agree to sell the estate, to let the orchard be cut down, they must also come to say goodbye and accept that things are sometimes better left alone. Anya, the daughter of the house, comforts her mother with these words:

> The cherry orchard is sold, it's no longer there, that's the truth, the truth, but don't cry, Mama, you have your life ahead of you ... We will plant a new orchard, more splendid than this one, you will see it, you will understand.

> *Anton Chekhov 1904: 332*

Out of the despair of these characters, as in all of Chekhov's plays, must come something new: a new orchard, a new dream. At the moment of greatest despair, just as in classical tragedy, there comes a realisation, an acceptance, the moment of **anagnorisis**. Where Chekhov set the template for much 20th-century tragedy that would follow, was in the reaction to this realisation.

It is in the responses of these characters to difficulty, in their acceptance of other forces – be it fate, or economics or tradition – that guide and influence their life, that Chekhov's characters attain a sainted, elevated air. The stoicism and the sacrifice on display in these plays is never far from heartbreaking, yet is always framed positively and even with humour. These are tragedies of the modern spirit through which Chekhov tells us to keep our chins up and just keep going.

SOME KEY IDEAS TO CONSIDER

- Whether there are heroes or villains in Chekhov's plays, or whether the distinction is more subtle.

- The fact that much of the meaning in Chekhov comes from subtext. Does this give the audience greater freedom when responding to the plays?

- Many people consider Chekhov to be a comic rather than tragic playwright. Do you agree with this?

- The way in which Chekhov uses time to create tragic and powerful effects.

MODERN

IRISH

TRAGEDY

OVERVIEW

Ireland has given English drama some of its greatest playwrights – Sheridan, Farquhar, Wilde and Shaw among others. Irish drama, however, is usually understood as writing by Irish dramatists that have their main impact on Irish culture and society. The most-studied of these writers are John Millington Synge, Sean O'Casey, and Brian Friel. These writers share two broad characteristics:

- their plays tend to reflect the fraught politics between Ireland, the colonised nation, and England, the coloniser and they do so in the language of the coloniser

- their plays frequently have wonderfully comic elements but also contain a deeper current of tragic feeling, often closely associated with the troubled politics between Ireland and England.

Synge and O'Casey were educated artists, as is Friel. All three take inspiration from their Greek and Shakespearean inheritance. The tragic rhythm of human error, death, and rebirth into a heightened state of learning, is present in the form and content of all their greatest work.

Although Irish born, Samuel Beckett does not deal in the same way with the Irish context and issues as the three playwrights considered in this chapter. His major contribution to tragic drama and his seminal play *Waiting for Godot*, are explored separately on page 177.

England and Ireland

The political relationship between these two countries has been bloodily contested for centuries. Ever since the 16th century, Ireland has been trying to assert its independence from England. In the years since, 'Protestant' came to be loosely identified with English-settler and, therefore, hostile to the 'Catholic' native Irish. The conflict in Ireland has often seemed to be a war of religions. In reality, it has more to do with struggles for independence from the United Kingdom than the particular worship practices of two branches of Christianity.

Historical and political tragicomedy

The Irish playwrights considered here – Synge, O'Casey and Friel – all mix up genres, a characteristic they share with other late 19th and early 20th-century dramatists, such as Ibsen and Chekhov. There is 'seriousness' in their work, and a recognition that the lives of their characters are often unhappy and apparently out of their control. In that respect they are tragic characters, but they are often foolish and find themselves in absurd situations that also make them figures of fun. Often they react to the slings and arrows of outrageous fortune with a shield of comic defiance. It would be a generalisation, but perhaps justifiable, to say that Irish drama deploys this tragicomic defence more frequently than most.

Something that makes good comedy is the gap between what people secretly aspire to be and do, and what reality forces on them. This is true of tragedy too, but unlike classical tragedy, 20th-century dramatists have tended to see that gap in the way that society as a whole is organised. The 'reality' that thwarts happiness in the modern world is not the gods, or **fate**, or some hero's **tragic flaw**, but the often absurd situations that politics and history seem to impose on people. The long struggle for Irish self-determination is, in the world view of many Irish playwrights, an underlying tragic situation that frequently causes their characters to raise that shield of comedy to deal with misery and worlds out of joint. Irish drama could, then, be characterised as historical and political tragicomedy.

The political background – some key events

1916 The Easter Rising. This was a failed attempt by armed nationalists to start a revolutionary war that would throw the British out of Ireland. It was put down by British troops and its leaders executed. Although a failure, it acquired the status of a heroic action that became an inspiration for later anti-colonial actions.

1922 Armed resistance to British occupation continued into the 1920s. The British government began to reconcile itself to an independent Ireland and in 1922, the Anglo-Irish Treaty came into effect. Ireland became an independent dominion within the British Commonwealth (as were Canada or Australia), apart from the north-eastern province of Ulster which was mainly Protestant but with a significant Catholic minority. Ulster became 'Northern Ireland', governed from London as part of the United Kingdom. (This is still the constitutional position today, although Ireland is no longer a dominion but an independent state.)

1972 A growing Civil Rights movement, modelled on the one black people created in America, had started in the 1960s. Aimed at establishing equality for Catholic citizens living in Northern Ireland, the movement's failure to achieve its aims led to a polarisation, with armed movements like the IRA (Irish Republican Army) and the UVF (Ulster Volunteer Force) confronting each other on behalf of their respective communities, and threatening to tip Northern Ireland into full-blown civil war. British troops were sent to protect the minority Catholic population but became embroiled in the region's complex politics. On January 30th (often named 'Bloody Sunday') British troops fired on a Civil Rights march in Londonderry, killing and wounding 13 people. Northern Ireland entered a period of violent communal conflict that provisionally ended in 1997 with the Good Friday Agreement.

THE PLAYWRIGHTS

J.M. SYNGE

Synge was fascinated by two contrasting elements: the new, socially-conscious European drama of writers like Chekhov and Ibsen, writing predominantly in the tragic mode; and the lives and culture of the Irish peasants who lived on the West coast of Ireland.

In The *Playboy of the Western World* (1907), his best-known play, he combines the two elements with a new tone that has come almost to define Irish drama, the mixing of tragic seriousness with comedy. This tragicomic form is different from the Shakespearean model, where serious action is relieved, or comically mirrored, by clowning. This dark comedy becomes a vehicle that can show the world's reality and confusion as accurately as tragedy.

SEAN O'CASEY

If Synge was mainly a writer of the countryside, another Abbey Theatre discovery, O'Casey, wrote mainly about the city. In particular, his work replaces romanticised ideas about the rural communities with harder-nosed politics about the city. His most famous plays form a tragic trilogy, all set in Dublin, and all dealing in the political and personal lives of people involved in the struggle for Irish independence. *The Shadow of a Gunman* (1923), *Juno and the Paycock* (1924) and *The Plough and the Stars* (1926) all deal with events between 1916 and 1924. This was a turbulent, often violent period in Irish history (**p.163**). These plays not only stand up against the injustice of occupation by the English, but also take a cool, often comic, look at the nationalists and their delusions and follies. Again, as with Synge, the comedy is the reality the playwright sees. It is not there just to give relief from more serious material. Nevertheless, the outcomes for the main characters are often disastrous. The deep tragic pattern of death and resurrection is ever-present, although the resurrection may only exist in what the audience takes away as new understanding rather than in the events of the play itself. For example, at the end of *Juno and the Paycock*, there is as clear a statement of tragic pessimism as you can get:

> I'm telling you…Joxer…th'whole worl's…in a terr…ible state o'…chassis!
>
> *Sean O'Casey 1924 in Three Plays 1994: 73*

However, it is uttered by a drunk character who has made us laugh at him and so his pessimism is contained and moderated.

BRIAN FRIEL

On the Bloody Sunday march of January 30th 1972 was a teacher-turned-playwright called Brian Friel. Of all the modern Irish playwrights, Brian Friel's ability to bring a dark humour to bear on Ireland's tragic history makes him particularly important. He had already had a significant hit with his 1964 play *Philadelphia, Here I Come!* Set on the night before a young man is about to leave Ireland to live in the United States, the play's themes reflect the realities of the time – that opportunities were few and far between for young Irish people unless they uprooted and left. This early success for Friel suggests that a country whose young generation has to leave to make meaningful lives elsewhere is damaged, and that this reality is tragic.

The play's American connection also points to a truth that many Irish people looked West across the Atlantic Ocean, rather than to Britain, for their future.

Events in Londonderry in 1972 led Friel to write another highly-regarded play, *The Freedom of the City* (1973), whose fictional world drew its inspiration from 'Bloody Sunday'. Friel's special skill has always been to combine a very sharp understanding of the complexities of Irish politics with a great generosity of spirit towards his characters and their worlds. He combines something of Synge's poetic relationship to the landscape and traditions of Ireland, with O'Casey's bittersweet comic analysis of the lives of people in moments of complex political and social upheaval. Friel's best-known plays are *Dancing at Lughnasa* (1990), *Making History* (1988), and *Translations* (1980), but he has been a prolific writer of plays since the 1960s. In most of these deeply humane plays, there is a tragic pattern in which ordinary people are offered up as sacrifices to the relentless pressures of encroaching modern living.

In Friel's work, the devastation and loss of the tragic experience is often made more optimistic by a softening that appears to lighten the end of his plays. However, there is a sting in the tail of these endings. For example, in *Dancing at Lughnasa*, the storyteller appears to end with an image of healing, of the dancing that has come through the radio to the isolated sisters in the heart of the countryside. The audience, however, has earlier witnessed the sisters' dancing as something fierce and angry, their lives destroyed by economic pressures and a powerlessness in the face of a brasher, more individualistic world on the horizon. Friel balances his tragedy with hope, but roots that hope in bleak social realities.

J.M. SYNGE

THE PLAYBOY OF THE WESTERN WORLD (1907)

SYNOPSIS

Into a fishing village on the wild Atlantic shore of Western Ireland stumbles a young man, Christopher 'Christy' Mahon. He seems to be a mysteriously romantic figure who flashes his linguistic seduction about the village, upsetting the men and beguiling at least some of the women. He boastfully claims to have murdered his father, a boast that proves hollow when his father turns up, battered but alive. The villagers react in different ways to this anarchic, violent duo in their midst. Sometimes they worship Christy and his dad. Later, as Christy's romantic fiction unravels, they attack him and try to get him hung. In the end, Christy and his father choose to leave the village, expelled like poison, but losing none of the defiant energy with which they have charmed and tricked the community.

When *The Playboy of the Western World* opened in Dublin in 1907, a section of the audience tried to shout the play down. This is an extraordinary tribute to the power of the play, and the ideas it brought into Irish society.

On the surface, some of the offence was caused by the flirtatious sexuality displayed by some of the female characters. There is an unmistakable teasing wit in the way the girls gather round Christy Mahon with their food offerings at the beginning of Act Two. Although close attention to the spoken text makes clear that Christy and the object of his love, Pegeen, never share a room let alone a bed, the general atmosphere of an open, realistic sexuality is so strong that elements of polite Dublin society probably saw more immorality than there is.

The line that caused greatest offence, however, seems to have been in Act 3 when Christy rejects an exaggerated sexual fantasy ('... what'd I care if you brought me a drift of chosen females, standing in their shifts itself maybe, from this place to the Eastern World.') for the love of Pegeen. Never mind that Christy is *turning down* a fantasy of thousands of girls in their underclothing, the straightlaced audience rioted at the very image spoken on a public stage.

This sexual prudery actually hides another, related, sensitivity. The period around the beginning of the 20th century was full of artistic, political and intellectual urging for the cause of Irish nationalism. Some of this was expressed as hostility to British occupation, but some was a positive championing of Irish culture. In Synge's case he became fascinated by the lives of peasants on the west coast of

Ireland. Some nationalists took Synge's interest in peasant life, particularly what he saw as its more natural sexuality, as an implied insult to their idealised, almost fundamentalist version of 'Irishness'. Merely suggesting that Irish peasant women could be sexual beings thus offended two sections of the audience – those who disapproved of any sexual suggestiveness on stage, and those who thought sexuality somehow damaged the image of proud Irish nationalism. The play dramatises, in tragicomic form, challenging realities that society finds unpalatable and attempts to repress.

The mixture of genres, typical of many modernist plays, means that its tragic elements are less obvious than in classical tragedy, yet there are formal elements from tragedy that the play draws on. There is, for instance, a sacrificial figure (**a scapegoat**), Christy (and his battered father). In the end, Christy escapes from the village, having escaped punishment and death, so his arc through the play moves from the tragic to the comic. It is as if the tragic energy he brings with him as the outsider stains others around him, particularly Pegeen, but he leaves strangely cleansed. There is social criticism in the play, another characteristic of modernist tragedy, shared by playwrights like Ibsen and Miller. The **tragic flaw** is lodged in the way a community runs itself, and the values it lives by. The wild Atlantic village that Christy and his father erupt into is tested by their presence. They fall under his spell (to varying degrees) and are revealed as at first gullible and, later, vengeful. It is as if Christy is like a modern-day celebrity who tricks his way into public favour then skips away again leaving hurt and damage behind him. It may be no accident that his name invokes the Biblical Christ, another stranger who enters the community to expose its hypocrisies and failures. In the Bible story, Christ is sacrificed. In Synge's story, Christy escapes and it is Pegeen Mike's life that is sacrificed, ironically to a man fearful of his religious masters.

It is that downbeat and troubled ending that shades an energetic comedy with tragedy. The 'playboy' is a trickster, a hustler, a story-teller, living off his wits, but he is not a conventional villain that we want to see punished. In some ways, Christy Mahon is a sacrificial figure whose arrival in the village exposes its values and assumptions, and he suffers because of them. There is great comedy in *The Playboy of the Western World*, but there is an underlying tragic pattern too. If the community cannot live with the Mahons' energies, and they have to be expelled, the tragic outcome is personalised in Pegeen Mike's loss of her dangerous love, and her confinement to a lifetime of marriage to a dull, religious obsessive. It is also imprisonment of a sort for the community as a whole. Their geographic horizons may be magnificent but their spiritual horizons, by the play's end, seem narrow and parochial. Here again the tragic form highlights the gap between aspiration and reality.

Critical perspective

Often they [Synge, O'Casey, Beckett] contravene traditional definitions. None, for instance, would meet the Aristotelian criteria as adumbrated in his *Poetics*. However, in a broader category, certain plays of Synge – *Riders to the Sea* (1904) and *Deirdre of the Sorrows* (1910) – and O'Casey – the Dublin trilogy, *The Silver Tassie* (1928) – might well fall within a canon of modern tragedy. More significant, perhaps, than the simple question of genre is the underlying tragic vision that informs a particular play. For instance, *The Playboy of the Western World* (1907), ending with Christy's triumphant exit, may not look much like a conventional tragedy, yet there is a sheer tragic quality to Pegeen Mike's belated recognition 'Oh my grief, I've lost him surely. I've lost the only playboy of the western world'. The same goes for the other ostensibly comic plays of Synge. Within the plays of each of the three dramatists, those aspects of tragedy that are asserted and those that are resisted illuminate his attitude to art and suffering, and the significance of these beliefs and dispositions to the cultural and political context within which he writes.

Ronan McDonald 2001: 3

SOME KEY IDEAS TO CONSIDER

- Who it is that experiences the greatest loss, and tragic outcome, in this play.

- The tragic pattern of death and rebirth – can you see this in Synge's play? Who, or what, dies and is re-born.

- The relationship between comedy and tragedy.

- The extent to which tragedy ceases to be about class and status in this play. What do you think Synge explores instead?

SEAN O'CASEY

THE SHADOW OF A GUNMAN (1923)

SYNOPSIS

In 1920, in the middle of a civil war caused by a power struggle before Ireland achieves its independence, two men share a room in a Dublin slum. Donal Davoren is a failed poet, shacked up with an unsuccessful salesman, Seamus Shields. When the neighbours in the tenement building start speculating that he might have connections with the IRA (Irish Republican Army), Donal plays along, excited by the effect this has on them, in particular the committed republican supporter Minnie Powell. In the play's second act, the British Army storms the tenement and Minnie is shot dead defending what she thinks is her brother-in-arms, Donal.

Context

Sean O'Casey was born into a poor lower-middle class family in 1880, and his most famous plays, the so-called 'Dublin' trilogy, are about class, his city, and most important of all, his times.

In Irish history, the years covered by these three plays, 1916 to 1922, are years when the centuries-old struggle for Irish independence came to a more-or-less final conclusion. The path to the Anglo-Irish Treaty of 1922, establishing an Irish Free State, was often bloody and violent. O'Casey's particular skill and insight was to write from the experience of ordinary working class people, caught up in the courageous but often (in his view) deluded heroics of the Irish resistance. His views are entirely Nationalist and anti the British occupation, but his sympathies are with the ordinary poor of Dublin.

The Shadow of A Gunman is set in 1920, in the last phase of British occupation. The Irish Republican Army is fighting a guerilla war against the British Army. Two young men living in a run-down Dublin tenement, are left with a bag of hand grenades by the IRA friend of one of them. They don't discover that it contains bombs until late in the play but the IRA connection proves fatal for at least one resident of the tenements, Minnie Powell.

Questioning heroism

Synge's Christy Mahon spins an heroic identity for himself, but O'Casey's Donal Davoren has an heroic identity thrust upon him. Neither he, nor his roommate

Seamus Shields are actually heroic, though Donal enjoys flirting with the role of resistance hero. Other people wrongly seem to assume he has IRA connections. In particular, Minnie Powell, the pretty and tough-minded girl who lives in a room at the top of the house, is captivated by the romantic aura of a noble, self-sacrificing national hero that she thinks him to be. In reality, he is very unheroic.

In Act One, we get to know the texture of life for people who live on the edge. There is a claustrophobic feeling, with the action confined to a dingy room in which nothing much happens apart from the banter between the two occupants, interrupted by occasional visits from a threatening landlord or strange neighbours, and once, significantly, by the real IRA man who lumbers them with incriminating weapons. Of all the people who fill the act, the one who seems least damaged either by poverty or cynicism, is Minnie. In Act Two, however, she pays a high price for this openness and naiveté.

The influence of Chekhov, Ibsen and Gorki

There is a very detailed stage direction at the start of the play. This is a play from the world of **Naturalism**, the world of Chekhov, Ibsen, and the Russian playwright Gorki, where the space and the objects in it are almost as important as the characters and the actions. The run-down tenement setting in some ways represents Ireland. Certainly, the mysterious bag holds an almost literally explosive symbolic significance: it represents all the responsibilities and challenges that confront the people of Ireland.

The absurd

If reality is outside the front doors, and on the streets, there is a touch of **the absurd** inside (**p.28** and **p.178**). The most famous 'absurdist' play of all, Samuel Beckett's *Waiting for Godot*, written in a later war, and in another occupied country, France, has echoes of O'Casey's play. Beckett's world is more abstract and symbolic, while O'Casey's is stage-directed to the hilt but both plays combine comedy with an underlying tragic spirit. Again, as in Synge's *Playboy of the Western World*, the surface texture is often comic, but the pattern of events is tragic, with the obvious fatal or **tragic flaw** in this case being Donal's need for love and admiration. By encouraging Minnie's illusion, he becomes responsible for her needless death. Minnie becomes the tragic sacrifice, not just to Donal's fantasies, but to the political realities caused by Britain's occupation of Ireland. Tragedy, as so often in Irish drama, is driven by historical circumstances, which act as the modern equivalent of classical fate.

Critical perspective

To Davoren is attributed authority partly owing to his superior education and partly to his imagined status as gunman on the run: the two are linked together. Donal has just the glamour for Minnie Powell that Christy Mahon has for Pegeen Mike (in *The Playboy of the Western World*) the potent combination of 'savagery and fine words'. The comedy of cross-purposes is similar in that neither Christy nor Davoren are the heroes they are thought to be by the strange community into which they come, the one only a pretend parricide, the other the mere shadow of a gunman. But they are made different by the class gap which is posited between Donal and the tenement people. Christy and Pegeen speak the same language, have the same points of reference, even if Pegeen initially misreads Christy as the playboy of her fantasy.

Nicholas Grene 1999: 122

SOME KEY IDEAS TO CONSIDER

- The death and rebirth pattern in tragedy. Can you see this in O'Casey's play? Who, or what, dies and is re-born?

- The fact that none of the characters is from a class with any power, whether political, social or economic. Can they be thought to be tragic in any sense?

- Whether Minnie is the main tragic character because she is sacrificed, or Donal, because he causes the death of someone he loves.

- What Donal's actions and Minnie's fate suggest about O'Casey's attitude to gender, at least as this play shows it.

BRIAN FRIEL

OVERVIEW

Brian Friel's father was a teacher and Friel himself trained as a teacher but became disillusioned with the authoritarian style 1950s Irish teachers were expected to adopt. As a pupil he had resented the way great works of literature were taught:

> pulling them apart, putting them together again, translating, scanning, conjugating, never once suspecting that these texts were the testimony of sad, happy, assured, confused people like ourselves.

Self-Portrait in Murray (ed.) 1999: 40

As a young adult, he eventually found a niche in primary school teaching and began to write short stories and plays.

The Friel family lived near what was known to Catholics/Nationalists as Derry and to Protestants/Unionists as Londonderry. Since 1929, this predominantly Nationalist city had fallen inside the borders of Unionist Northern Ireland. Friel's father was elected a Nationalist city councillor, and his son seems to have inherited a sense of being an outsider: while his roots (and his actual family) were in Ireland, he lived a few miles down the road in the United Kingdom. Certainly his play *Translations* shows the importance of names in the process of colonising a people. (His own birth certificate name was even changed from Brian to Bernard, the registrar deeming Brian to be too Irish.)

Friel's playwriting career blossomed after an internship in America, observing the work of the Irish theatre director Tyrone Guthrie in Minneapolis. In 1964 he returned from America and began to write *Philadelphia, Here I Come!* This is the first of several plays for which Friel invents a fictional Irish town in which to locate his stories. The place is Ballybeg. The Gaelic original of this anglicised name means 'Small Town'. It allows Friel a fictional location that also has the imaginative solidity of a place and a history. In *Philadelphia, Here I Come!*. Gar O'Donnell leaves 1960s Ballybeg for the States and the sisters in *Dancing at Lughnasa* struggle to survive in 1930s Ballybeg. In *Translations* the British Army succeeds in mapping 1830s Baile Beag, in the process changing its name, to suit English ears better, to Ballybeg.

Brian Friel began writing plays at a time when some English contemporaries – Arden, Pinter, Bond, Wesker – were influenced by the socially conscious and politically informed playwriting of the German Bertolt Brecht. Friel resists the 'political' label, fearing the lack of subtlety in what might be seen as political propaganda. Yet most of his mature plays are rich with a sense of particular social and political life.

TRANSLATIONS (1980)

SYNOPSIS

Set in 1833, the play starts in a rural Irish 'hedge' school, an unofficial centre of self-education for local people. For them, English is a foreign language, as much as the Latin and Greek they study in books. The school is run by Hugh O'Donnell and his son Manus. Another son, Owen, newly returned from Dublin, is helping the occupying British Army by translating between Gaelic and English.

The Army is helping to make maps of the country, in the process anglicising place-names to make their task as occupiers easier. Owen has forged a working relationship with the English soldier Yolland, admiring his culture and sophistication. Yolland in turn falls for the local girl Maire. Neither he nor Maire speak each other's language. As tension between the local Gaelic-speakers and the British soldiers grows, the two love affairs – Owen's for English culture, and Maire's for the English soldier – move towards a terrible conclusion. Yolland disappears, a presumed victim of violent resistance to the occupation. In revenge, the village is attacked and burned by the English.

Brian Friel's 1980 play *Translations* is very important in Irish drama (and in English-language drama) for two reasons. One is the effectiveness and power of the play itself, and the other is the historical moment in Anglo-Irish relations at the time of the play's creation.

Political and social tragedy

Translations contains a tragic love-story, like *Romeo and Juliet*, about doomed love across barriers of social convention and language. But it's also about a love affair between an English soldier, Yolland, and the Irish language he has been sent to suppress. His job is to make maps of the colony and to change the Irish place names into ones that colonising English soldiers and bureaucrats can read and understand. This relationship is, in its way, equally tragic. In neither case is there a particular character flaw that dooms the relationship, whether sexual or cultural. These characters cannot be accused of anything more than expressing their ordinary humanity. What makes their relationships tragic, and invokes the underlying tragic pattern, is the social and political trap that they all find themselves in. The question that lives deep in this play is whether social change is possible without doing terrible damage to individual people.

The play's historical period is one where the world is opening up to new scientific and economic developments. Mapping is part of that – with accurate maps and a standardisation of names, transport of goods and services becomes easier, and, more cynically, populations can be more easily controlled by a more mobile military. At the same time, this modernisation undermines and weakens a settled, traditional culture, embodied in language, and the sense of community made possible by shared language and ways of living. It is this conflict of cultures that creates a context for tragedy. The modern-day equivalent of the gods or of **fate**, dooming otherwise decent people to terrible endings, is the triangulation of history, politics, and culture. Within that dramatic space, there is no easy escape and well-meaning men and woman are pitched into tragic conflict with one another.

The re-naming of the fictional Baile Beag, anglicised by the military map-makers as Ballybeg, may seem a small, inevitable bureaucratic convenience. In its impact on the local Irish culture, however, it threatens to be catastrophic, taken together with all the other modernising changes transforming the world. Map-making, like the arrival of radio in the later Ballybeg of *Dancing at Lughnasa*, looks like progress but has a sinister subtext. Hugh O'Donnell, the old teacher, recognises that his old, coherent, organic way of life, embodied in the words of the Gaelic language, and the names of places in that language, may inevitably have to give way to something new and less humane:

> But remember that words are signals, counters. They are not immortal. And it can happen – to use an image you'll understand – it can happen that a civilisation can be imprisoned in a linguistic contour which no longer matches the landscape of ... fact. Gentlemen. (*He leaves.*)

> *Brian Friel 1980 in Plays One 1996: 419*

A tragic form?

There are formal ways in which Friel's play evokes the spirit of Greek drama. In the ancient form, there would be a **chorus** of citizens, commenting on, reacting to, and anticipating new developments in the plot. In *Translations*, the members of the hedge school to some extent do the same job. It is one of Friel's delicious ironies that these peasants, patronised by the English, seem to have a closer cultural connection to the roots of Western civilisation in Athens and Rome, than with their colonisers. The language in which the original Greek tragedies was written is read in the tiny hedge-school, and the lessons of ancient Greek culture discussed and applied to the present-day of the 1830s. Even the humour in the play points up the overall intensity of tragic feeling, not least in the love scene between the English soldier and the Irish peasant. Neither speaks the other's language, and they are thrown together by the so-called universal language of music – the dance. (There are surely echoes here of Leonard Bernstein's *West Side Story*, itself a re-working of *Romeo and Juliet*.) As in so much Irish drama, humour is tinged with poignancy and a sense that there is a great deal at risk.

The impact of the play

Translations has a special place in Northern Ireland history, not just in the arts world, but in the social and political life of the province. It opened up a debate about the politics and power of language from a Northern Irish perspective. It has long been a journalistic cliché to add the word 'tragic' to the phrase 'Irish history', but in the drama, that word is fully realised. As in all tragic drama, there is a resolving and a healing momentum that is discernable beneath the stories of suffering. If anything, civil life got worse after *Translations*. As the play was rehearsed, Republican prisoners were planning hunger strikes to back their claim that they were political prisoners rather than 'ordinary' criminals. The following year, 1981, ten slowly starved to death. The anger and bitterness that followed marked a new low in the province's fortunes. But art works more subtly, over a longer time-span. Some have claimed that the Good Friday Agreement of 1998 was rooted in a climate for understanding that *Translations* had helped to foster. The play came from Republican sympathisers but it wasn't Republican propaganda. It moved its audience's hearts with a love story at the same time as it engaged their minds.

Critical perspective

> The crisis he is concerned with is a crisis both of language and of civilization and it is experienced directly by people who are trapped within the confines of a place and an attitude of mind from which there is no escape. It is, thus, a tragic play. Military and cultural imperialism, provincial rebellion and cultural fantasy collide with such force that the worst aspects of each are precipitated into a permanent and deadly confrontation. It is a play about the tragedy of English imperialism as well as of Irish nationalism. Most of all, it is a play about the final incoherence that has always characterized the relationship between the two countries, the incoherence that comes from sharing a common language which is based upon different suppositions ... What is most characteristically tragic about the play is the sense of exhilaration which it transmits to the audience. Language lost in this fashion is also language rediscovered in such a way that the sense of loss has been overcome.
>
> *Seamus Deane 1996: 21*

SOME KEY IDEAS TO CONSIDER

- Which character suffers the most in *Translations*, and whether there is any point at which that suffering was avoidable.

- Whether there is a single tragic hero in *Translations* and why/why not.

- Where, apart from the Yolland-Maire scene, you find comedy, and why it is used.

- Where you feel a rhythm that ends with some sort of enlightenment or reconciliation (a tragic rhythm).

SAMUEL

BECKETT

OVERVIEW

NELL: [*Without lowering her voice.*] Nothing is funnier than unhappiness, I grant you that. But –

Samuel Beckett: Endgame 1957: 101

In the 20th and 21st centuries tragedy has come to mean something rather different than it did to the classical Greek dramatists (**p.37**). The work of Irish playwright Samuel Beckett exemplifies some of these new and shocking developments in our understanding of the role drama – and tragedy in particular – might play in society. Intense, bewildering and often lacking a clear message or conclusion, his plays are tragedies of the 20th century, juxtaposing the bleak and depressing with the funny and angry. Beckett was a fiercely inventive and revolutionary dramatist. He tackled head on the pain and resilience of the human condition, in plays that sought to express the supposedly inexpressible meaninglessness of their world.

Existentialism and the Theatre of the Absurd

Beckett's work was a major strand in what came to be known as the **Theatre of the Absurd**. This loose, unconventional movement sprang up in the years after the Second World War and followed the theories of the **Existentialist** movement, led by famous philosophers like Albert Camus and Jean-Paul Sartre. These writers tried to make concrete the mood of a world brought almost to destruction by two World Wars in which there was a belief that man was lost in a sea of meaningless choices and dead-end ideas, a godless world in which simple explanations and rational thought no longer made sense.

The Theatre of the Absurd was an extension of this mood, an attempt to convert complex philosophy into practical form, to make such a nihilistic world view into challenging yet consumable dramatic events. It was drama that tapped into the prevalent attitude of the time. Martin Esslin, the critic who first referred to these playwrights as the 'Absurdist movement', claimed that:

> The hallmark of this attitude is its sense that the certitudes and unshakeable basic assumptions of former ages have been swept away, that they have been tested and found wanting, that they have been discredited as cheap and somewhat childish illusions.

Martin Esslin 2001: 23

This is the environment in which Beckett wrote; in which his theatre created a strong and complex notion of the meaningless circularity and comedy of existence. In a world without meaning, the most appropriate mode for theatrical exploration was tragedy and Beckett was to reinvent the genre and make it resonant for the 20th century.

Meaningless meanings

The majority of Beckett's work for theatre was written in a spell between around 1950 and 1965, before he turned increasingly towards the supposedly more 'fixed' media of radio, television and film. He was an obsessive dramatist, always looking to control his text and its presentation. He often wrote plays and novels in French first before translating them into English, believing that writing in a second language required greater discipline, leading to greater precision and exactitude in his work. He fought long and hard to avoid easy interpretation of his works, claiming that he did not know what his plays 'mean', only that he had written the words and if he knew what they meant then he would have said so at the time. Charles Lyons, speaking of *Endgame*, has observed this avoidance of meaning throughout Beckett's work. 'Eventually', he observes,

> one has to give up the comfort or security of a single interpretation of
> *Endgame*, recognising that the play does not work towards the clarification
> of a meaning but, rather, towards the clarification of the impossibility of
> meaning.
>
> *Charles R. Lyons 1983: 61*

Beckett, along with many critical thinkers at the time, believed that meaning in all forms of life had become unstable and unreliable. In Ancient Greece, tragedies were assumed to tell the truth of the way of the world. In the 20th century Beckett was aware that truth had become a shifting entity. As a result he wrote plays with a conscious lack of meaning, asking his audiences instead to decipher the meaning for themselves.

Facing up to reality

Beckett's most famous plays are complex exercises in understanding and interpretation. Where some critics and audiences interpret them as bleakly tragic, others find humour. Plays such as *Waiting for Godot* (1955), *Act Without Words I & II* (1956), *Endgame* (1957), *Krapp's Last Tape* (1958), *Happy Days* (1961) and *Play* (1962) all contain moments of pure slapstick and farce despite dealing with situations that seem hopeless and tragic (in both the everyday and dramatic sense). Vladimir and Estragon, the two tramps in *Waiting for Godot*, appear doomed to re-live the same situation, never able to go where they want. Hamm and Clov in *Endgame* play out another seemingly endless battle, knowing that 'something is taking its course', but unable ever to establish what it is. Beckett's characters are almost always trapped in some way, whether it is an imperceptible, unknown entrapment like those of *Godot* and *Endgame*, or a more literal, physical one – the huge urns that contain the three heads in *Play*, or Winnie in *Happy Days*, 'stuck up to her diddy's in the bleeding ground' (Beckett, *Collected Works* p.156). Beckett's characters seem bound endlessly and repetitively to play out their existence, with any hope of change or development shown to be cruelly misplaced.

Martin Esslin notes that:

> The Theatre of the Absurd has renounced arguing about the absurdity of
> the human condition; it merely presents it in being.
>
> *Martin Esslin 2001: 25*

Towards the end of *Endgame*, Hamm, the wheelchair bound central figure, violently proclaims to no-one in particular that 'you're on earth, there's no cure for that!' (Beckett, *Collected Works*, p.118), directing us how to interpret these plays in terms of modern tragedy. These characters are all trapped in some way or another, all must accept their fate and get on with things – gleefully, in the case of Winnie, wistfully in the case of Krapp. Like Chekhov before him Beckett adapts tragedy into a new form for the paranoid, nihilistic world in which he found himself after World War 2. For Beckett the tragedy of great gods and heroes was irrelevant. The greatest tragedy of all was harder to define – these are plays about facing up to the tragedy of just being alive.

WAITING FOR GODOT (1955)

Nothing happens, nobody comes, nobody goes, it's awful.

Beckett 1955: 41

SYNOPSIS

Waiting for Godot revolves around two old men – possibly tramps – named Vladimir and Estragon. They sit by a tree on a country road and attempt to pass time, waiting for the arrival of a man named Godot who may, or may not, be able to help them in some unspecified way. During the course of the day they are visited by a man named Pozzo and his servant, Lucky, along with a small boy who brings a message announcing that Godot will not be coming that day. Act One describes the action of one such day. Act Two describes the action of another such day, possibly the next, possibly months later. The action of the second act is a condensed and reduced version of the action of the first, and both acts end with an identically repeated promise of departure that, we now assume, is not to be fulfilled.

> VLADIMIR: Well? Shall we go?
>
> ESTRAGON: Yes, let's go.
>
> [*They do not move.*]

The rest of the action is taken up with exactly what the title implies – waiting. Vladimir and Estragon play out a series of routines and games, evidently with some experience, merely to pass the time, in order to be able to move on to the next day in which, once again, nothing will happen, nobody will come.

Waiting for Godot caused a storm on its first performance and has continued to do so ever since. It emerged – first of all in French as *En Attendant Godot* in 1952 and later in an English version in 1955 – out of nowhere and caused anger, delight and incomprehension in equal measure. It almost single-handedly ripped up the idea of theatre being driven by plot, and it sealed the reputation of Samuel Beckett as a dramatist before his career had even really begun. It is hard to over-estimate the importance of this play in the progression of theatre in the 20th century. So what can we learn about modern tragedy from 'a play in which nothing happens, twice'? (Mercier, V., *Irish Times*, 18 Feb 1956, p.6)

Context

After World War 2 a new generation found itself unable to rely on the beliefs such as God or the State, having seen these very structures bring them close to total annihilation. Tragedy, in these circumstances, was not a specific event but everywhere, a condition of being alive. This idea of universal tragedy was vital to the **absurdists** who created from it open-ended plays like *Waiting for Godot* in which the sense of tragedy is implicit.

The play

Waiting for Godot is a key text of the absurdist movement, having arrived at the very height of the post-war crisis in meaning and beliefs. Vladimir and Estragon's repeated and apparently pointless routine can be interpreted as a metaphor for the pointlessness that Beckett and the **Existentialists** saw in life. From this meaninglessness, however, the only justifiable meaning that could be found was for the individual. Beckett's plays, argues Martin Esslin:

> present their author's intuition of the human condition that is essentially polyphonic; they confront their audience with an organized structure of statements and images that interpenetrate each other and that must be apprehended in their totality.
>
> *Martin Esslin 2001: 45*

The repeated action, the comic interludes to pass the time and the cyclical nature of *Waiting for Godot* all build to create an idea of futility yet empathy which raises questions about the wisdom (or otherwise) of mankind's resolute belief that the future can be different – and better – regardless of any evidence to the contrary.

In the English version of the text, Beckett gave the play a subtitle – 'A tragic-comedy in two acts'. There is something about this phrase that implies being stuck between positions, of being neither one nor the other and so being nothing at all. As the two men practise their timeworn routines we see in them a stoic resistance, a refusal to buckle and yet a yearning to do so. The play begins with an acceptance of fate – 'Nothing to be done' – and yet, throughout, the two men must remind themselves of why they stay: 'We're waiting for Godot', says one before the other replies 'Ah!' Whether we see in them a stubborn, foolhardy refusal to escape or a stirring refusal to buckle says, in the end, as much about us as it does about Beckett or the play itself. Christopher Innes notes that:

> Godot's meaning is in the image created by its performance ... the only progression is entropy, the stripping away of hope, material objects, even extended speech.

> Christopher Innes in John Russell Brown (ed.) 1995: 426

That Vladimir and Estragon never come to realise the repetition, or become aware of their wider predicament, would seem to make the play less a tragedy as far as the characters are concerned, and more a tragedy of the audience itself as they watch and experience the circular, grasping nature of existence enacted before their eyes.

This is tragedy played out at the rawest of levels, where despite every crutch of normal existence having been removed, the body must continue to function. When sense, logic, plot and action have all been stripped away, all that is left is to pass the time. And to wait.

SOME KEY POINTS TO CONSIDER

- What Godot may represent.

- The role humour plays in *Waiting for Godot* and how this effects the experience of it as a tragedy.

- Whether it is necessary for someone to die for a play to be considered a true tragedy. Or is the position the two men find themselves in just as bad as death?

- The significance of the boy. Does his reappearance represent a sense of hope for you, or a sense of despair? Why?

MODERN

AMERICAN

TRAGEDY

OVERVIEW

FAMILIES AT THE FRONTIER

Consider two phrases associated with modern America: 'The American Century' and 'The American Dream'.

'The American Century' was what the American publisher Henry Luce called the 20th century. He wanted the United States to use its military and financial power to spread an American idea of freedom and democracy all around the world. Back home, 20th-century America lived with a myth called 'The American Dream', where anybody and everybody has equal possibilities to climb out of poverty, be treated with respect, and the right (says the American Declaration of Independence) to 'life, liberty and the pursuit of happiness.' There are big, idealistic ideas inside these two phrases. In the tragic drama of writers like Arthur Miller, Tennessee Williams, and Eugene O'Neill, there is a set of challenges to such high, vague, ideals.

The family as a place of safety/place of danger

American tragic drama seems to be all about families. Arthur Miller's *All My Sons*, Tennessee Williams' *Cat on a Hot Tin Roof* or Eugene O'Neill's *Long Day's Journey into Night* are intense narratives about what we now might call 'dysfunctional families'. In this they remind us that since classical times family dynamics have been at the heart of tragic drama: *Hamlet* is about families – mothers, fathers, uncles, girlfriends, and their peculiar relationships. Sophocles' *Oedipus Rex*, is about a man who makes love to his mother, and the repercussions of this tragic error throughout the state and universe.

Family looms large in American culture because it fits well with American visions of self-reliance and independence from the state. When the first Europeans, the Pilgrim Fathers and others, landed on the East Coast, they were faced by many dangers, as well as untold opportunities. Understandably, the people who lived there, native Americans, resented being colonised, exploited, even massacred by the newcomers, and sometimes responded violently. For the immigrant newcomers, the challenge of a new world, with no infrastructure (social networks or roads or markets) such as they had known in England, or Europe, was frightening. The weather was unpredictable and so was the wildlife. What you had to protect you was your family. The central importance of family to American culture and consciousness is reflected in everything from Arthur Miller's plays to *The Godfather* movies, and innumerable numbers of American sitcoms and teen shows. Family is what, in an ideal world, keeps you safe (and, therefore, family becomes what it seems necessary to defend, sometimes to absurd lengths).

But tragedy is the art form that knows that the world is not ideal. Because the heart of American culture is the idea that 'all are created equal', old ideas of tragic drama as a form that relies on the upper class or the monarchy for its tragic heroes is not appropriate for telling the American tragedy. There is no monarchy, and the American Dream says that there must be no caste of rulers from which ordinary people are barred.

THE PLAYWRIGHTS

ARTHUR MILLER

A tragedy of modern America

Arthur Miller is perhaps the best known of all American playwrights, writing a series of plays which prove that in the democratic 20th century, the tragic hero could be an ordinary guy – a travelling salesman, an Italian immigrant, or a factory owner.

Miller was a son of Jewish parents, his father a clothing manufacturer. When America fell into the Great Depression of the 1920s and 30s, the family had to move from prosperous Manhattan to the bleak back end of Brooklyn. The certain promise of the American Dream was undermined, its **tragic flaw** being greed and exploitation. While the Second World War contributed to the end of the Depression, the post-war prosperity also had its victims, as embodied in the character of Willy Loman. This failed salesman kills himself so that his two sons and his wife can claim the insurance and stop paying out on the fridge. Prosperity and consumerism can be tragic flaws too.

Written in the late 1940s and early 1950s, Miller's greatest works sit in a period right in the middle of the 20th century. Miller acts like a sensor of what most disturbed American society during and following World War 2, registering the huge shocks of a changing post-war culture and politics. He exposes the fear of Depression-haunted economic collapse (*All My Sons*, 1947), touches the sensitive points in the story of how the American state became established (*The Crucible*, 1953) and, again in *The Crucible*, responds to the atmosphere of postwar paranoia, channelling protest against the anti-left-wing purges of artists and intellectuals, in a tragedy about literal witch hunting. Three years later life would mirror art as Arthur Miller found himself the subject of a metaphorical witch hunt, hauled before the House Un-American Activities Committee (HUAC), accused of communist (i.e. pro-Soviet Russian) sympathies. In front of the HUAC, he refused to denounce his fellow citizens, just as his fictional hero John Proctor had done, thus positioning himself, in the eyes of literary history, in the role of tragic hero, prepared to risk himself for his beliefs.

EUGENE O'NEILL

A personal tragedy of addictions

From early on in the 20th century, the playwright who provides a foundation stone of American drama is Eugene O'Neill. Coming, like so many Americans, from immigrant stock, O'Neill often took his characters and narratives from the margins of society. In his earlier work, he sometimes broke with the naturalistic conventions of earlier tragic playwrights such as Ibsen and Chekhov and in plays like *The Emperor Jones* (1920) introduced **Expressionist** staging techniques. In *Desire under the Elms* (1925) and *Mourning Becomes Electra* (1931) he deliberately draws on Greek tragic patterns to write about very American family themes. O'Neill helped set up a theatre company called The Provincetown Players, which not only provided him with a stage for his plays but also introduced some of the more radical European playwrights like Strindberg to American audiences.

In 1941 O'Neill wrote *Long Day's Journey into Night*, a tragic drama based closely on his own life. His father was a stage actor-manager, who had fraught relationships with his children. His mother became addicted to narcotics after his birth, leaving O'Neill with lifelong feelings of guilt. O'Neill's last wife, Carlotta Monterey, also had serious problems with drug addiction. This play concentrates all this biographical material into a time period of one day, observing one of the **classical unities (time)**. The claustrophobic tension gains extra oppressiveness by being set on the Atlantic sea-coast, with sea mist cutting off the real world as injected morphine cuts off Mary Tyrone from reality.

Although written during World War 2, *Long Day's Journey into Night* wasn't staged until 1956, after O'Neill's death. Despite being written in wartime, O'Neill's tragic gaze seems very much inward, with no sense of political or military conflict in the play's nervous system. This contrasts with Arthur Miller's stand against political persecution and for freedom of speech, marking him as a public, socially-active, politically-aware, artist.

TENNESSEE WILLIAMS

A radical politics of the soul

A third great American writer, Tennessee Williams, sits somewhere nearer O'Neill than Miller. Williams too struggled with ill-health, addiction and family traumas. His life was made harder by his inability to live comfortably with his gay identity.

However, it was Miller who described Williams' 'radical politics of the soul' recognising that Williams, in a different way, was also a political writer. Like O'Neill, he created characters who come from marginalised parts of society. Often they are imaginative and sensitive, and become damaged by a hard, industrialised, dog-eat-dog society. Many of Williams' characters are female. Some critics have claimed that these characters are projections of gay personal and social crises and that Williams was forced to represent these tragic issues through female characters because of the period's public intolerance of homosexuality.

Williams sometimes calls upon a social archetype, the 'Southern Belle', a white woman from the old, slave-owning, aristocracy of the southern states. Characters like Blanche DuBois in *A Streetcar Named Desire*, whose social and economic power has gone, remind us of the ugly history of Civil War and slavery. In *The Glass Menagerie* and *A Streetcar Named Desire*, his central female characters also seem to reflect his sister Rose, who suffered from mental health problems.

THE 1950S AND BEYOND

Like Miller, Williams' great plays were written and performed in the 1950s. After this period, new social and political realities appeared. The Cold War confrontation between the United States and the Soviet Union became dangerously hot in Vietnam, and the Civil Rights Movement for black equality became violently polarised after the assassination of Martin Luther King. Tragic American drama began to give way to more **absurdist** styles of drama on stages, and cartoon-like agitprop protest on the streets and in cafes and parks. The following plays are interesting examples of plays of this period.

- Edward Albee: *Who's Afraid of Virginia Woolf?* (1962): The tragic-comic collapse of a middle-class marriage, reflecting feelings of fear, illusions, and mistrust at the height of the Cold War.

- Amiri Baraka: *Dutchman* (1964): A violent confrontation between a black man and a white woman on a subway train, anticipating shifts in racial and gender politics of the time.

- Sam Shepard: *Buried Child* (1978): A dysfunctional Midwestern farming family gradually offer up their dark secret to a visiting outsider.

- August Wilson: *Ma Rainey's Black Bottom* (1984): The racial and gender politics at the heart of the music business in the 1920s, based on the real life of blues singer Gertrude 'Ma' Rainey.

- Suzan Lori-Parks: *In The Blood* (1988): In the 'Greed is Good' America of the 1980s, a homeless black woman struggles to bring up her children in a space under a city bridge.

The 1990s

The 1990s finished on a high note with a play by Tony Kushner, who worked with the tragic form in his magnificent two-part drama *Angels in America*. The family theme is still there but these families are fluid and flexible, as when a Mormon mother takes a dying New York gay man under her wing. The **tragic flaw** in these plays is now social and clinical rather than personal. It is the AIDS pandemic and the American state's cruel indifference to it. Above all, the plays end with a sense of renewal after trauma, of qualified hope for the future, both for America and for the world. The ancient tragic rhythm of harsh human experience, of learning from it, of death and resurrection, is returned to American drama.

TENNESSEE WILLIAMS

OVERVIEW

> I write about violence in American life only because I am not so
> well acquainted with the society of other countries.
>
> *Tennessee Williams: New York Times 1959 in Williams 2000: 11*

Thomas Lanier Williams III knew a thing or two about tragedy. The son of a travelling shoe salesman in America's Deep South he grew to become one of America's foremost dramatists of the 20th century. His plays deal in a modern, social kind of tragedy – the tragedy of relationships in turmoil, of lovers on the edge, of ambitions thwarted, of families in despair – yet his own life, too, was never far from pain, suffering and loss. The ghosts of greed, depravity and uncontrollable desire haunted the life of the man just as they haunt his characters. The director Elia Kazan, who famously worked with Williams many times, once observed that 'everything in his life is in his plays, and everything in his plays is in his life'.

A career backwards

Tennessee Williams' career followed a strange and, ultimately, disappointing trajectory. Fêted and admired for his early work, he became a hugely successful and influential force in the years immediately following World War 2. However, his career saw a steady decline until his death in 1983, as his signature style of lyrical, passionately intense drama fell gradually out of favour. He often cut a lonely, troubled figure in his final years, no longer appreciated artistically and tormented both by substance addictions and by the very demons we see enacted in the drama of his plays. Indeed Williams' own character, family and background provided the largest and most pervasive pool of material behind his plays. His mismatched parents – the daughter of an Episcopal Minister and a womanising drunkard – fought terribly throughout his youth. Their violent rows had such an effect on his sister, Rose, that she was finally driven insane. His mother's failed pretensions to Southern gentility, his father's open disapproval of his son's sickly, sensitive ways, his sister's fragility and descent into broken, tormented madness – all these aspects and more recur frequently throughout his intensely personal plays. As Williams once confessed:

> I can't expose a human weakness on the stage unless I know it through
> having it myself.
>
> *Tennessee Williams: New York Times 1959 in Williams 2000: 12*

Williams in his work

In his most famous works Williams returned frequently to those themes and factors he knew best – arresting female characters and the American Deep South. In many of his plays Williams places a strong female character at the centre of the drama and these women are complex, vital creations. Sometimes the aggressor and sometimes the victim in the tragedies played out, they all bear a clear lineage back to Williams' mother (the faded Southern Belle, wronged by her man) and sister (the shy, delicate flower, on the verge of collapse). Allean Hale notes:

> Growing up in [a] female-dominated environment doubtless gave Tom
> the empathy shown in the women characters created by the playwright
> Tennessee.

Allean Hale in M.C. Roudané (ed.) 1997: 11

Yet this empathy was paired with a searing honesty that would not allow Williams simply to place these women on a pedestal. He sought to explore the psychology behind the flaws in his family as much as he sought to celebrate the women he loved. In this difficult relationship, at the very least, lay the foundations for some of the strongest female characters of the last century.

Williams also had a troubled relationship with his native South. Having been given the nickname Tennessee at college due to his distinctive Southern drawl, many of his plays have the stamp of the South on them, in their setting, in their characters and in their resolute adherence to codes of honour, gentility and pride. These codes and the South itself, however, are not always presented with admiration. According to Albert J. Devlin:

> Williams seemed to address an audience well accustomed to the bizarre
> ethnicity of the South. Their expectations of 'a unique moral perversity'
> in Dixie would help them to find the familiar and invidious social critique
> within the so called 'Southern grotesque'.

Albert J. Devlin in M.C. Roudané (ed.) 1997: 103

The South is a fertile ground for Williams, a home from home in his imagination, but also a strongly mythological arena, symbolic of the decay and demise of what many would consider to be 'old' America.

Cleansing through tragedy

In many of the works from Williams' golden period – including *The Glass Menagerie* (1944), *A Streetcar Named Desire* (1947) and *Cat on a Hot Tin Roof* (1955) – he utilised the form of classical tragedy to try and explore the psychological reasons for his characters' flaws. In these characters Williams sought to present unabridged the sheer force of desire or masculinity or ambition or greed. The effects of these traits are almost universally seen to be negative and, as such, characters like Brick Pollitt, Blanche DuBois and Laura Wingfield could all be interpreted as representing aspects of the classical **tragic hero**. Aristotle insisted that:

> the movement of a tragedy should involve a reversal (**peripeteia**) in the hero's circumstances, not from unhappiness to happiness but from happiness to unhappiness. It should arise not from wickedness but from **hamartia** in the hero.

> *K. McLeish 1998: 31*

Williams' central characters all experience, or have already experienced, a shift toward unhappiness – whether through crushing of ambition, through failure of desire or through acts of physical violence.

In putting these characters on stage, Williams is also dramatising characters who incorporate strong elements of his own personality. They populate what Williams called his 'memory plays', re-enacting stages of the writer's life in such a way as constantly to try to offer solace, solution or hope. As Williams observed:

> if there is any truth in the Aristotelian idea that violence is purged by its poetic representation on a stage, then it may be that my cycle of violent plays have had a moral justification after all. I know that I have felt it.

> *Tennessee Williams: New York Times 1959 in Williams 2000: 12*

The tragedies presented in Williams' plays are the tragedies of the writer himself, but they are magnified by the power, the poetry and the force of the passions he puts on the stage. It is doubtful that they truly helped to purge his own demons but, in the process of cleansing, he not only produced some of the most startling American drama ever written, but gave new life to tragedy, a genre which forces the audience to engage with the unravelling lives they see depicted before them.

THE GLASS MENAGERIE (1944)

SYNOPSIS

Tom Wingfield lives with his mother, Amanda, and his fragile, crippled younger sister Laura in a small apartment. He dreams of escape and his mother dreams of a better life for them all. Amanda is desperate for Laura to be wooed by a 'gentleman caller' and so Tom arranges for an old school friend, Jim, to visit.

The pressure of the visit sends Amanda into a frenzy and fills Laura with sickness and fear. She retreats to attend to her glass collection whilst Amanda desperately prepares for the visitor.

When Jim arrives, he is greeted extravagantly by Amanda, but Laura feigns sickness to avoid him. Jim joins her and, as they talk, Amanda reveals to him that she felt strongly for him in high school. A powerful bond is formed and seems to promise more, but Jim finally reveals that he is engaged to be married and makes a swift exit. Laura and Amanda are crushed and Tom retreats further into his desire for escape.

JIM	Let me give you a hand.
AMANDA	Indeed you will not!
JIM	I ought to be good for something.
AMANDA	Good for something? [*Her tone is rhapsodic.*] *You*? Why, Mr O'Connor, nobody, *nobody's* given me this much entertainment in years – as you have!
JIM	Aw, now, Mrs Wingfield!
AMANDA	I'm not exaggerating, not one bit!

Tennessee Williams 1944 in Williams 2000: 290

The Glass Menagerie was first produced in 1944 and gave Tennessee Williams his first taste of real success. It is probably the most personal work Williams ever wrote and it is also the one that encapsulates many of the great themes and characters to which he would return over the course of his career. It is a powerfully expressed play which deals in a very minor-key type of social tragedy: those small-scale, crushing disappointments that happen to families in the gap between ambition and reality.

A family under pressure

From the very beginning of the play a stifling sense of failed-betterment permeates the text. This sense is vividly personified in the desperate attempts of the mother, Amanda Wingfield, to see her fragile, troubled daughter Laura (closely related to Williams' own sister, Rose) courted and won by a 'gentleman caller', in the traditional Southern style. Her son, Tom, a failed and dream-filled artist, arranges for his workmate Jim to fulfil this ambition. The pressures of anticipation and fear, however, bear heavily on both mother and daughter. Amanda's vulgar, oppressively garish attempt at bonhomie – 'I guess this is what they mean by Southern hospitality' (Williams, p.310) says Jim uncertainly as he departs – only serves to increase the difficulty for the shy, awkward Laura. Her attempts to avoid the meeting at any cost make her eventual disappointment all the harder to bear. Williams builds on the contrast between Laura's fragility and her desperately driven mother to create a strongly tragic sense of defeated dreams, both old and new, at the play's end.

The memory play

In his introduction to the text Williams describes *The Glass Menagerie* as a 'memory play'. In employing the character of Tom as self-appointed narrator, he skilfully updates the function of the Greek **chorus**, relaying the action to us second-hand and thereby distancing us from it, placing it in a different reality to our own. 'I give you truth in the pleasant disguise of illusion' (Williams, p.234), announces Tom, creating for an audience the sense of a heightened, semi-imagined reality. This 'dreamed' type of drama is intended by Williams to be non-naturalistic, to present a world not accurately representative of real life or real emotional behaviour. Williams describes the style as:

> attempting to find a closer approach, a more penetrating and vivid expression of things as they are.
>
> *Tennessee Williams: Production Notes 1944 in Williams 2000: 229*

As such Williams allows his characters to act in ways that may otherwise seem to be too grand, too highly-strung, too exaggerated because, as he says in the opening stage directions to scene 1:

> Memory takes a lot of poetic license. It omits some details; others are exaggerated, according to the emotional value of the articles it touches, for memory is seated predominantly in the heart.
>
> *Tennessee Williams 1944 in Williams 2000: 233*

The characters in the text, as in many of Williams' works, are specifically intended to be larger than life. They function as archetypes, ciphers used by Williams to express concerns about larger groups or tracts within American society. Each of the four characters represents a favourite theme for Williams – the creative spirit, the damaged flower, the faded South and the flawed, masculine hero. The interaction between these forces is what interests Williams, and the play's ultimate stifling of both the South and the artistic spirit could be interpreted as a damning indictment of the ruthless progress demanded by modern American society.

Small tragedies

The tragedy here is, as elsewhere in Williams' plays, classically structured yet quintessentially modern – it is the tale of a poor family, strung up by failed ambitions and lost hopes. Christopher Bigsby sees 'a kind of heroism' in Amanda at the play's close:

> Deserted and betrayed, she stays and continues her losing battle with time in the company of her doomed daughter and, in what is virtually the play's final stage direction, Williams finds a 'dignity and tragic beauty' in that sad alliance. It is no longer the absurdity of this abandoned woman he chooses to stress.

Christopher Bigsby in M.C. Roudané (ed.) 1997: 42

As Tom explains at the very outset, the gentlemen caller is 'the long-delayed but always expected something that we live for' (Williams, p. 235). His arrival, flushed with promise, only makes his departure seem to be a final nail in the coffin of the Wingfields' eternal longing. It may only be a small tragedy but, as Williams understands all too well, it is not the size of the action that matters, but the size of the impact.

SOME KEY IDEAS TO CONSIDER

- How Williams creates a sense of Amanda's crushed ambition and desperation for her children to succeed.

- What Williams is trying to imply when Tom accidentally breaks one of Laura's glass pieces.

- To what extent, and how, Tom fulfils the role of the classical Greek chorus.

- Whether all – or indeed any – of the characters could be considered to be tragic.

- Whether the tragedy hinges on character flaws or social context.

CAT ON A HOT TIN ROOF (1955)

SYNOPSIS

Gathering on the family's vast Mississippi plantation to celebrate patriarch Big Daddy's birthday, the Pollitt family spend one long evening arguing, fighting and revealing hard truths to one another.

Big Daddy's younger – and favoured – son, former football hero Brick, drinks heavily and rejects all advances from his wife Margaret, refusing even to share a bed with her. Margaret is desperate for a child, since Brick's brother Gooper and his wife Mae have many children and show them off wherever possible. Margaret reveals that tests have shown Big Daddy has cancer, and tries to persuade Brick to impregnate her so as to secure an heir to the plantation.

As the family gather, Big Daddy, having been told he does not have cancer, is gregarious and brash, rejecting his wife violently and keen to make up for lost time. He talks with Brick and tries to find a cause for his son's drinking, implying a deep homosexual desire for Brick's now dead school friend, Skipper. Brick responds by telling Big Daddy the truth about his medical condition.

As the truth of Big Daddy's condition is broken to Big Mama, Gooper and Mae produce legal papers, attempting to assume control of the plantation. Margaret, finally, announces that she is pregnant, delighting Big Daddy. She then pours away all of Brick's alcohol and approaches the bed as the curtain falls.

BIG DADDY	**Who's been lying to you, and what about?**
BRICK	**No one single person and no one lie…**

Tennessee Williams 1955 in Williams 2001: 71

If *The Glass Menagerie* deals in family tragedy on a small-scale then so, ostensibly, does the play Williams wrote ten years later. Much like the earlier work it tells the tale of a family falling apart under various pressures and strains, yet the difference between the two plays could not be more marked: *Cat on a Hot Tin Roof* is a big play in every way. From the size of the cast to the scale of the setting the play seems never to be anything less than vast in energy, scope and power. Characters talk over one another constantly, they argue, they drink. Children run in and out, voices drift at the periphery and – in the midst of it all – a family reaches breaking point as greed, secrets and bitterness come to the surface of a family celebration.

Unity of time, place and action

One striking thing about *Cat on a Hot Tin Roof* is that it features no change of scene or break in time across its three-act duration. The action on stage is played out in real time, within one room and building, toward a single (potentially) decisive conclusion. These factors place *Cat on a Hot Tin Roof* firmly in the realms of classical tragedy described by Aristotle in *The Poetics* as being 'an imitation of an action that is complete, and whole, and of a certain magnitude'). Aristotle's concept of tragedy developed into what became known as the **classical unities of time, place and action**, wherein the concentration of a drama on one single, unbroken event was thought to give it a higher magnitude and to amplify the work's dramatic effect. With *Cat on a Hot Tin Roof* in mind this is certainly the case, the feeling of claustrophobia and rising tension adding immeasurably to the drama, and the play has great claims to stand as a tragedy to rival the Ancients.

As the play unfolds, however, it becomes clear that there are many different potentially tragic plots playing themselves out. Big Daddy learns that he is dying whilst Big Mama suffers a brutal rejection at the hands of her beloved. The plantation is fought over bitterly by Gooper, Mae and Margaret whilst Brick quietly and calmly drinks himself towards oblivion and 'the click'. So is the play really a tragedy in the classical sense of the term, with one central, heroically flawed tragic figure?

Brick by name...

In his introduction to the updated, Broadway version of the play's final act, Williams offers us a clue as to his own view. He describes how he was initially averse to changing his text as:

> I felt that the moral paralysis of Brick was a root thing in his tragedy, and to show a dramatic progression would obscure the meaning of that tragedy in him.

> *Tennessee Williams: Notes of Explanation 1957 in Williams 2001: 107*

Whether he saw the play as 'Brick's Tragedy' is open to debate, but the emphasis is clear – Brick presents the sympathetic centre of the play for Williams. But can we place Brick in the role of the classical tragic hero, brought low by fate, design and his own personal flaws? His tragedy is hard to engage with as he is such a consciously passive/aggressive type, obviously flawed but not noticeably warm or courageous. He scorns his wife ('Maggie, you're spoiling my liquor', Williams, p.30), drinks wilfully to excess and is clearly in some kind of denial about his own sexuality ('I had friendship with Skipper. – You are naming it dirty!', Williams, p.42). His tragedy, rather than occurring during the action on stage, could be argued to be deep-seated and long-standing, it has preceded him and he is now just a victim in its grip. He is, as Albert J. Devlin argues, in an advanced state of evasion and denial. Devlin notes that Williams referred to Brick as having 'the poetry of the man who is not competing', and it is this passivity which negates Brick's potential for heroism. Devlin argues that:

> With [his] measured, alienating speech Brick deflects the family politics, economic aspiration, and sexual allure that Maggie would use to re-centre her husband's interest in his patrimony. His broken ankle, devout drinking, and mocking self-detachment … display Williams' skill in producing in his protagonist the intense and surprising effect of silence and reserve.
>
> *Albert J. Devlin M.C. Roudané (ed.) 1997: 109*

In classical terms, his stubbornness and refusal to accept help mean that he lacks the moment of realisation, known as **anagnorisis**, by which the hero comes to realise the truth of his predicament. The tragedy here lies, instead, on a much wider scale, and it is bigger than one man or, indeed, the whole family altogether.

A multitude of tragedies

The form of the play seems to hint at an unresolved, more total kind of tragedy. Williams' tragedies are concerned with both the impact of social pressures on the traditional family and the impact of moral and political pressures on society itself, including belief in the great American Dream. In this play Big Daddy is the very embodiment of that Dream, what Devlin calls:

> the exemplar of a rather crude domestic order that had pioneered for wealth since launching its economy after the Civil War.
>
> *Albert J. Devlin M.C. Roudané (ed.) 1997: 104*

He is a man with great wealth but an inability to connect fully with the world around him. His cancer is a powerful symbolic device, and is pointedly described by Gooper in Act Three:

> right now he is sinkin' into uraemia an' you all know what uraemia is, it's poisonin' of the whole system due to th' failure of th' body to eliminate its poisons.
>
> *Tennessee Williams 1955 in Williams 2001: 97*

The cancer affects not only Big Daddy. It also represents the creep of avarice, greed and depravity in American society. It affects every aspect of the family until they are finally unable to face each other, to communicate at any level or even to accept the faults within themselves.

Williams' broader, all-encompassing outlook successfully shifts the traditional focus of tragedy away from the flaws and faults of one great figure, thereby denying an audience the moment of realisation, the acceptance of flaws and fate which will, in turn, provide the sense of **catharsis** that allows them to leave the theatre fulfilled. Instead, *Cat on a Hot Tin Roof* remains resolutely a big play: by refusing to resolve the tragedy of any one person, it instead displays the outcomes wrought when the faults and flaws exist within the society itself.

SOME KEY IDEAS TO CONSIDER

- The purpose of the many long interjections and stage directions added by Williams. What do they add or achieve for a reader? Is it possible to see such stage directions as a **chorus**, with Williams himself providing some sort of commentary on the action?

- What Williams is trying to achieve by having no completely sympathetic characters in the play. How does this impact on our interpretation of the play as tragedy?

- How Williams' use of the classical **unities** creates a sense of rising tension and violence. Is this tension ever fully released?

- Which character might be considered to be the tragic hero of the piece.

A STREETCAR NAMED DESIRE (1947)

SYNOPSIS

Blanche DuBois arrives in New Orleans' French Quarter, having travelled on a streetcar destined for 'Desire', to stay with her pregnant sister Stella and recover from a nervous breakdown. Her young husband has killed himself and the family plantation, Belle Reve, has been lost due to financial mismanagement. Blanche claims to be taking a break from her position as an English teacher.

Stella lives in a small apartment with her husband, Stanley Kowalski, a hard, blunt, powerful child of Polish immigrants. Suspicious of Blanche and resentful of her affected, delicate presence in the house, Stanley turns against her and the two swiftly become enemies. Stanley has a group of male friends with whom he spends evenings playing poker and drinking. One such evening is disturbed by Blanche, and Stanley resolves to find out the truth of her stories. Meanwhile one of his poker friends, Mitch, begins to show an interest in Blanche, only later to reject her.

Discovering that Blanche has had to flee her hometown because of various sexual scandals, Stanley finally confronts her. The violent nature of the confrontation culminates in a rape and this in turn leads to Blanche's breakdown. Stanley has her committed to an asylum and the play ends with her being led away as Stella holds her newborn baby and all the local neighbourhood watches on in shock and pity.

The most powerful tragedies from the ancient Greeks onwards have the force of myth. The idea that the mythology of a nation or a culture presses hard on any great tragedy, giving it greater depth and resonance for a wide audience, has long been prevalent. In the case of Tennessee Williams' culturally concerned works, it is especially true.

A stage icon

In 1947 Williams followed up his first great success, *The Glass Menagerie*, with *A Streetcar Named Desire,* one of the great, canonical touchstones of American theatre and, arguably, American mythology. It is revered for its power, its lyricism, its broadminded view of a cross-section of American society. It encompasses, notes Christopher Innes:

> all his [Williams'] major themes: the ambiguous nature of sexuality, the betrayal of faith, the corruption of modern America, the over-arching battle of artistic sensitivity against physical materialism.

> *Christopher Innes in John Russell Brown (ed.) 1995: 422*

It has been referenced countless times in popular culture – not least in *The Simpsons* – and it clearly holds a vital place in modern American culture. Yet in spite of all this, the iconic status of *A Streetcar Named Desire* could well be argued to have been sealed after the fact by the now legendary performance of one man – Marlon Brando.

Brando occupies a key place in the mythology of American Theatre. He was revered for his dedication to a role, for his virility, his power and the sense of charming danger he brought to the stage. His performance as Stanley Kowalski in the original production of *Streetcar* is said to have been of such persuasiveness, power and passion as to seal the place of Williams and his play in the American pantheon almost single-handedly. His interpretation certainly cast the mould for the iconic Williams' anti-hero – rough, masculine, deeply alluring but also fatally flawed and cowed by circumstances, by fate, by desire.

All-American male?

With his first appearance onstage, during a kind of overture detailing the life and vibrancy of the setting, Williams gives us a number of visual and verbal clues as to Stanley Kowalski's basic character. He appears, 'roughly dressed in blue denim work clothes… [carrying] his bowling jacket and a red-stained package from a butcher's' (Williams, p.116). This package contains, as Stanley monosyllabically registers, 'Meat!' He 'heaves the package' up to his unsuspecting wife in what is a graphic demonstration of blunt masculinity – the hunter-gatherer male flinging the carrion to his partner, then heading off to drink and bowl. With this small vignette, Williams skilfully sets up the broad sweep of Stanley's character creating, in effect, a cipher for the American, working male. Here is the mythological all-American – an immigrant of Polish descent, embracing American culture and American women, working hard, playing hard and attempting to succeed as his constitutional rights allow. Innes sees Stanley as:

> representing the norms of a soulless society, crude and ruthlessly competitive as well as uncultured, yet sexually vital and dynamic.
>
> *Christopher Innes in John Russell Brown (ed.) 1995: 422*

The darkness in his character belies the myth of the American Dream, revealing the desires and urges that drive so much of the American way. This is a popular theme with Williams, who raises the tragic stakes in this play by questioning and critiquing this image of the roughhouse Yankee who always gets his man. That the character has become so synonymous with Brando – an actor of unnervingly equal charm and darkness – has only gone to emphasise this facet even more.

Blanche DuBois – heroine, aggressor or victim?

Stanley, however, is not the only highly symbolic character in the text. The themes of the play, argues Innes, 'are given archetypal shape in the protagonists' with Blanche representing:

> the decaying South, neurotic and corrupted, hiding from herself behind artificial illusions

Christopher Innes in John Russell Brown (ed.) 1995: 422

Blanche is running away from a past that we slowly learn about during the play. Frail, highly strung, ethereally dressed in white, she seems always to be out of place in her surroundings. She is the visible manifestation of Southern gentility, thrust into the seething modern world, unable to cope either emotionally or financially, having lost both her young husband and her family plantation. In this respect she can be seen to represent one side of what Felicia Hardison Londré calls:

> the evolution of the social system from the old agrarian South, burdened by its past… to the post-war urban-industrial society in which Stanley's class has gained leverage.

Felicia H. Londré in M.C. Roudané 1997: 54

Her final defeat – taken away by officials of an asylum, still outdatedly relying 'on the kindness of strangers' (Williams, p.225) – is arguably the play's tragedy and yet, partly through Marlon Brando's powerful performance, the line between Blanche as victim and aggressor has become ever more blurred.

It has been argued that Brando's performance, and the subsequent perception of Stanley's character, led to audiences 'rooting for his [Stanley's] victory over Blanche' (Londré, in Roudané, 1997: 50). And so where does the tragedy lie? Is it Blanche's rape, her defeat and her eventual institutionalisation, or elsewhere? Londré argues that Williams

> intended a balance of power between Blanche and Stanley, to show that both are complex figures whose wants and behaviours must be understood in the context of what is at stake for them.

Felicia H. Londré in M.C. Roudané 1997: 50

At stake for both is something essentially selfish – escape for Blanche, sexual satisfaction and dominance for Stanley – and the inference of this is that none of these old or new social forms is equipped to be anything other than, essentially, self-serving and vicious. So again, as elsewhere in Williams, we must look outside the central characters themselves, if we want to find the true, heroic/tragic centre of the piece.

Melting pot

At the play's conclusion, nearly every character is onstage. Indeed, outside of the Southern Blanche and the Polish Stanley, the whole cast takes in a wide range of ages, colours and ethnic backgrounds to paint a picture of a particular swathe of American society. These are the down-at-heel newcomers, the lower depths working hard to better themselves the American way, in the troubled pursuit of an(y) American Dream. The tragedy in this play, just as in *Cat on a Hot Tin Roof*, lies not in personal circumstances, but in the lives and the losses of the culture and the society itself. In the final scene Eunice, comforting Stella, says that 'Life has got to go on. No matter what happens, you've got to keep on going.' (Williams, p.217) As the play ends, the men return to their cards and Stella receives her baby from Eunice. Life and the community are still going to go on. In the face of great struggles this must always be the case and here, in this melting pot of people trying to better themselves, Williams is showing us that just to carry on is sometimes the hardest, most tragic thing of all.

The original Broadway production of *A Streetcar Named Desire* showcased vividly Williams' desire to create plays that exist in a clearly living, fully-realised world. As his notes for *The Glass Menagerie* show, he wanted to create theatre that had the fluid quality of imagination, allowing an audience to see, hear and feel more than just one flat, dimensionless aspect of his character's lives. The design for *A Streetcar Named Desire* allows for this beautifully, showing not only both rooms of the Kowalski apartment, but also elements of the apartment above, the alleyway, the street and the bars nearby. In creating a world so fully-layered and complex, he succeeds in stripping away binary certainties from his drama, creating instead a vibrant, dense and complex world where the only true goodness lies in a sense of social equality and togetherness. All human life is here, and alive it certainly is.

SOME KEY IDEAS TO CONSIDER

- The role that offstage music plays in representing Blanche's breakdown.

- Whether you see Stanley or Blanche as the tragic hero – and what this suggests about your interpretation of the play.

- How Williams uses each scene of the play to reveal one more element about Blanche and her past. What does this mean for a reader's perception of Blanche?

- The place names Williams chooses – Elysian Fields, Desire, Cemeteries. What effect do they create for a reader?

ARTHUR MILLER

> I believe that the common man is as apt a subject for tragedy in
> its highest sense as kings were.
> *Arthur Miller: 'Tragedy and the Common Man' New York Times: 1949*

OVERVIEW

In the middle decades of the 20th century Arthur Miller became an icon in the American cultural landscape. Through his involvement in the anti-Communist McCarthy trials of the 1950s, he gained an international reputation. Through his marriage to Marilyn Monroe he gained fame and glamour. Through his essays and novels, his writing for newspapers and the screen he established himself as a vigorously independent-minded voice within the arts. But, most of all, through his plays he sought to redefine the notion of tragedy, to re-energise classical traditions and to re-engage major drama with the facts of life for the common American man. Miller's works were informed and influenced by all aspects of his life and beliefs, creating theatre which was both strikingly personal and engagingly universal:

> The plays are my autobiography. I can't write plays that don't sum up
> where I am. I'm in all of them.
>
> *Arthur Miller in Christopher Bigsby (ed.) 1997: 1*

In the dramatic transformation of his own experiences and philosophies, Miller moved to centre stage the plight of ordinary American men in mythologically grand scenarios and, consequently, brought into being some of the most quintessentially American epic drama of the last hundred years.

Making a stand – Miller's tragic heroes

In his essay of 1949, Miller defines the tragic hero as being:

> a character who is ready to lay down his life, if need be, to secure one
> thing – his sense of personal dignity.
>
> *Arthur Miller: 'Tragedy and the Common Man', New York Times 1949*

He argues that this can apply to any person from any walk of life, not merely to kings, and certainly it applied to Miller in his dealings with the so-called 'McCarthyism' of the mid-20th century. Senator Joseph McCarthy was a key figure in 1950s America, a leader in the naming and denouncing of perceived Communist spies and sympathisers within American Government. His proclamations contributed significantly to the creation of a fervent public fear of Communism in American society. This fear generated a massive interest in the organisation known as the

HUAC – the American Senate's 'House un-American Activities Committee' – which was investigating alleged Communist leanings in people of influence throughout society at large. Miller, amongst many others, was called before the 'House un-American Activities Committee' in 1956 and asked to name friends and colleagues involved in supposedly Communist activities. Miller refused, claiming that:

> I am trying to, and I will, protect my sense of myself. I could not use the name of another person and bring trouble on him. I take the responsibility for everything I have ever done, but I cannot take the responsibility for another human being.
>
> *House Committee on Un-American Activities 'Testimony of Arthur Miller'*
> *in Griffin 1996: 7*

Miller's experience with HUAC was to have a great effect on him. He believed strongly that the individual must make a stand against society if it is for committed and justifiable means. His standpoint in the HUAC trials can be seen to reflect much of what he had attempted previously and would go on to achieve in the creation of tragic and heroic figures who were 'common men'.

Tragedy was to become the most apt form for Miller's drama. As Brenda Murphy observes:

> Miller was trying to define a tradition that would encompass both the psychological and the social. He found this in classical Greek drama.
>
> *Christopher Bigsby (ed.) 1997: 11*

Many of Miller's plays feature a central character, usually male, striving to face up to a testing situation in a manner that he perceives to be right and proper. Whether this action is seen to be so by an audience is open to debate, with Miller simply allowing the situation to speak for itself. In this manner, he argues, the tragic mode is inevitably brought into being. In the very act of risking all for principle – 'in this stretching and tearing apart of the cosmos' as Miller puts it:

> the character gains in 'size'… the commonest of men may take on that [tragic] stature to the extent of his willingness to throw all he has into the contest, the battle to secure his rightful place in the world.
>
> *Arthur Miller: 'Tragedy and the Common Man', New York Times 1949*

In each of his major plays – *All My Sons* (1947), *Death of a Salesman* (1949), *The Crucible* (1953) and *A View from the Bridge* (1955) – there is a hero figure, a man who may be seriously flawed, who may or may not be correct in his assumptions and yet who acts wholeheartedly and with commitment in defence of his own honour. For Joe Keller, Willy Loman, John Proctor and Eddie Carbone the outcome is necessarily tragic and final and yet, in the process of arriving at the outcome, each play makes interesting use of tragic elements in an exploration of what Miller refers to as 'the belief – optimistic, if you will, in the perfectibility of man.'

A VIEW FROM THE BRIDGE (1955)

SYNOPSIS

Eddie Carbone is a lifelong dock-worker, living in the run down Red Hook area of New York with his wife Beatrice and his orphaned niece Catherine. The family agree to take in two of Beatrice's Italian cousins – Marco and Rodolpho – who are entering the country illegally in order to escape from poverty back home.

Following the Italian code of family loyalty, Eddie believes it is an honour to take the two men in and they both come to work with him on the docks. When Rodolpho takes an interest in Catherine, Eddie begins to think suspiciously of the blonde haired, good-looking Italian who sings, dances, makes dresses and cooks. Eddie proclaims repeatedly that Rodolpho is 'not right' as his true, less than paternal, feelings for his niece become clear.

When Catherine and Rodolpho reveal their feelings for each other, Eddie tries to find a way to stop their union legally, calling on the lawyer Alfieri. When this fails and the couple announce they are to marry, Eddie calls the immigration department and gives his relations up. This act brings shame on Eddie who, in a final confrontation with Marco, draws a knife to defend his honour. Marco is too strong and turns the blade on Eddie, killing him in front of his family, in the street.

Many of Miller's plays evoke elements of tragedy whilst exploring aspects of the writer's own life or beliefs. Of all his works, *A View from the Bridge* stands out as the most intensely personal and the most uncompromisingly tragic.

Contexts

Written in 1955, the play was a response to Miller's experience with the HUAC Communist trials and, more specifically, a response to the film *On the Waterfront*, directed by Miller's former friend Elia Kazan. Upon testifying to the HUAC trials, renowned director Elia Kazan named names of supposed Communist sympathisers in order to avoid being 'blacklisted', which would have resulted in him being unable to continue working in Hollywood. This decision alienated him from many friends, including Miller, and in response Kazan directed the film *On the Waterfront*. In the film a dockworker testifies against a corrupt union boss, his action being presented as noble, selfless and for the greater good. In Miller's play a dockworker, Eddie Carbone, also informs against those to whom he is supposedly loyal – in this case he 'shops' to the authorities the illegal Italian immigrants who are related to his wife, and who are both hiding in his house and working with him on the docks. Yet this time the outcome is more complex. Eddie's actions are presented not as being for the greater good, but rather as self-serving and weak: it is his improper feelings for his niece Catherine, rather than a more morally justifiable motivation, that leads him to betray his family. Rather than leading to his elevation within the society, his decision to betray the immigrants precipitates his fall from grace and eventually his death.

A Greek tragedy for modern times

Written as an 'intentional allusion to Greek dramatic architectonics' (B. Murphy in C.W. Bigsby, ed., 1997: 12), the play was conceived as a one-act verse play narrated, in the style of a **Greek chorus**, by the lawyer Alfieri. With this script Miller wanted to see 'whether we could in a contemporary theatre deal with life in some way like the Greeks did' (Miller, quoted by B. Murphy in C.W. Bigsby, ed. 1997: 12). The original version was not a success but the script was revised a year later to become a more conventional two-act prose drama. Miller retained many of the classical features of the original, not least the choric function of Alfieri. In the play's gradually rising action and the complexity of the protagonist's motives there is a strong case for this play to be seen as the blueprint for Miller's notion of the tragedy of the common man.

Eddie's self-inflicted tragic fall is classically framed. Miller experimented with a number of different endings for the play, exploring for himself the different effects that each conclusion brought. But, in the end, he settled for the most classical of endings, whereby the faults inherent in the protagonist inevitably cause his death at the hands of those he was apparently trying to protect. Eddie's self-serving actions, presented as they are within this rhetoric of self-sacrifice, can be interpreted as a rejection of Elia Kazan's attempt to justify himself, to present betrayal as admirable, in *On the Waterfront*. However it is also a clear attempt by Miller to solidify a sense of his belief in the individual's right to self-justification, even in the face of understandable opposition from society as a whole. The play nakedly displays what Murphy refers to as 'the psychological and social forces that lead inevitably to Eddie's destruction' and it is this inevitability that leads Miller to most exploit the Greek tragic form.

Miller draws on the structure of Greek tragedy and in doing so he suggests to the audience that Eddie's fall is not only a result of a **flaw** within his character (his improper feelings towards Catherine) but is also pre-ordained. In this use of the tragic form the character of the lawyer Alfieri acts as both **chorus** and catalyst in the downfall of the hero. 'Every few years,' he tells us in his opening speech,

> there is still a case, and as the parties tell me what the trouble is ... the thought comes that in some Caesar's year, in Calabria perhaps or on the cliff at Syracuse, another lawyer, quite differently dressed, heard the same complaint and sat there as powerless as I, and watched it run its bloody course.

> *Arthur Miller 1955 in Miller 2000: 12*

From the outset, with the pointed use of the word 'bloody', Miller prepares his audience for a tragic event. He has said that he:

> wanted to reveal the method nakedly to everybody so that from the very beginning of the play we are to know that this man can't make it, and yet might reveal himself somehow in the struggle.
>
> *Arthur Miller in B. Murphy, Christopher Bigsby (ed.) 1997: 13*

Alfieri, the narrator and confidant of the audience, prepares the ground for a tragic exploration leading to pity, terror, catharsis and death. In alerting the audience to the inevitable end at the very beginning, Miller locks Eddie Carbone into a tragic scheme from which it is impossible to escape.

Having originally created notes for the play under the title 'An Italian Tragedy', Miller clearly wanted to explore the complexities that tragedy involves. In this play he closely explores conflicting codes of honour in the society of Italy and America. What might seem honourable behaviour in America – upholding the law of the land and turning in illegal immigrants – is entirely dishonourable in terms of the codes of family loyalty and kinship in the Sicilian society from which these immigrants come. The play introduces a rich exploration of ideas about heroism and honour across different cultures. Honour in tragedy is a complex and shifting concept and Eddie is caught in the middle of this conflict between history and the present, between family and society. His final status as tragic hero depends, to some extent, on whose values, laws and codes of honour you seek to uphold.

Eddie – a tragic hero for 20th-century America?

Miller was looking to explore a classically complex tragic figure. Eddie is just that figure – an upstanding, moral, popular man whose own drives and suspicions overtake him, bringing the inevitable violence and blood. His jealousy echoes the unquenchable rage of Othello, his inappropriate affection for Catherine has echoes of Hamlet's Oedipal complex. And yet Eddie is a longshoreman in a poor area of New York. In raising this man to the role of the fallen hero, Miller trusts that the need to justify one's own beliefs, and an unswerving faith in one's own motivations will reveal itself to an audience as, finally, a grand and sympathetic notion. Ultimately, Miller says, he came to realise that:

> however one might dislike this man, who does all sorts of frightful things, he possesses or exemplifies the wondrous and human fact that he too can be driven to what in the last analysis is a sacrifice of himself for his conception, however misguided, of right, dignity and justice.
>
> *Arthur Miller: Notebooks 1940s*

For Eddie, justice may bring death, this fact may be necessary for the restoration of order in the society of the play, but Miller tells us that his tragedy is no less powerful for the fact that we may not agree with his beliefs.

SOME KEY IDEAS TO CONSIDER

- The effect of Miller's use of a chorus figure, revealing the fate of the protagonist from the very beginning.

- The role of women in the play. Are Catherine and Beatrice largely marginalised figures, only passive in the action, or are they fully involved in it?

- Why Miller experimented with different endings. What, for you, would be the most satisfactory ending to the play?

- What Miller is trying to say about heroism in different societies and cultures.

THE CRUCIBLE (1953)

SYNOPSIS

It is 1692 in Massachusetts, a devoutly Puritan area of the 'new' America. When a group of young girls fall ill after claiming to have danced and chanted in local woods, the town of Salem is gripped by a fear of witchcraft. A judge is sent for to set up trials in order to find and punish anyone guilty of involvement in dark arts.

John Proctor, a local farmer, has previously been unfaithful to his wife, Elizabeth, with their former servant Abigail, one of the girls accused. As the trial gets underway Elizabeth's name is mentioned by the girls and she is arrested on suspicion of witchcraft and a small doll given to her by another servant, Mary Warren, is used as evidence of voodoo practice. Proctor believes the girls are lying out of malice and resolves to testify against them.

As the trial progresses many local men are arrested for protesting about the injustice of the proceedings. To try and prove the maliciousness of the girls' actions, Proctor confesses his infidelity, but Elizabeth will not confirm his story, preferring to save his good name. When the girls all go into violent fits, Mary Warren panics, accusing Proctor of Devil worship in an attempt to save herself.

Proctor is imprisoned for his crime and Elizabeth tries to persuade him to confess. Finally he agrees and signs a confession in order to save others. He tears this confession up, though, when he realises that it will be used publicly to blacken his name. The play closes as Proctor and another accused witch, Rebecca Nurse, are led to the gallows.

Context

Where *A View from the Bridge* can be interpreted as Miller's response to the HUAC trials, then the play that preceded it had a big part to play in first bringing him within the radar of Senator McCarthy and his friends. *The Crucible* was the only play Miller ever wrote set outside the modern era and it was very clearly intended as a direct theatrical response to the Communist trials and the so-called 'witch-hunt' of which they were a part. It is a remarkable piece of work taking, as its base, the story of the Salem Witch Trials of the 1692 and creating from it a scrupulously observed, factually-based metaphor for the arbitrary nature of the HUAC accusations and the public frenzy created by it. As ever with Miller the sword is double-edged: as a piece of stand-alone historical drama it is both powerful and resonant; as a piece of tragedy applied to the state of 20th-century American society, it is savage and apt.

The individual and his conscience

Like *A View from the Bridge*, *The Crucible* is morally challenging and, as a result, a difficult play to read or watch. Miller avoids making direct judgement on proceedings, allowing our sympathies to fluctuate throughout as the scenario shifts and alters. The play chronicles a single male protagonist – John Proctor – battling against a series of external forces in defence of something very personal and private. Proctor wants, above all else, to rescue his name from disgrace and, as with other Miller heroes, his actions have a wider relevance with which he is ultimately unconcerned. Miller has said:

> The longer I worked the more certain I felt that, as improbable as it might seem, there were moments when an individual conscience was all that could keep a world from falling.
>
> *Miller: Notebooks 1940s*

The personal morality of the hero is often at odds with what we might consider to be an heroic ideal and it is in this conflict between intention and goodness that Miller tries to interrogate the idea of tragedy in common life. In the form of John Proctor he has created another difficult character, a man whose power is palpable yet whose motives are blurred, a man who stands for a sense of justice that may not be legally right but which, morally at least, obeys a different set of laws altogether.

A feminist view of the drama

The play focuses on the claims of witchcraft made by a group of young girls in the Puritan town of Salem, an early and devoutly religious American settlement. It has troubled some critics who feel that it presents a world and a system in which women are marginalised. Indeed it is often observed that many of Miller's plays feature strong and powerful male characters in the lead, but his female characters often lack depth or perform only a passive role within the drama. Critic Betty Caplan was scathing in her review of *The Crucible*, feeling that Miller had presented only weak and unromantic female characters. Considering Abigail, Caplan addresses Miller directly:

> How do you describe her when she first appears? 'a strikingly beautiful girl, an orphan, with an endless capacity for dissembling.' That's it. She never develops. Face being fortune, this one's a bad 'un. What do you understand about her?
>
> *Betty Caplan: The Guardian quoted in Bleiman, Broadbent et al 1993: 40*

She suggests that Abigail is too one-dimensional a character to be fully believable and that Miller is using her and the other girls as a **scapegoat** for the fate that befalls John Proctor. Caplan also feels that Proctor's wife, Elizabeth, is held responsible by Miller for his plight: 'When Proctor salts the soup Elizabeth has cooked at the beginning of Act Two, the message is clear: 'This woman is not tasty enough'' (Caplan, quoted in Bleiman, 1993: 41). Clearly Caplan is making an extreme case but the role of women in Miller's plays is often little more than peripheral as the male characters play out their tragedies in a world familiar to their author. In *The Crucible*, however, Miller transposed the action to a world in which women were considered unequal and so, in the fevered claims of the young girls and Miller's sceptical response to them, we possibly find the situation magnified.

Name and reputation

The claims of witchcraft and devil worship made by the young girls directly affect John Proctor and his wife and bring his personal reputation into question. Proctor himself, however, is not a man without blemish. Having previously made lustful advances towards Abigail, the leader of the accusers, it becomes unclear whether he stands against the trial for reasons of love or reputation. Consider his famous plea to the court, when asked why he will not let his 'good name' be tarnished by a signed confession against his own community:

> Because it is my name! Because I cannot have another in my life! Because I lie and I sign myself to lies! Because I am not worth the dust on the feet of them that hang! How may I live without my name? I have given my soul; leave me my name.

Arthur Miller 1953 in Miller 1968: 124

This is a strikingly similar argument to Miller's own, when questioned at the HUAC trials (**p.186** and **p.204**). Proctor, finally, accepts his own sins, accepts his status as a flawed, trapped man. In laying down his life he finally attempts to effect a greater good. 'You have your magic now', he tells the court, 'for now do I think I see a shred of goodness in John Proctor. Not enough to weave a banner with, but white enough to keep it from such dogs' (Miller, p.125). At the very last – and in the face of a continuing mania in his society – Proctor finds that he can make a difference. Miller declines to reveal whether his action has a positive effect after all and yet, at the close of the play, the 'perfectibility' of one flawed man brings about a triumph of the individual in the face of incomprehensible social ill.

SOME KEY IDEAS TO CONSIDER

- Whether this is a tragedy of its time or for all time.

- Whether this tragedy leads to a purging of fear and sadness as defined by Aristotle in relation to classical tragedy.

- Whether Proctor is a tragic hero with whom a modern audience can identify.

TRAGEDIES OF THE FATHER

All My Sons (1947) and Death of a Salesman (1949)

Miller's first two great plays of the mid-century – *All My Sons* (1947) and *Death of a Salesman* (1949) – also deal with the notion of a tragic hero drawn inevitably to his downfall and death. In contrast to *The Crucible* and *A View from the Bridge*, however, both of these plays are focused far more roundly on the family and the pressures that this unit can come under when the social forces acting on the hero cause the flaws and the transgressions that must ultimately and violently surface in the drama. Miller still treats his subject with a degree of moral detachment and, arguably, both Joe Keller in *All My Sons* and Willy Loman in *Death of a Salesman* demonstrate just as much of a troubling moral focus as do Eddie Carbone and John Proctor. Yet, in both these plays, the purpose of the tragedy seems to be more focused on the true Greek spirit of **catharsis** and redemption. These are the tragedies of fathers and sons who must live by their mistakes, learn from their mistakes and, finally, die by them in the name of a greater good that finally and positively reveals itself in the action.

ALL MY SONS (1947)

SYNOPSIS

The Keller family, led by the father Joe, has run a successful manufacturing business for many years. Their eldest son, Larry, went missing as a fighter pilot in the Second World War and is presumed dead by all in the family except the mother, Kate, who passionately clings to the hope he will return one day. Chris, the younger son, returns home with Larry's former fiancée, Ann, hoping to announce their engagement and – as a result – end the speculation over Larry's fate.

Joe becomes suspicious of Ann, the daughter of his former business partner Steve who was disgraced when jailed during the war for allowing defective plane parts to be sent to the US Air Force. This action resulted in the death of twenty one pilots. The reason for Joe's suspicion becomes clear as it transpires that Ann's brother, George, has come to suspect that it was Joe himself rather than Steve who was responsible for the shipping of the faulty parts.

As Joe attempts to defend his finances and his reputation, Chris becomes suspicious himself and finally forces Joe to confess his culpability. Disgraced in the eyes of his family and responsible for the twenty one deaths, Joe finally accepts his guilt. He goes into the house and shoots himself, leaving Chris to reveal the news as the curtain falls.

All My Sons was Miller's first great stage success and deals with a single family suffering the consequences of past sins, a feature of tragedy from Aeschylus' *Oresteia* onwards. Much has been made of the play's similarity in form and content to the work of Ibsen, a playwright Miller admired immensely. It is certainly the most Ibsenesque of Miller's plays, dealing with 'bringing the past into the present' (Arthur Miller, *Collected Plays*, p.20 quoted by Stephen R. Centola in C.W. Bigsby, 1997: 50) as Joe Keller must accept his responsibility for chasing too hard after success and causing the death of many fighter pilots during the Second World War. Pushed by his son's growing realisation of the truth of his culpability, Keller tries to hide behind the idea that he always wanted to provide a good life for his children. Chris Keller, his eldest son, responds violently to this idea:

> What the hell do you mean, you did it for me? Don't you have a country? Don't you live in the world? What the hell are you? You're not even an animal, no animal kills his own, what are you? ... I ought to tear the tongue out of your mouth.

Arthur Miller 1947 in Miller 2000: 158

As the full extent of his guilt sinks in, Keller must realise his mistake (his moment of **anagnorisis**) and admit that he catastrophically prioritised his own and his family's needs above those of the wider community. This tension between the family and the community is fundamental to the tragic form, resolving itself in this play in Joe's recognition that, 'I think to him they were all my sons. And I guess they were, I guess they were' (Miller, p.170). He departs the stage and shortly a shot is heard – Keller's suicide is the final tragic requirement of the story. Having realised his error, the hero must take the fullest responsibility and for Keller there is clearly no other option, having caused so many to die by his negligence.

The women in the play

Although the female characters are arguably only peripheral to the action, both Ann and Kate have a key role to play in the establishment of Joe's tragedy. Both women drive certain elements of the plot – Ann brings with her the sense of suspicion that is eventually turned into accusation by George and Chris, Kate tries to hold the family together with her painful faith in Larry's survival – and yet both are ultimately also helpless to halt the process at work. The argument at the centre of the play is clearly seen by Miller as being between a father and his son and, as such, neither Ann (whose motivation is never fully articulated by Miller) nor Kate can ever hope to effect a change in the plot. This is not an unfamiliar trait in Miller's plays but, here, the sense of family is crucial to the final reckoning of Joe.

The play demonstrates what Murphy calls 'the individual's responsibility to society even when that means the sacrifice of the claims of family' (Murphy, in Bigsby, ed., 1997: 19). Joe has lived for many years trying – rightly or wrongly – to protect and support his family. His wife has held his secret for the same reasons and Ann seeks to come into the family in spite of previous events. Both women support the men in the play and yet, in this case, they also solidify the sense of what Miller places at stake – the family unit. *All My Sons* is the tragedy of a man who must finally acknowledge that sometimes the family unit cannot come first. In acknowledging that responsibility, Joe Keller finally performs an act truly for the benefit of his son – to accept his blame and to absolve him from the sins of the father and, by extension, set him free.

SOME KEY IDEAS TO CONSIDER

- Why this play continues to be revived. Why might it still be relevant today?

- Whether Joe really is the tragic hero in this play. Is there an argument that says it could be Chris? Or even Kate?

- Why Miller makes such a detailed description of the setting, especially the fallen apple tree. What does this symbolism seek to tell us?

- The ways in which play follows the patterns of classical tragedy.

DEATH OF A SALESMAN (1949)

SYNOPSIS

The play is told through a series of scenes over the course of about twenty four hours at the end of the life of Willy Loman, a travelling salesman from New York. Willy has not been well for some time and some of the scenes are played out in flashback as Willy tries to reconcile elements of his life that have led to his current, unsuccessful state.

Willy is in continual denial about his lack of success, often imagining his brother, Ben, who made millions mysteriously in Africa. His sons, Biff and Happy, attempt to lift his spirits by agreeing to set up a sports goods firm, allowing Willy to experience the success he so craves. Happy, though, is naïve and Biff has spent many years since high school as a dropout in Texas. Biff had been a football star at school but failed Maths and did not get to college.

As the play continues it becomes clear that Willy has had at least one affair on his travels and feels great guilt for this. He is fired by his boss and meets his sons to discuss their plans. Biff has failed to get any money for the business from his boss and, finally, confronts Willy about his fantasies, his affair and his recent suicide attempts.

Willy is forced to face up to his failure and begins to think of the worth of his life insurance. The voice of his brother calls him to his car and he drives away, ostensibly to kill himself. The play ends with a funeral scene and his long-suffering wife announces that she has just made the last payment on their house, meaning that 'We're free.'

Absolution is a key factor in what is probably Miller's most famous play *Death of a Salesman*. For some, it is also the most classically tragic of all Miller's dramas. Matthew C. Roudané notes that:

> the play embodies, for many, the peripeteia, hamartia, and hubris that Aristotle found essential for all great tragedies.

Matthew Roudané in Christopher Bigsby (ed.) 1997: 61

Certainly in Willy Loman's last twenty-four hours there is evidence of all these tragic elements. Loman is the typical tragic protagonist who fails to realise the shortcomings of his life and refuses to acknowledge culpability for them. Yet as an audience sees scenes from his past played out we come to realise that the affair, the desperation and the inflated sense of self-worth all contribute to a tragic examination of denial. Christopher Bigsby argues that this denial:

> lies at the heart of Miller's work. Time after time he explores the lives of those who fail to acknowledge their freedom to act. They are observers of their own fate, unwilling, often through guilt, sometimes through fear, to intervene on their own behalf or to acknowledge their responsibility toward others.

Christopher Bigsby (ed.) 1997: 4

215

Willy Loman has watched as his situation has grown increasingly desperate over many years, creating multiple illusions of success and ambition for himself and his sons. These fantasies have only deepened his denial and detached him further from the truth. His flashbacks all relate to this denial and reveal elements of all the things he refuses to admit to himself.

The salesman and the dream

It is not a coincidence that Miller made his main character a salesman – central to the idea of the American Dream is the notion that any man can become something great; he just has to have confidence and sell himself. Willy Loman has sold his own idea of himself for so long that the truth and the dream are fatally divided. It is in this failure to recognise one's own predicament – in the excess of self-belief and importance that the Greeks called **hubris** – that all tragedy arises. As such, *Death of a Salesman* can be seen as a quintessentially American tragedy, a stinging critique of a society that encourages confidence, belief and betterment without always rewarding those qualities. Willy has spent his whole life hoping to achieve wealth in the same way as the brother he idolises, yet he 'exists in a world that increasingly detaches itself from him, reminding him daily of his insignificance' (Bigsby, ed. 1997: 80), as Roudané puts it. He exists in a gap that has existed in American culture for centuries – the gap between the expectations of wealth that are generated by a capitalist, consumerist society and the realities of families unable to pay their mortgage, update their insurance or fix the fridge. Willy, as a salesman, is complicit in the selling of dreams and of consumables all across the north east of the United States, and yet he is also as much a victim as anyone, cast out and rejected after thirty four years by a system and a dream that he has idolised. His is a tragedy created by a society of dreams and played out in families across America even today.

The end – recognising the truth

It could be argued that Willy Loman has been absent from reality for so long, his fantasies have become so ingrained, that his return to earth seems impossible. And yet at the very last, his eldest son Biff finally makes him realise the truth – screaming at him that 'I am not a leader of men, Willy, and neither are you. You were never anything but a hard-working drummer who landed in the ash-can like all the rest of them!' (Miller, p.105). Willy Loman, the archetypal 'little man' (signalled even in his name), finally assesses his worth and finds more value in his death than in his life. 'Can you imagine that magnificence with twenty thousand dollars in his pocket?' (Miller, p.107) he asks, thinking of the value of his death insurance, making the decision to protect the life of others by taking his own. In this moment he takes on that 'stature' to which Miller has referred; he becomes in one action, a tragic and complex hero. 'We're free' sobs his wife at the play's conclusion, as Willy Loman's attempt to absolve himself creates a **cathartic** and powerful moment for both his family and the audience.

SOME KEY IDEAS TO CONSIDER

- The significance of the staging and the ways in which the scenes from the past and the present are represented.

- The significance of the names Miller gives to his characters. Do characters like Willy Loman, Happy and Biff live up to them?

- Why Miller made his central character a travelling salesman. What does this job tell us about the pursuit of the American Dream?

- Why Miller added the 'requiem' at the play's end. How does this fit into a wider tragic scheme?

MILLER'S TRAGEDIES OF THE ORDINARY MAN

All of Miller's protagonists die trying to right a wrong or to better the lot of others. They each arrive at this point in different ways but, as Stephen Barker observes:

> in Miller no successful path to right choice and actions exists; it is a matter of choosing the correct incorrect path to an idea, and that idea is always the failure and betrayal of the purity and perfection for which his characters strive.

Stephen Barker in Christopher Bigsby (ed.) 1997: 237

Each of these men, for different ideals and different values, dies in trying to make something better, to make themselves or their world more perfect. Miller admires these men, no matter their background, and sums up their predicaments in 'Tragedy and the Common Man' (1949) by arguing that 'tragedy, then, is the consequence of a man's total compulsion to evaluate himself justly.' We all strive to be perfect, Miller argues in these plays, but perfection is never fully achievable. Instead, we can only hope to acknowledge our own faults and take responsibility for the problems we have created. In embracing this ideal, Miller's tragedies of the ordinary man push us one step closer to the perfectibility of man.

MODERN
BRITISH
TRAGEDY

OVERVIEW

Since 1945 tragic drama in Britain has explored, and been provoked by, political conflict and institutional change. Politics has been a central concern of British dramatists: in the 1960s, 70s and 80s class conflict and the struggle for women to gain greater equality had prominence. In the last thirty years the changing face of Britain as a more multicultural society and the nature of Britain's place in a globalised and increasingly dangerous world have also been a matter for the stage. All of these topics are fraught with intractable and urgent conflicts, making them ideal subjects for tragic drama.

CONTEXTS

Freedom of expression

Two Acts of Parliament have had a major impact on the British theatre in the years since 1945. The Arts Council, founded in 1946, ensured that government finance would be made available for the development of the theatre, free from conditions about how the money should be distributed. Stage freedom was further enhanced by the abolition of censorship in 1968. Since 1737 an unelected official of the royal household, the Lord Chamberlain, had possessed the power to decide what could be shown on stage. He had banned, amongst other matters, anything which he had thought to be 'indecent', anything which might 'do violence to the sentiment of religious reverence' or which might 'be calculated to impair friendly relations with a Foreign Power' (Shellard 1999: 9).

The introduction of funding and the abolition of censorship gave theatre the freedom to stage plays which would not otherwise have been financially viable, as well as those which tackled controversial and difficult topics, particularly on political and sexual matters. Although these freedoms were challenged during the 1980s under the Thatcher government, they nonetheless enhanced the ability of the stage to act as a critic of power and of conventional beliefs, two key features of tragic drama since classical times.

Influences

A major strand of British theatre in the second half of the 20th century was dominated by left-wing, and especially Marxist politics. The visit of Bertolt Brecht's company, the Berliner Ensemble, to London in 1956 to perform *Mother Courage* was the beginning of a long period when Brechtian ideas exercised a powerful influence over British writers, directors and designers. Brecht's plays sought, by a variety of means, to dramatise the conflicts and contradictions in society so that the audience could identify the political choices at stake in their own lives and to understand how and why the world needed to be transformed. Brecht's **Epic theatre** did not represent the world **naturalistically**; rather, it refused to let the audience forget that they were watching actors at work. Brecht did not want the audience so emotionally involved that they lost a sense of objective judgement about what they were watching. This did not mean, however, that his theatre was not emotionally affecting. The action proceeds episodically, rather than in a smooth continuous narrative, inviting the audience themselves to make connections between the different scenes. Before 1956 British theatre had, on the whole, presented the mainly middle-class audience with a reflection of itself, with working-class people often appearing as servants, or comic figures, or individuals marginal to the main action. Brecht showed all classes on stage, with the plight of working people often in the foreground.

Theatre Workshop – drama for the working class

> Tragedy is not about reconciliation. Consequently it is the art form of our time.
>
> *Howard Barker 1989:13*

This awareness of social class in the theatre was evident in Joan Littlewood's Theatre Workshop company. From 1953 until the late 1960s Littlewood worked principally from an impoverished old theatre in the East End of London, producing a mixture of reinvigorated classics and political drama for a working-class audience. Theatre Workshop's style was energetic and irreverent, drawing on physical theatre. The theatre critic Michael Billington describes their 'trademarks' as 'a fluid mixture of speech and song, expressive use of light and sound, the suggestion of the stage as a metaphorical world' (Billington 2007: 25). For Littlewood tragedy was not a high culture art form, but for everyone.

Raymond Williams and the tragedy of class conflict

The most influential British left-wing literary theorist of this time, Raymond Williams, described how class conflict, and indeed revolution, is a tragic situation in as much as ultimately real individuals are caught in inescapable conflicts with each other.

Writers who have expressed the tragedy of the individual caught in historical conflict in this way include David Hare (b.1947), who was a student of Williams at Cambridge. Hare's dramas explore the impact of historical forces on individuals who are striving to live well in a world of conflict and compromise. Caryl Churchill (b.1938), a playwright whose earlier work shows the influence of Brecht, has written, amongst many other things, of the tragic position of individual women in contemporary society.

> Because they have bled life out of the word freedom, the word
> justice attains a new significance. Only tragedy makes justice its
> preoccupation.
>
> *Howard Barker 1989: 14*

In left-wing tragedies of the late twentieth century such **catharsis** (emotional response to the tragedy's conclusion) as exists may be an increased consciousness of injustice, its sources and its remedies. The emotion which the audience feels for those who suffer is experienced in the context of the political events and human actions which have caused it. Those events are shown not to be the operations of fate: the world could be different if we were able to act to change the human actions which bring about tragic suffering. Those further actions which seek to right – or avoid – injustice may well, as Williams noted, bring even more suffering, which adds to the tragedy. For Williams, tragedy was not 'just' a literary from, but part of the nature of modern life itself which finds its expression in our art (**p.24**).

Probably the most genuinely **Epic** of contemporary dramatists, in the mould of Brecht, is Edward Bond (b.1934), in as much as many of his plays are spare, episodic, enigmatic and sometimes brutal. Bond wrote that 'theatre must talk of the causes of human misery and the sources of human strength'. Both Brecht and Littlewood were formative influences on his work. Bond's own concern with the violence inherent but often hidden away in modern life is challengingly developed by his clearest heir Sarah Kane (1971-99), who herself died young.

Apolitical tragedy?

A different continental influence on British theatre came from France, in the form of **absurdism**. Following the catastrophes and genocide of the mid-century, and with the threat of nuclear annihilation hanging over the world, some writers felt that life was indeed a tragedy, but with no apparent hope of any kind of meaning or redemption. Rather than seeing politics as offering a means of bringing about a just world, as the Marxist critic Raymond Williams and political playwrights might argue, absurdist tragedy suggests that politics may in fact be the cause of our insoluble predicament. The play which had the greatest impact here was Samuel Beckett's (1906-89) *Waiting for Godot* (1955) (**p.180**). Tragedy is rooted in the fact that life has no meaning or purpose; no hope that the lot of humanity will get better, and no God to validate our desire for justice or need for ultimate explanation. But in this rejection of faith in both God and humanity, there is an authentic honesty which confers some dignity to those who confront the tragic predicament of mankind without illusion.

> They give birth astride of a grave, the light gleams an instant,
> then it's night once more.
>
> *Samuel Beckett 1955: 83*

Harold Pinter's (1930-2008) early work was initially regarded by some as absurdist. Much of it, however, has come to be seen as both tragic and political, not least by the dramatist himself. In this reading of his work the forces that render life intolerable are not ultimately mysterious and, in the destruction of the protagonist(s), the vulnerability of those forces is revealed. Examples may include *The Birthday Party* (1958) and *Mountain Language* (1992). In *The Birthday Party* the mysterious figures of Goldberg and McCann are brutal representatives of social conformity. They silence and remove the cantankerous and unpleasant Stanley Webber, but not before he has deeply unsettled their confidence through his resistance, even when the power of speech has been taken from him.

DAVID HARE

David Hare displays Raymond Williams' concern to present the 'whole action' of the drama, that is to show how larger historical and political events have an impact on people's lives, but also to understand those events and the reasons behind them. As with Williams, an optimism about our shared human values emerges clearly, alongside a sense of rage against an injustice which is presented as never necessary. Whereas Greek tragedy often sought to bring into the open contradictions in the beliefs and ideas of the citizen community, modern political tragedy seeks to demonstrate a common humanity which must be respected in a divided and conflicted society.

THE TRILOGY (1990-1993)

Racing Demon, Murmuring Judges, The Absence of War

In the 1990s Hare wrote a trilogy of plays which examined the state of key British institutions under pressure from unleashed market forces: The Church of England (*Racing Demon*, 1990), the legal system (*Murmuring Judges*, 1991) and the Labour Party *(The Absence of War*, 1993). More recently he has produced in effect dramatised documentaries written almost entirely from the reported speech of real people. *The Permanent Way* (2003) dealt with the disasters which followed the privatisation of the railways, and *Stuff Happens* (2004) with the deceptions which led to the US-led invasion of Iraq in 2003.

PLENTY (1978)

The tragic woman

Although most of Hare's plays might be seen to have tragic figures – good men brought down by an error of judgement (for example the Labour leader George Jones in *The Absence of War*, and US Secretary of State Colin Powell in *Stuff Happens*) – the female protagonists of his earlier work are perhaps more obviously tragic. Hare has always been a close observer of the contradictory pressures on women in an era of increasing female emancipation, and the costs of these social changes on individual women.

In *Plenty* (1978), Susan Traherne has served as a very young undercover agent in Nazi-occupied France during the Second World War, and is filled with optimism about how England will change after the experience of war. She cannot accommodate herself, however, to the compromises of the peacetime world and England's self-deceptions about itself and its place in the world and in this she is a tragic figure of the same form, at least as *Hamlet* or Ibsen's *Hedda Gabler*.

She makes an unwise marriage to the diplomat whom she met when her married lover died in Brussels, and tries to have a child by another, working-class man whom she barely knows. By the end of the play she is psychologically broken, and back in the arms of an agent from her French resistance days. The eleven episodic scenes tell the story of Susan's life between 1947 and 1962, interrupted by flashbacks to her time in France.

FRENCHMAN	The English ... have no feelings, yes? Are stiff.
SUSAN	They hide them, hide them from the world.
FRENCHMAN	Is stupid.
SUSAN	Stupid, yes. It may be ... (Pause)
FRENCHMAN	Huh?
SUSAN	That things will quickly change. We have grown up. We will improve our world.

David Hare 1978: 207

THE SECRET RAPTURE (1988)

A woman's integrity

The Secret Rapture is set very precisely at the height of Conservative rule in Britain in 1988. Isobel is a woman who strives always to act morally in a world where selfish individualism has become sanctified. The demise of the values of the old Left is symbolised by the death of Isobel's socialist father at the play's beginning. Isobel's stepmother Katherine is a troubled alcoholic her own age. Isobel attempts to look after her and gives her a job in her own graphic design firm, an act which eventually costs her not only her marriage, but eventually also her life. Isobel's principal antagonist is her sister Marion, an ambitious junior government minister with a smug Christian husband.

MARION	Because you can't understand there are actually more important things in life than your wretched sense of honesty.

Isobel looks at her, not rising to the charge.

ISOBEL	Well in that case why won't you offer her [Katherine] a job?
MARION	Don't be ridiculous. I'm in the Conservative Party.

David Hare 1988: 25-6

While neither Isobel's husband nor her sister can understand her sense of duty or of love, Marion is troubled by her own lack of understanding of what other people feel, acting as a dramatic foil for Isobel whose own individuality is destroyed by such an ability. It is a moving and insightful play with a genuinely tragic central figure. Isobel acts throughout with honesty and generosity, but without compromising her own integrity and right to have her opinions heard. The tragedy lies in the fact that she lives in a society where those qualities are not valued. In contradiction to the Aristotelian and **Idealist (p.22-23)** views of tragedy, it is the protagonist's virtues rather than failings, that lead to her downfall in a fundamentally unjust world.

SKYLIGHT (1995)

A polarised society

The clash of values in modern Britain is even more sharply drawn in *Skylight* (1995). Kyra's affair with Tom, a successful businessman, ended when his wife was diagnosed with cancer. She becomes a primary teacher in a tough London school. The action takes place in her small, cold flat several years later, after his wife's death. He is hoping they may be able to rekindle the relationship. Kyra is from a middle-class background, but Tom is working class. When Tom accuses her of making herself a martyr to no purpose, Kyra defends herself passionately:

> I'm tired of these sophistries. I'm tired of these right-wing fuckers. They wouldn't lift a finger themselves. They work contentedly in offices and banks. Yet now they sit pontificating in parliament, in papers, impugning our motives, questioning our judgements. And why? Because they themselves need to feel better by putting down everyone whose work is so much harder than theirs. (*She stands, nodding*) You only have to say the words 'social worker ... probation officer' ... 'counsellor' ... 'for everyone in this country to sneer'.

David Hare 1995: 79

They argue fiercely, despite the fact that they still love each other. It is far from clear at the end that the relationship has a future. Both are tragic figures: eloquent, energetic, but unable to find a meeting place in a society too sharply polarised for happy endings. Characteristically, modern British tragedy locates its source in a society in conflict, not finally in the individual. Kyra and Tom cannot escape the identities written for them by the divisions of Britain in the 1990s.

SOME KEY POINTS TO CONSIDER

- The relationship between political/social comment and tragedy.

- The use Hare makes of classical ideas about tragedy.

- The role of women in these tragedies.

CARYL CHURCHILL

TOP GIRLS (1982)

SYNOPSIS

The first act features a dinner party of different women from history, art and legend. They have all gathered together to celebrate Marlene's appointment as the boss of the Top Girls Employment Agency in London. They are all women for whom family life with children has been very difficult, to say the least, because of male behaviour in the society in which they lived.

In the second act we see Top Girls in action, in a series of scenes where women are interviewed for possible job opportunities and the firm's female employees discuss their personal lives. In all cases the need to defer to how the unseen men wish women to be is a powerful factor. Marlene's sixteen year-old 'niece' Angie suddenly arrives from Suffolk, hoping to stay with her. We have previously seen Angie with her younger and cleverer friend Kit in scene which shows her to be unhappy, not to say a little disturbed, and at odds with her 'mother' Joyce. Marlene treats Angie with little consideration, despite Angie's idolisation of her 'aunt'.

Act Three takes place a year before Act Two. Marlene arrives at her sister Joyce's house. We discover that Angie is actually Marlene's daughter, secretly 'adopted' by the childless Joyce who is trapped in an unhappy marriage. Marlene left Angie behind so that she could pursue her career. The two quarrel bitterly. At the end it is unclear whether Angie has overheard the truth about her real mother.

Top Girls (1982) is perhaps Churchill's best-known play. In its remarkable first act, five women, both historical and fictional, meet in a restaurant to celebrate Marlene's elevation to manager of the Top Girls employment agency. The party includes an Emperor's concubine from medieval Japan, a Scottish Victorian traveller, a legendary female Pope, a woman depicted in a 16th-century Brueghel painting fighting devils, and Chaucer's much put-upon heroine Patient Griselda.

As the highly entertaining and increasingly drunken party progresses, the bemused audience come to see that all of these women were remarkable in some sense, but none was able to have a happy or sustained family life with children because of the demands, mostly violent, made upon them by men. What, then, of Marlene, who has achieved the kind of professional status which feminists have fought for women to have the opportunity to achieve?

'Unnatural' women

JOYCE   What good's first woman if it's her? I suppose
         you'd have liked Hitler if he was a woman. Ms
         Hitler. Got a lot done, Hitlerina.

Caryl Churchill 1982: 84

Act Two shows Marlene and her colleagues to be selfish and unsympathetic to their clients and each other. Top Girls is an employment agency where women are made to accommodate the demands of men whose power remains unimpaired. Even the resentful wife of the man who failed to obtain Marlene's position repeats male clichés about successful women:

MRS KIDD   You don't care. I thought he was going too far but he's
            right. You're one of these ballbreakers/ that's what you
            are. You'll

MARLENE   I'm sorry but I do have some work to do.

MRS KIDD   end up miserable and lonely. You're not natural.

MARLENE   Could you please piss off?

Caryl Churchill 1982: 59

In the longest scene in Act Two we see Marlene's niece Angie, an angry, immature and barely qualified school leaver in her Suffolk village. She idolises her aunt, resents her mother Joyce and, in the act's final scene, arrives uninvited at the employment agency, unwelcome and initially unrecognised by Marlene, hoping to stay with her. As Angie lies asleep in the office at the end of the act, Marlene's brutal verdict on Angie is that 'she's not going to make it' (Churchill, p.66).

The brilliance of the dramatic writing is sustained throughout Act Three, which is set a year before Act Two. Marlene has suddenly paid a visit to her sister Joyce. This is another drunken female gathering, but now Marlene reveals to the audience that she, too, has a disturbing tale to tell, if not on the scale of Griselda or Pope Joan. Angie is Marlene's daughter, abandoned to the care of the childless and unhappily married Joyce so that Marlene could pursue her career. Joyce's resentment of her sister erupts in a vicious argument, where their political differences about the first woman Prime Minister, Margaret Thatcher (1979-90) are emphatically expressed. There is no resolution or reconciliation at the end of the play. In the play's last lines it seems as if Angie may have overheard the truth of her maternity, but Marlene refuses to acknowledge her. These two sisters cannot reconcile the mutual conflict caused by the society which has inscribed them into its structures, nor can they resolve the clash between their social roles and their own deepest feelings. As such Marlene and Joyce are tragic figures.

As tragic figures, both Marlene and Joyce have positive qualities: the former has an energy and desire to make her way in a man's world, and the latter has compassion and intelligence. Marlene is ruthless and emotionally damaged, Joyce embittered and near despair. *Top Girls* identifies brilliantly that individual freedom is an illusion in a society where gross economic inequality persists. Despite the advances made by middle-class women, poverty and limited life experiences are still most prevalent amongst women, even twenty-five years on. The violent argument with which the play ends, in the context of what we know will happen a year later to the initially sympathetic figure of Marlene, invests the play's conclusion with a typically contemporary form of **catharsis**: a complex emotional connection with a main character, combined with political insight.

Breaking the unities

It is important to recognise here Churchill's use of a non-linear time scheme in the play in producing the tragic effect. The audience knows the effect of the action before its cause. Other 21st-century dramatists have employed this technique, for example David Hare in *Plenty* (**p.224**) and Harold Pinter in *Betrayal* (1978) which tells the story of an adulterous affair from its ending backwards. In contrast with Aristotle's idea of the **unity of time** in classical tragedy, where the plot moves forwards over the course of a single day, here it is the lack of temporal unity which makes the experience tragic for the audience. The onlookers know more than the play's characters do about their fate.

SOME KEY POINTS TO CONSIDER

- Whether it makes more sense to say that Churchill depicts a tragic society rather than tragic protagonists.

- Whether *Top Girls* has a tragic **catastrophe**. Does it matter if a catastrophe is implied rather than presented?

- Whether the play's political anger makes it less effective as a tragedy.

- How Churchill presents female lives as tragic.

- How Churchill combines historical and fictional characters.

EDWARD BOND

> Art is always sane. It insists on the truth, and tries to express the justice and order that are necessary to sanity but are usually destroyed by society. All imagination is political.
>
> *Edward Bond 1987: 5*

OVERVIEW

When the 14 year-old working class schoolboy Edward Bond saw Donald Wolfit as Macbeth in 1948 he felt that 'for the very first time in my life I met somebody who was actually talking about my problems, about the life I'd been living, the political society around me' (Bond 1983: v). Bond's work is a powerful attempt to express the tragic nature of our alienation from ourselves. His work explores the consequences of living in, and being shaped by an irrational and contradictory society; consequences which include emotional suffering and the loss of mental and intellectual freedom. Tragedy is a means whereby we can get a clearer understanding and a 'rational' emotional grasp of the historical forces which produce suffering in the world. When interviewed in 1997 he remarked that:

> If you want to live in an inhuman world and accept it you become inhuman. You need to say why that world is inhuman, why it matters to you, and why you want to change it. It all relates to ownership. What I aim at is a kind of socialism in which people can own themselves.
>
> *Edward Bond in Michael Mangan 1998: 2*

Violence – a central concern

Although he has written, and continues to write, a wide range of different kinds of drama, violence has always been a principal concern of Bond's plays:

> Violence occurs in situations of injustice. It is caused not only by physical threats, but even more significantly by threats to human dignity. That is why, in spite of all the physical benefits of affluence, violence flourishes under capitalism.
>
> *Edward Bond: 'Introduction' to Lear 1971 in Bond 1977: 13*

Bond's most notable early play, *Saved* (1965), features a notorious scene in which a group of youths stone a baby to death in its pram. The infant's murder is the dramatic focus of the tragedy, but all of the callous, inarticulate, angry working-class characters in the play are tragic figures, trapped by historical forces which deny them the ability to express themselves and understand their predicament. Yet the principal character, Len, ends the play by mending a broken chair; a symbol of the possibility of some kind of putting back together of their lives. Violence has always been at the heart of tragedy from the Greeks onward, but Bond seeks to render it newly shocking, and refuses to allow the audience to encounter stage violence as merely ritual or conventional.

The Shakespeare connection

A Shakespearean, epic sweep and episodic method are most evident in Bond's retelling of *King Lear* as a tale or revolutionary violence, *Lear* (1971), and his version of the Trojan War, *The Woman* (1978). In one of his most powerful tragedies, *Bingo* (1973), Bond turns his attention to Shakespeare himself.

BINGO (1973)

SYNOPSIS

Shakespeare has retired from London to his garden in Stratford. He is depressed. He agrees to allow some land over which he has rights to be enclosed for sheep farming, even though it will entail the eviction of the poor people who live there.

A young woman who comes begging is at his gate is turned away and later whipped for vagrancy. When the evictions come she is hanged for her part in violent rioting. Shakespeare visits her gibbeted body, and gets drunk with his old friend the playwright Ben Jonson, who tries to borrow money from him. Shakespeare later quarrels with his own daughter.

A mentally ill old man who works for Shakespeare is accidentally shot by his own son, an evangelical preacher who is out at night filling in the ditches of the enclosers.

Neither the son, nor Combe, the encloser, believe they have done anything wrong in the play. Both visit Shakespeare who is now confined to bed.

Shakespeare, appalled by the suffering he sees and by what he takes as his own culpability in it, kills himself with poison which he took from the drunken Jonson. His daughter bursts in as he dies trying to find a copy of his will.

Bond deals with a controversial episode in Shakespeare's own life. In 1613, Shakespeare offered no resistance to the unpopular enclosure of lands around Stratford-upon-Avon in which he had a financial interest. In return for agreeing to the enclosure which would allow sheep farming, Shakespeare's income was guaranteed by the enclosers; for some of the poorest residents of Stratford, the cost of the enclosure was hunger and destitution. As a prominent citizen of the town Shakespeare could have helped to prevent the enclosures and consequent suffering. However, he chose not to. How, asks Bond, could the man who had such insight into the truth of how we live in an irrational and violent society behave in such a way? How can a writer's life and work be so at odds? Bond's Shakespeare faces up to this contradiction, and in despair, commits suicide. Bond says:

> if he didn't end in the way shown in the play then he was a reactionary blimp or some other fool. The only more charitable account is that he was unaware or senile

> *Edward Bond 1973 in Plays: Three 1987: 4*

Thus Shakespeare himself becomes himself a tragic protagonist, unable in his own life to live up to the need for justice so eloquently expressed in his writing. As Bond says:

> His behaviour as a property-owner made him closer to Goneril than Lear. He supported and benefited from the Goneril-society.

> *Edward Bond 1973 in Plays: Three 1987: 6*

As Shakespeare says in the play's final scene:

> Absurd! Absurd! I howled when they suffered, but they were whipped and hanged so that I could be free. That is the right question: not why did I sign one piece of paper? – no, no, even when I sat at my table, when I put on my clothes, I was a hangman's assistant, a gaoler's errand boy.

> *Edward Bond 1973 in Plays: Three 1987: 63*

'Scenes of Money and Death'

Bingo is subtitled 'Scenes of Money and Death', and a recurrent idea is that when money takes the place of human relationships some kind of death is the outcome. When, in the first scene, a young vagrant woman begs at Shakespeare's garden gate, he offers her money, only for her to be frightened away. The Old Man, a servant of Shakespeare's who has been rendered childish by a war wound, becomes the young vagrant's lover to the disgust of both Shakespeare's embittered and hostile daughter Judith and of the Old Man's son. The Old Man nevertheless offers more comfort and friendship in his sexual exploitation of the vagrant than anyone else in the play.

> In *Bingo*, Shakespeare takes on the role of the typical Bond hero, watching and trying to understand a world distorted by cruelty.

> *Michael Mangan 1998: 34*

A tragic eloquence

Shakespeare's business partner and local magistrate William Combe orders the young woman to be whipped for vagrancy. She subsequently suffers a breakdown, sets fire to some hay ricks and is hanged as a consequence. Shakespeare is drawn to her gibbeted body in the third of the six scenes, and, having been frustratingly silent, finds his eloquence at last.

In the following scene the playwright Ben Jonson visits him in local tavern. Jonson asks for a loan while Shakespeare becomes increasingly drunk and taciturn. Money, not friendship, is what the envious Jonson wants and he is revealed as the inferior writer when a group of dispossessed peasants enter, led by the old man's son. Jonson can only babble idealised pastoral lyrics, literature divorced from the reality of rural life. Poetry written for money will also be artistically dead.

On the way home the drunken Shakespeare walks across a snowy field, which stands for the tragic failure of his writing to connect with his life; for the fact that making money is the antithesis of telling the truth as a writer. The field is as blank as a piece of paper with nothing written on it, reproaching him by representing his real achievement. It is here that finally he expresses what he sees as truth on stage: 'the truth means nothing when you hate. Was anything done?' (Bond, 1973 in *Plays: Three,* p.57) As he says these lines the Old Man's son accidentally shoots his father upstage, mistaking him for one of Combe's men.

The play's last scene is icy but very moving. The son and Combe visit the depressed and bedridden playwright. The son uses his evangelical faith to talk himself out of his responsibility for his father's death. Combe unwittingly hands Shakespeare the poison which Shakespeare had earlier stolen from Jonson (the money-obsessed Jonson and Combe are the possessors of death). Thus only Shakespeare, in his suicide, takes full responsibility for his actions, asking of his plays, to the last, 'Was anything done … was anything done?' (Bond 1973 in *Plays: Three,* p.66). As he dies Judith ransacks his room hoping to find a will more favourable than the one Shakespeare had pushed under the door to his frantic, demented mother.

The form of the tragedy

The play makes very effective use of montage in its episodic structure and in its use of a double-focused stage action in several scenes. As Shakespeare confronts his own complicity in the suffering caused by the enclosure of the fields, a son kills his father, a mocking echo of an event in one of his earliest works, *Henry VI Part 3* (2.5.54). As Shakespeare takes responsibility for his actions in his anguished suicide, Combe and the Son explain how neither of them are really responsible for the old man's death. In the style of Brecht, the audience is challenged to think, make connections and judge in order to comprehend the tragic action. The **catharsis** of tragic pity is, as in much contemporary British tragedy, political: it encourages its audience to think critically about money, power, cruelty, community and family both on the stage and in their own lives by making connections between events. The play also enacts its own central concern, the tragic concern: the responsibility of the artist to speak truthfully about suffering and injustice.

SOME KEY IDEAS TO CONSIDER

- Whether the play's episodic structure makes it hard for the audience to become involved with the tragedy.

- The importance of silence to its tragedy and what is left unsaid in the play.

- Whether there is anything positive in the play's conclusion. 'Was anything done'?

MODERN BRITISH TRAGEDY – SOME KEY IDEAS TO CONSIDER

- Whether tragedy can exist in a society where there is little belief in God.

- The relevance of tragedy to a world threatened by nuclear war or environmental catastrophe.

- Whether the emergence of female dramatists in the twentieth century has changed our understanding of tragedy.

- Why socialist dramatists have been drawn to tragedy in the late twentieth century.

CITY AND ISLINGTON
SIXTH FORM COLLEGE
283 - 309 GOSWELL ROAD
LONDON
EC1
TEL 020 7520 0652

GLOSSARY

GLOSSARY

Absurd

> The Theatre of the Absurd was an attempt to convert the complex philosophy of Existentialism into practical form, to make such a nihilistic world view into challenging yet consumable dramatic events.

Anagnorisis

> The point at which the protagonist recognises their tragic error/the reality of their situation.

Brechtian

> 'Epic theatre' which aims to distance the audience emotionally from the action in order to understand how and why characters behave as they do, politically and morally.

The catastrophe

> A 'turning up-side down', the calamitous action which precipitates the denouement or conclusion. It is the catastrophe which provokes the catharsis, the emotional response from its audience.

Catharsis

> A Greek medical term literally meaning 'purgation'. Aristotle used catharsis in *The Poetics* to describe the emotional experience of the audience at the end of a tragedy. The term has come to mean the response of the audience, both intellectual and emotional, to tragic suffering.

Choral ode

> In Greek tragedy a song which is sung and danced by the chorus.

Chorus

> The chorus watches the action unfold, offering comments to the characters and the audience and giving their reflections on the action. In Greek tragedies, the chorus is explicit. In other plays (for example Tennessee Williams' *The Glass Menagerie*) there may be a character who fulfils the function of a chorus.

Deus ex Machina

> Literally means 'a god from the machine' and in classical drama referred to a god who intervened in a play to sort out all the complications and bring it to an end. The term is now used to describe any artificial means of resolving the plot of a play.

Dionysus

> The Greek god of wine and theatre, the god of ecstasy or leaving behind one's normal identity, and the god of festivity and joy.

Epic theatre

> See Brechtian.

Episode

> In Greek tragedy a scene of dialogue between the characters in the play.

Existentialism

> A philosophy based on the belief that man is lost in a sea of meaningless choices and dead-end ideas, a godless world in which simple explanations and rational thought no longer make sense. It is, however, a world in which human beings make their own identity through authentic choice.

Expressionism

> Expressionism is in some ways a revolt against Naturalism. Expressionist drama sought to put emotional and physical intensity back on the stage directly rather than through the subtext, dramatising the inner chaos and violence of disturbed psychologies in an edgy, anxiety-ridden style.

Fate

> The idea that human action is somehow predetermined. Not all writers and cultures have regarded this as incompatible with human free will.

Fear (or awe)

> According to Aristotle, fear is one of the emotions the audience experiences through tragic drama.

Foil

> A character whose situation parallels that of the protagonist and so acts as a point of contrast and comparison.

Hamartia

> The protagonist's error of judgement which brings about their downfall. NB hamartia is different from the tragic flaw: hamartia is a matter of action, not character.

Hubris

> Excessive human pride, self-belief or self-importance.

Idealist

> In philosophy, the belief that ideas, not physical matter, are the ultimate reality.

Materialist

> In philosophy, the belief that physical matter is the ultimate reality.

Megalopsychia

> A Greek word meaning 'greatness of soul' used by Aristotle to describe the characteristics of the tragic protagonist.

Naturalism

> Theatre which aims to depict human action and feeling in a 'realistic' way.

GLOSSARY

Pathe mathe
> A Greek term translated as 'through suffering comes understanding'.

Pathos
> The quality of a play that excites pity in an audience.

Peripeteia
> The moment at which events of the play turn in an unexpected direction for the protagonist. The moment of reversal may coincide with the protagonist's moment of recognition (or anagnorisis).

Pity
> According to Aristotle, pity is one of the emotions the audience experiences through tragic drama. For Aristotle pity seems to have meant something rather different from simply sympathy for the suffering person. It also included a sense of relief that the events are happening to someone else. Through feeling pity for another person's loss, members of the audience learn something which benefits their lives.

Providence
> The idea that all actions are part of a pre-ordained pattern which will see the good rewarded and the bad punished, or that the universe is working towards the best possible outcome, even if humans cannot see it now.

Protagonist
> The main character in the play. The term is used instead of 'hero' to avoid the positive associations that this word has.

Reversal
> See peripeteia.

Scapegoat
> Someone who is made to bear the guilt of a community or population and is punished for it.

Stasimon
> A choral ode sung and danced by the chorus while not entering or leaving the stage.

Stoicism
> A philosophical movement which believed that humans' only 'natural' and rational response to their fixed fates was not to let their emotions take control of their minds.

The Theatre of the Absurd
> See Absurd.

Tragic flaw (sometimes called 'fatal flaw')

> The idea proposed by the critic A.C. Bradley in *Shakespearean Tragedy* (1904) that the tragedy is a result of a flaw in the psychological make-up of the protagonist who he believed embodied greatness in conflict with evil. The concept of the tragic flaw is different from Aristotle's hamartia which refers to an action not the character of the protagonist.

Tragic hero/Tragic protagonists

> A man with a nobility about him, a man both of high birth and courageous and generous character, but not perfect. (See above for distinction between hero and protagonist.)

The unities

> According to Aristotle, writing in 330 BC, a century, the action of a tragedy must be self-contained, with a single plot line (unity of action), located in a single place (unity of place) and confined to a single day (unity of time).

INDEX

S

T

BIBLIOGRAPHY

Aristotle (1965), 'On the Art of Poetry', in *Classical Literary Criticism*, trans. T.S. Dorsch, Harmondsworth: Penguin Books.

Barker, Howard (1989), *Arguments for a Theatre*, London: John Calder.

Beckett, Samuel (1986), *The Complete Dramatic Works*, London: Faber and Faber.

Belsey, Catherine (1985), *The Subject of Tragedy: Identity and Difference in Renaissance Drama*, London: Methuen.

_____ (1991), 'Making histories then and now: Shakespeare from Richard II to Henry V', in F. Barker, P. Hulme and M. Iversen (eds), *Uses of History: Marxism, Postmodernism and the Renaissance*, Manchester: Manchester University Press.

_____ (2007), *Why Shakespeare?*, Basingstoke: Palgrave Macmillan.

Bigsby, Christopher, 'Entering The Glass Menagerie' in Roudané, Matthew C. (1997), *The Cambridge Companion to Tennessee Williams*, Cambridge: Cambridge University Press.

Bigsby, Christopher, (1997), *The Cambridge Companion to Arthur Miller*, Cambridge: Cambridge University Press

Billington, Michael (2007), *State of the Nation: British Theatre Since 1945*, London: Faber and Faber.

Bleiman, B., Broadbent, S. et al (1993), *Arthur Miller*, London: English and Media Centre

Bond, Edward (1977), *Plays: One*, London: Methuen.

_____ (1983), *Lear*, ed. Patricia Hearn, London: Methuen.

_____ (1987), *Plays: Three*, London: Methuen.

Boon, Richard (2003), *The Cambridge Companion to David Hare*, Cambridge: Cambridge University Press.

Bradley. A.C. (1991), *Shakespearean Tragedy*, Harmondsworth: Penguin Books.

Brown, John Russell (1997), *The Oxford Illustrated History of Theatre*, Oxford: Oxford University Press.

Bushnell, Rebecca (2008) *Tragedy: A Short Introduction*, Oxford: Blackwell Publishing.

Carter, D. M. (2007), *The Politics of Greek Tragedy*, Exeter: Exeter University Press.

Ceresano, S. P. (2004), *William Shakespeare's 'The Merchant of Venice': A Sourcebook*, London: Routledge.

Chaucer, Geoffrey (1957), *The Complete Works*, ed. F.N. Robinson, Oxford: Oxford University Press.

Chapman, George (1964), *Bussy D'Ambois*, ed. N. S. Brooke, Manchester: Manchester University Press.

Chekhov, Anton (2002), *Plays: 'Ivanov', 'The Seagull', 'Uncle Vanya', 'Three Sisters', 'The Cherry Orchard'* ed. Richard Gilman, Harmondsworth: Penguin Books.

Churchill, Caryl (1982), *Top Girls*, London: Methuen.

Clark, Sandra (1987), *John Webster 'The White Devil' and 'The Duchess of Malfi': A Critical Study*, Harmondsworth: Penguin Books.

Conacher, D.J. (1983), 'The Trojan Women' in *Oxford Readings in Greek Tragedy*, ed. Erich Segal, Oxford: Oxford University Press.

Coult, Tony (2003), *About Friel: the Playwright and the Work*, London: Faber and Faber.

Cuddon, J. A. (1976), *A Dictionary of Literary Terms*, Harmondsworth: Penguin Books.

Deane Seamus (1999), 'Introduction', *Brian Friel: Plays One*, London: Faber and Faber.

Devlin, A.J., 'Writing in 'A Place of Stone': Cat on a Hot Tin Roof' in Roudané Matthew C., (1997), *The Cambridge Companion to Tennessee Williams*, Cambridge: Cambridge University Press.

Dillon, J., (2007), *The Cambridge Introduction to Shakespeare's Tragedies*, Cambridge: Cambridge University Press.

Dodds, E.R., 'On Misunderstanding the Oedipus Rex', in *Oxford Readings in Greek Tragedy* (1983), ed. Erich Segal, Oxford: Oxford University Press.

Dollimore, Jonathan (1984, 2004 3rd edition), *Radical Tragedy*, Basingstoke: Palgrave Macmillan.

Drakakis, John (1994), (ed.) *New Casebooks: 'Antony and Cleopatra'*, Basingstoke: Palgrave Macmillan.

Eagleton, Terry (1986), *William Shakespeare*, Oxford: Basil Blackwell.

_____ (2003), *Sweet Violence: The Idea of The Tragic*, Oxford: Blackwell Publishing.

Easterling, Pat, 'Form and Performance' in *The Cambridge Companion to Greek Tragedy*, (1997), Cambridge: Cambridge University Press.

Eaton, Sara (1991), 'Beatrice-Joanna and the Rhetoric of Love', in *Staging the Renaissance*, ed. David Scott Kastan and Peter Stallybrass, London: Routledge.

Eliot, T.S. (1951), *Selected Essays*, London: Faber and Faber.

Empson, William (1969), 'Mine Eyes Dazzle', in G.K. and S.K. Hunter (eds.) *John Webster*, Harmondsworth: Penguin Books.

Esslin, M. in Brown, John Russell (1995), *The Oxford Illustrated History of Theatre*, Oxford: Oxford University Press.

Euripides (1998), *'Medea' and Other Plays*, trans. James Morwood, Oxford: Oxford University Press.

_____ (2004), *Women of Troy*, trans. Kenneth McLeish, London: Nick Hern Books.

Fernie, Ewan (2002), *Shame in Shakespeare*, London: Routledge.

Forker, Charles R. (1986), *The Skull Beneath the Skin: the Achievement of John Webster*, Carbondale: Southern Illinois University Press.

French, Marilyn (1992), 'Macbeth and Masculine Values', in *New Casebooks: 'Macbeth'*, ed. Alan Sinfield, Basingstoke: Palgrave Macmillan.

Friel, Brian (1973), *The Freedom of the City*, London: Faber and Faber.

_____ (1990), *Dancing at Lughnasa*, London: Faber and Faber.

_____ (1988), *Making History*, London: Faber and Faber.

_____ (1980), *Translations*, London: Faber and Faber.

_____ 'Self-Portrait' in ed. Murray, Christopher (1999) *Brian Friel: Essays, Diaries, Interviews 1964-1999* London: Faber and Faber.

Goldhill, Simon (1986), *Reading Greek Tragedy*, Cambridge: Cambridge University Press.

_____ (2004), *Love, Sex and Tragedy: Why Classics Matters*, London: John Murray.

_____ (2007), *How to Stage Greek Tragedy Today*, Chicago: University of Chicago Press.

Gottlieb, Vera and Allain, Paul (eds) (2000), *The Cambridge Companion to Chekhov*, Cambridge: Cambridge University Press

Grene, Nicholas (1999), *The Politics of Irish Drama: Plays in Context from Boucicault to Friel*, Cambridge: Cambridge University Press.

Griffin, Alice (1996), *Understanding Arthur Miller*, Columbia: University of Carolina Press.

Gross, John (1992), *Shylock*, London: Vintage.

Hadfield, Andrew (2003), *William Shakespeare's 'Othello': A Sourcebook*, London: Routledge.

_____ (2004), *Shakespeare and Renaissance Politics*, London: Thomson.

Hale, Allean 'Early Williams: the Making of a Playwright' ed. Roudané Matthew C., (1997), *The Cambridge Companion to Tennessee Williams*, Cambridge: Cambridge University Press.

Hanssen J.M. 'Ibsen and Realism' www.ibsen.net

Hapgood, Robert (1999), *Shakespeare in Production: 'Hamlet'*, Cambridge: Cambridge University Press.

Hare, David (1995), *Skylight*, London: Faber and Faber.

_____ (1984), *The History Plays*, London: Faber and Faber.

_____ 1988), *The Secret Rapture*, London: Faber and Faber.

Hazlitt, William (1906), *Characters of Shakespeare's Plays*, London: J.M. Dent.

_____ (1969), 'Lectures on the age of Elizabeth' in *Marlowe: 'Dr Faustus', A Casebook*, ed. John D. Jump, London: Palgrave Macmillan.

Healey, Margaret (1998), *Richard II*, Plymouth: Northcote House.

Holderness, Graham (1989), 'Are Shakespeare's tragic heroes 'fatally flawed'? Discuss', *Critical Survey 1*.

Homer (1987), *The Iliad*, trans. Martin Hammond, Harmondsworth: Penguin Books.

Hopkins, Lisa (2008), *Christopher Marlowe, Renaissance Dramatist*, Edinburgh: Edinburgh University Press.

Ibsen, Henrik (1965), *A Doll's House and Other Plays,* Harmondsworth: Penguin Books.

Innes, C. in Brown, John Russell (1995), *The Oxford Illustrated History of Theatre*, Oxford: Oxford University Press.

Ioppolo, Grace (2003), *William Shakespeare's 'King Lear': A Sourcebook*, London: Routledge.

Jardine, Lisa (1983), *Still Harping on Daughters: Women and Drama in the Age of Shakespeare*, Hemel Hempstead: Harvester Wheatsheaf.

_____ (1996), *Reading Shakespeare Historically*, London: Routledge.

Johnson, Samuel (1989), *Samuel Johnson on Shakespeare*, ed. H.R. Woudhuysen, Harmondsworth: Penguin Books.

Jones, Nesta (2000), *Brian Friel*, Faber Critical Guides, London: Faber and Faber

Kermode, Frank (1969), (ed.) *'King Lear': A Selection of Critical Essays*, London and Basingstoke: Palgrave Macmillan.

Kerrigan, John (1996), *Revenge Tragedy: Aeschylus to Armageddon*, Oxford: The Clarendon Press.

Kitto, H.D.F. (1966), *Greek Tragedy*, London: Methuen.

Knox, Bernard M. W. (1983), 'The Hippolytus of Euripides' in *Oxford Readings in Greek Tragedy*, ed. Erich Segal, Oxford: Oxford University Press.

Kott, Jan (1974), *Shakespeare Our Contemporary*, New York: W. W. Norton.

Kyd, Thomas (1959), *The Spanish Tragedy*, ed. Philip Edwards, Manchester: Manchester University Press.

Leavis, F.R. (1952), *The Common Pursuit*, London: Chatto and Windus.

Leggatt, Alexander (2006), *William Shakespeare's 'Macbeth': A Sourcebook*, London: Routledge.

Londré, Felicia Hardison 'A Streetcar Running Fifty Years' in ed. Roudané Matthew C., (1997), *The Cambridge Companion to Tennessee Williams*, Cambridge: Cambridge University Press.

Luckyj, Christina (1989), A *Winter's Snake: Dramatic Form in the Tragedies of John Webster*, Athens GA and London: University of Georgia Press.

Lyons, Charles R. (1983), *Samuel Beckett*, London: Macmillan.

McDonald, Ronan (2001), *Tragedy and Irish Literature: Synge, O'Casey, Beckett*, Basingstoke: Palgrave Macmillan

McEvoy, Sean (2006), *William Shakespeare's 'Hamlet': A Sourcebook*, London: Routledge.

_____ (2006a), *Shakespeare: The Basics*, second edition, London: Routledge.

_____ (2008), *Ben Jonson, Renaissance Dramatist*, Edinburgh: Edinburgh University Press.

McIlwraith, A.K. (1971), (ed.) *Five Elizabethan Tragedies*, Oxford: Oxford University Press.

McLuskie, Kathleen (1985), 'The patriarchal bard: feminist criticism and Shakespeare: *King Lear* and *Measure for Measure*', in *Political Shakespeare*, ed. Jonathan Dollimore and Alan Sinfield, Manchester: Manchester University Press.

Madelaine, Richard (1998), *Shakespeare in Production: 'Antony and Cleopatra'*, Cambridge: Cambridge University Press.

Mangan, Michael (1998), *Edward Bond*, Plymouth: Northcote House.

Marlowe, Christopher (1964), *Dr Faustus*, ed. John D. Jump, Manchester: Manchester University Press.

_____ (1997), *Edward II*, ed. Martin Wiggins and Robert Lindsey, Manchester: Manchester University Press.

_____ (2003), *Tamburlaine Parts I and II*, ed. Anthony B. Dawson, London: Methuen.

Middleton, Thomas and William Rowley (1964), *The Changeling*, ed. Patricia Thomson, Manchester: Manchester University Press.

Middleton, Thomas/Cyril Tourneur (1996), *The Revenger's Tragedy*, ed. R. A. Foakes, Manchester: Manchester University Press.

Middleton, Thomas (2007), *Women Beware Women*, ed. J. R. Mulryne, Manchester: Manchester University Press.

Miller, A. (1949), 'Tragedy and the Common Man', *New York Times*. See http://www.nytimes.com/books/00/11/12/specials/miller-common.html

_____ (1961), *Death of a Salesman*, Harmondsworth: Penguin Books.

_____ (1968), *The Crucible*, Harmondsworth: Penguin Books.

_____ (1996), *The Theater Essays of Arthur Miller*, ed. Robert A Martin and Steve Centola, New York: Da Capo Press.

_____ (2000), *A View from the Bridge/All My Sons*, Harmondsworth: Penguin Books.

Mills, Sophie (2002), *Euripides: 'Hippolytus'*, London: Duckworth.

Mulryne, J. R. and Margaret Shewring (1989), *This Golden Round: The Royal Shakespeare Company at the Swan*, Rugby: Jolly & Barber.

BIBLIOGRAPHY

Murray, Christopher (ed.) (1999), *Brian Friel: Essays, Diaries, Interviews 1964-1999* London: Faber and Faber.

Newman, Karen, ''And wash the Ethiop white': femininity and the monstrous in Othello', in *Shakespeare Reproduced*, (2005), ed. Jean E. Howard and Marion F. O' Connor, London: Routledge.

Nuttall, A.D. (2007), *Shakespeare the Thinker*, New Haven and London: Yale University Press.

O'Callaghan, Michelle (2009), *Thomas Middleton, Renaissance Dramatist*, Edinburgh: Edinburgh University Press.

O'Casey, Sean (1957), *Three Plays*, London: Macmillan.

O'Toole, Fintan (2002), *Shakespeare is Hard, But So is Life*, London: Granta Books.

Otway, Thomas (1969), *Venice Preserved*, ed. Malcolm Kelsall, London: Edward Arnold.

Palmer, D. J. (1972), 'The unspeakable in pursuit of the uneatable: language and action in Titus Andronicus', *Critical Quarterly 14*.

Adrian Poole (2005), *Tragedy – a very short introduction,* Oxford: Oxford University Press.

Ryan, Kiernan (2002), *Shakespeare*, third edition, Basingstoke: Palgrave Macmillan.

Seneca (1966), *Four Tragedies and 'Octavia'*, trans. E. F. Watling, Harmondsworth: Penguin Books.

Shakespeare, William (1984), *Othello*, ed. Norman Sanders, Cambridge: Cambridge University Press.

_____ (1984a), *Titus Andronicus*, ed. Eugene M. Waith, Oxford: Oxford University Press.

_____ (1990), *Macbeth*, ed. Nicholas Brooke, Oxford: Oxford University Press.

_____ (1990a), *King Richard II*, ed. Andrew Gurr, Cambridge: Cambridge University Press.

_____ (1995), *Titus Andronicus*, ed. Jonathan Bate, London: Thomson.

_____ (1995a), *Antony and Cleopatra*, ed. John Wilders, London: Thomson.

_____ (2002), *King Richard II*, ed. Charles R. Forker, London: Thomson.

_____ (2005), *Antony and Cleopatra*, ed. David Bevington, Cambridge: Cambridge University Press.

_____ (2005a), *King Lear*, ed. Kiernan Ryan, Harmondsworth: Penguin Books.

_____ (2006), *Hamlet*, ed. Ann Thompson and Neil Taylor, London: Thomson.

_____ (2007), *Complete Works*, ed. Jonathan Bate and Eric Rasmussen, Basingstoke: Macmillan.

Shellard, Dominic (1999), *British Theatre Since The War,* New Haven and London: Yale University Press.

Smith, Emma (2007), *The Cambridge Introduction to Shakespeare*, Cambridge: Cambridge University Press.

Sidney, Sir Philip (1966), *A Defence of Poetry*, ed. Jan Van Dorsten, Oxford: Oxford University Press.

Sophocles (1982), *The Three Theban Plays: 'Antigone', 'Oedipus the King', 'Oedipus at Colonus'*, trans. Robert Fagles, Harmondsworth: Penguin Books.

Spurgeon, Caroline (1936), 'Leading Motives in the Imagery of Shakespeare's Tragedies', in *Shakespeare Criticism 1919-35*, ed. Ridler, Anne, Oxford: Oxford University Press.

Stewart, Victoria (2003), *About O'Casey: the Playwright and the Work*, London: Faber and Faber.

Tycer, Alicia (2008), *Caryl Churchill's 'Top Girls'*, London: Methuen.

Taplin, Oliver (1978), *Greek Tragedy in Action*, London: Routledge.

Tourneur, Cyril (1969), *The Atheist's Tragedy, in Jacobean Tragedies*, ed. A. H. Gomme, Oxford: Oxford University Press.

Vaughan, Virginia Mason (1994), *'Othello': A Contextual History*, Cambridge: Cambridge University Press.

Wallace, Jennifer (2007), *The Cambridge Introduction to Tragedy*, Cambridge: Cambridge University Press.

Webster, John (1996), *'The Duchess of Malfi' and Other Plays*, ed. Weis, René, Oxford: Oxford University Press.

Wheatley, Christopher J. (2000), 'Tragedy', in *The Cambridge Companion to English Restoration Theatre*, ed. Fisk, Deborah Payne, Cambridge: Cambridge University Press.

BIBLIOGRAPHY

Wickham G. (1992), *A History of the Theatre* 2nd Edition, London: Phaidon

Wilders, David (2004), *Shakespeare in Production: 'Macbeth'*, Cambridge: Cambridge University Press.

Wiles, David (2000), *Greek Theatre Performance*, Cambridge: Cambridge University Press.

Williams, Raymond (1979), *Modern Tragedy*, London: Verso.

Williams T. (2000), 'The *Glass Menagerie*' and '*A Streetcar Named Desire*' in *A Streetcar Named Desire and Other Plays*, Harmondsworth: Penguin Books.

_____ (2001), *Cat on a Hot Tin Roof*, Harmondsworth: Penguin Books.

Winnington-Ingram, R.P. (1980), *Sophocles: An Interpretation*, Cambridge: Cambridge University Press.